# MAKING OUT
# IN THE MAINSTREAM

# MAKING OUT

## IN THE MAINSTREAM

*GLAAD and the Politics of Respectability*

Vincent Doyle

McGill-Queen's University Press

Montreal & Kingston · London · Chicago

© McGill-Queen's University Press 2016

ISBN 978-0-7735-4678-3 (cloth)
ISBN 978-0-7735-9858-4 (ePDF)
ISBN 978-0-7735-9859-1 (ePUB)

Legal deposit first quarter 2016
Bibliothèque nationale du Québec

Printed in Canada on acid-free paper that is 100% ancient forest free
(100% post-consumer recycled), processed chlorine free

This book has been published with the help of a grant from the Canadian
Federation for the Humanities and Social Sciences, through the Awards
to Scholarly Publications Program, using funds provided by the Social
Sciences and Humanities Research Council of Canada.

McGill-Queen's University Press acknowledges the support of the Canada
Council for the Arts for our publishing program. We also acknowledge
the financial support of the Government of Canada through the Canada
Book Fund for our publishing activities.

Library and Archives Canada Cataloguing in Publication

Doyle, Vincent A., 1970–, author
Making out in the mainstream : GLAAD and the politics of respectability /
Vincent Doyle.

Includes bibliographical references and index.
Issued in print and electronic formats.
ISBN 978-0-7735-4678-3 (bound). – ISBN 978-0-7735-9858-4 (ePDF).
– ISBN 978-0-7735-9859-1 (ePUB)

1. Mass media and gays. 2. Gay & Lesbian Alliance Against Defamation.
3. Gay rights – Press coverage. 4. Gay liberation movement – Press coverage. 5. Gays in mass media. 6. Gays in popular culture. 7. Sexual
minorities in mass media. 8. Gay rights. 9. Gay liberation movement.
10. Gay activists. I. Title.

P94.5.G38D69 2016        302.23086'64        C2015-907124-0
                                             C2015-907125-9

To my mother, Marie-Paule Doyle, and in memory
of my father, Raymond Doyle (1936–2012).

# Contents

Acknowledgments | ix

Introduction
LGBT Cultural Politics in Neoliberal Times | 3

1
Rags to Riches: GLAAD's Rise to the National Stage | 30

2
"We Want In": The Politics of Access and Inclusion | 77

3
Insiders – Outsiders: The Dr Laura Campaign | 124

4
Sex, Race, and Representation | 176

Conclusion
Mainstreaming's Ambivalent Embrace | 229

Notes | 261
Bibliography | 273
Index | 281

# Acknowledgments

A book's unity is an illusion conjured up via the labour of many people. Some of them leave their mark clearly and others do so less visibly. I assembled and reassembled the fragments of thought, observation, conversation, and writing in this book over a long period of time, which makes it difficult to adequately recognize everyone who has, in one way or another and at one time or another, contributed. Therefore, to everyone who has supported the making of *Making Out in the Mainstream*, I extend my heartfelt appreciation.

I am especially indebted to my mentors: Tom Waugh, who, in addition to introducing me to the field of LGBTQ media studies, facilitated my first contact with McGill-Queen's University Press; Will Straw, whose courses in the graduate programme in communication at McGill University all those years ago expanded my horizons immeasurably; and Lisa Henderson, whose grace, generosity, and awesome intellect I deeply admire. I am lucky to have had them as teachers, and luckier still to count them among my friends.

Larry Gross remains a guiding influence and was instrumental in securing my entrée to GLAAD. He also provided a thorough assessment of a late draft of this book. I would like to thank him, Lisa Duggan, and the anonymous reviewers for their helpful feedback. My editor at MQUP, Jonathan Crago, was generous with his time and expertly guided me as to what needed to be done. Sarah Banet-Weiser provided editorial assistance and championed the book. Eric O. Clarke (1963–2010), Mary Gray, Jonathan D. Katz, David Valentine, Viviane Namaste, John Erni, Kevin Barnhurst, and Suzanna Walters were important interlocutors at early stages of the project, as were my dissertation committee members Jacqueline Urla, Briankle Chang, and Justin Lewis. My dear friend Katherine Sender's input helped me weather the storms and find the gravitational centre of the book. Melissa González gave me superb advice on a troublesome chapter (and life in general) when I really needed it. Diane di Mauro instigated and directed the Sexuality Research Fellowship Program of the Social Science Research Council (US), without which it would not have been possible for me to conduct full-time fieldwork in New York City and Los Angeles. A Mellon Postdoctoral Fellowship in Humanities and Media and Cultural Studies at Macalester College, Minnesota, and the friendship and kindness of faculty colleagues Leola Johnson and Clay Steinman, helped ease my entry into professional academic life.

IE University, my academic home in Spain since 2008, has given me more opportunities to grow, both personally and professionally, than I could have imagined. For their warmth, encouragement, and collegiality, I am thankful to my friends and colleagues Begoña González-Cuesta; Laura Illia; Magdalena Wojcieszak; Pedro Cifuentes; Ruth Palmer; Maria José Ferrari; Javier Garcia; and my fellow Canadian, confidant, and sometimes sparring partner, Rolf Strom-Olsen.

The love and support of so many friends and chosen family have carried me onward as I moved from Montreal to Massachusetts to Minneapolis to Madrid: Neil Hartlen; the Petoussis-Wrights, Elana, Hélène, and Stelio; John Custodio; James Allan; Gildas Illien, Robbie Schwartzwald; Sean Holland (1964–2010); Steve Dahl; Mathieu Derouin; Maura Tarnoff; and Luis Ruiz, to name but a few. Many others will recognize themselves in the acknowledgement that my participation in certain groups has brought me needed balance and joy over the years: UMASS CommGrads, Camp Gilmour, the Twin Cities Gay Men's Chorus, and Club Gastronómico.

This book could not have been written without the participation of GLAAD staff and board members, and especially Jason Heffner, who somehow managed to get me in; Joan Garry, who allowed me to stay and trusted me to be fair, accurate, and inclusive; Steve Spurgeon, Cathy Renna, and Dilia Loe, who made themselves extraordinarily available; and Michael Lopez and Wonbo Woo, who were great friends to me in the field. Sarah Kate Ellis, GLAAD's president and chief executive officer since 2014, kindly agreed to be interviewed for the book's conclusion.

Finally, just as I was entering the last stages of writing, Carlos Crespo landed in my life as though sent from heaven and quickly became a treasured collaborator, interlocutor, and companion. This book is better for his manifold contributions to it, as is my life.

## Permissions

Portions of this book were originally published as "But Joan! You're My Daughter! The Gay and Lesbian Alliance Against Defamation and the Politics of Amnesia," in *Radical History Review* 100: 209–21. (Copyright MARHO: The Radical Historians Organization, Inc, 2008.) All rights reserved. Republished by permission of the copyright holder, and the present publisher, Duke University Press.

Portions of chapter 3 were originally published as "Insiders – Outsiders: Dr Laura and the Contest for Cultural Authority in LGBT Media Activism," in *Media/Queered: Visibility and its Discontents*, ed. Kevin Barnhurst (New York: Peter Lang Publishers, 2007).

# MAKING OUT
# IN THE MAINSTREAM

# LGBT Cultural Politics in Neoliberal Times

The Gay and Lesbian Alliance Against Defamation, since 2013 known simply as GLAAD, was founded in 1985 by a small group of writers and academics who were angry with how the *New York Post* was covering the AIDS crisis. It has since grown into a professional media activist organization with close ties to the cultural industries, offices in New York City and Los Angeles, dozens of staff members, and a multi-million dollar budget. This book is the first full-length ethnographic study of gay and lesbian media activism and is based on eighteen months of participant observation carried out in 2000–01 at GLAAD's New York City and Los Angeles offices.[1] At the time of my fieldwork, GLAAD's mission was to advocate for "fair, accurate and inclusive representation of people and events in the media as a means of eliminating homophobia and discrimination based on gender identity and sexual orientation" (Khan 2012).

When I began this study in 2000, I encountered an organization that, by its own account, was riding wave after wave of success. Under the leadership of Joan Garry, a former executive at MTV and Showtime Networks, GLAAD had significantly increased its ability to attract large donors and corporate money, become one of the most visible organizations of the gay and lesbian movement, and established itself as a widely respected and influential media activist organization.[2]

By June 2011, GLAAD's ship appeared to be sinking. Its president, Jarrett Barrios, a former Massachusetts state senator, had been forced to resign along with eight board members over allegations that AT&T had recruited GLAAD to lobby the Federal Communications Commission (FCC) in support of the telecom giant's proposed $39-billion merger with T-Mobile. One of the board members to resign, Troop Coronado, was a former AT&T executive and lobbyist who had previously worked for the right-wing and anti-gay Heritage Foundation. GLAAD had also reportedly received a $50,000 donation from AT&T.[3]

GLAAD was not the only organization to be implicated in lobbying the FCC on behalf of AT&T: the National Association for the Advancement of Colored People, a number of important labour unions, and the National Education Association also issued letters in support of the proposed merger (which did not receive government approval). *Politico* pointed out that, in order to sway Democratic appointees to the FCC, AT&T had secured letters "from a slew of liberal groups with no obvious interest in telecom deals – except that they've received big piles of AT&T's cash."[4] In other words, in an apparent case of quid pro quo, all of these organizations had been convinced to sign on to a letter whose language AT&T had provided.

The scandal hit GLAAD particularly hard, in part because a number of notable gay bloggers and other lesbian-, gay-, bisexual-, and transgender-focused media outlets followed up on the story with the revelation that GLAAD had sent a letter to the FCC in 2009 in support of AT&T's position against net neutrality (the principle that Internet service providers should treat all data equally, regardless of their source). Under pressure from bloggers and journalists, Barrios withdrew the 2009 letter and blamed the episode on an administrative error committed by his assistant. Later, as the pressure continued to build, he took personal responsibility for the letter and its contents, but it was already too late. On an Internet radio program hosted by gay activist and journalist Michelangelo Signorile, Laurie Perper, who had been co-chair of GLAAD's board of directors during part of Barrios's tenure, suggested that GLAAD should be dissolved over concerns that its reputation was tarnished beyond repair.[5] Even mainstream media took notice. A damning editorial in the *Boston Globe* stated: "Clearly, some activist groups have grown a little too fond of their corporate backers, at a cost to their credibility ... Shilling for AT&T makes them seem more like paid lobbyists than clarions of justice; it carries more than a whiff of hackery."[6]

Was the AT&T debacle an isolated incident? Or was it symptomatic of broader trends in the evolving relationships between corporations and areas of social life, like the non-profit sector, which had previously been afforded some protection from market forces? Many social theorists have noted that neoliberalism's ascension since the 1980s has significantly reconfigured how the relationships between individuals, civil society, the state, and the economy are understood and enacted. As political economist and geographer David Harvey (2007, 2) explains, "neoliberalism is in the first instance a theory of political economic practices that proposes that human well-being can best be advanced by liberating individual entrepreneurial freedoms and skills within an institutional framework characterized by strong private property rights, free markets and free trade." For cultural studies scholar Stuart Hall (2011, 728), it constitutes a "hegemonic project" that appeared to be in crisis in the immediate wake of the financial debacle of 2008–09, but "keeps driving on," in large part because it has colonized Western societies' common sense. This colonizing dimension is key to neoliberalism's enduring influence. As political theorist Wendy Brown (2005, 39–40) argues, neoliberalism is best understood as an ideology whose "rationality, while foregrounding the market, is not only or even primarily focused on the economy; it involves *extending and disseminating market values to all institutions and social action*, even as the market itself remains a distinctive player" (italics original).

As fundamentalist beliefs about the putatively emancipatory outcomes of so-called free markets have spread to more and more areas of social life, including the LGBT non-profit sector, they have produced what queer scholar Lisa Duggan (2003, 42) calls a new brand of "equality politics," which are "compatible with a corporate world order" and the upward redistribution of resources that neoliberalism produces. This new equality politics, which is oriented to the "greater acceptance of the most assimilated, gender-appropriate, politically mainstream portions of the gay population" (44), has tended "to redefine gay equality against the 'civil rights agenda' and 'liberationism,' as access to the institutions of domestic privacy, the 'free' market, and patriotism" (50–1). Duggan further argues that, starting in the 1990s, the large organizations of the LGBT movement "have nearly all moved away from constituency mobilization and community-based consultation," followed "the national political culture to the right," and "adopted neoliberal rhetoric and corporate decision-making models" (45). In the process, she concludes, the movement's dominant organizations have become "the lobbying, legal, and public relations firms for an increasingly narrow gay, moneyed elite" (45). As international relations scholars Peter Dauvergne and Genevieve LeBaron (2014, 156) suggest in *Protest, Inc.*, the "corporatization of activism" is not without its advantages, except that "achieving current gains is requiring activist organizations to conform with, rather than work to transform, global capitalism." The "resulting compromises and pragmatism," they say, "are legitimising a world order where the health of corporations and economies is what 'matters the most.'"

The former executive director of the National Gay and Lesbian Task Force, Urvashi Vaid (1995), in *Virtual Equality*, was among the first to critique the movement's increasing emphasis on inclusion within dominant institutions, a development she terms "mainstreaming." In aiming to integrate LGBT people within the status quo, she claims, mainstreaming required strategies oriented to arguing that homosexuality is legitimate and respectable, and the abandonment of earlier goals to dismantle the oppressive structures that made it appear illegitimate and unworthy of respect in the first place. Vaid (1995, 54) notes that respectability "is limited by race, class, and gender assumptions," and argues that mainstreaming could only lead to partial and uneven accommodations with dominant society. The equality that mainstreaming promises, she suggests, is "virtual" at best, "a state of conditional equality based more on the appearance of acceptance by straight America than on genuine civic parity" (xvi).

Drawing on Vaid and Duggan, I understand the mainstreaming of the LGBT movement as a response to not only the challenges but also the opportunities (however limited and limiting) created by the movement's neoliberal turn since the 1990s, in two key senses that the title *Making Out in the Mainstream* captures. "Making out" is rich with connotations, one of which is to succeed or fare as well as possible in a given situation.[7] In this first sense, to make out in the mainstream is to attempt to derive maximum advantage from what dominant institutions allow to the privileged few to whom inclusion is granted. For

GLAAD, as I show in this book, this meant seeking to maximize what could be gained from forging closer relationships with corporate entities, and particularly large media companies. This sense of making out also captures an important dimension of what it means to be a subject of neoliberalism. As Brown (2005) argues, "classical liberalism articulated a distinction, and at times even a tension, among the criteria for individual moral, associational, and economic actions." Neoliberalism, by contrast, "normatively constructs and interpellates individuals as entrepreneurial actors in every sphere of life," thus erasing "the discrepancy between economic and moral behavior by configuring morality entirely as a matter of rational deliberation about costs, benefits, and consequences" (42). Put differently, neoliberalism produces subjectivities oriented to an economic calculus that privileges making out as well as possible above other considerations (an insight that helps explain why the leaders of so many ostensibly progressive organizations were eager to take AT&T's money despite any misgivings about the proposed merger with T-Mobile).

The second key sense of making out relates to its multiple connotations with regards to visibility, meaning, and representation. To make out the meaning of something is to interpret its signification on the basis of available linguistic codes and conceptual maps, but the expression can also connote the process of constructing meaning in particular ways to highlight and/or conceal certain characteristics, as in to make oneself out to be richer (or more attractive, or more successful, etc.) than one actually is. This sense of making out links up with the tendency of mainstreaming strategies to deploy a cultural politics of respectability, such as by promoting the idea that gay and lesbian people in the United States, in the words of a gay market researcher, feel "all the same emotions about life, God, and country as Americans of heterosexual orientation" (Lukenbill quoted in Chasin 2000, 48).

These interconnected senses of making out, referring to economic and symbolic processes, connect the various parts of this book. *Making Out in the Mainstream* explores key aspects of the cultural politics and political economy of gay and lesbian representation since GLAAD's founding in 1985. I describe and analyze some of the implications of the LGBT movement's increasing emphasis on inclusion within dominant institutions through a detailed ethnographic account of GLAAD's media activism in 2000–01. Through case studies of the GLAAD Media Awards, and of the organization's responses to *Dr Laura*, Eminem, and *Queer as Folk*, I argue that earlier coming out strategies – the dismantling of the closet, the right to sexual privacy, the creation of a mass movement and of a gay public sphere – were largely supplanted by the politics of making out: a desire to derive maximum (personal, political, and economic) advantage from the legitimation of homosexuality within mainstream institutions and to promote representations of gay and lesbian people that are compatible with a social order that defines good citizenship in terms of market-based values of self-betterment through consumption, middle-class respectability, professionalism, and entrepreneurialism.

This way of framing my interrogation of GLAAD constitutes a response to questions first posed by Vaid (1995, 203): "Who has been mainstreamed, to what extent, and why?" In attempting to answer these questions (to which I add, "how?"), I also want to provide an empirical basis from which to imagine a new politics of sexual representation beyond mainstreaming that might productively exploit the contradictions inherent in "neoliberalism's erosion of liberal democracy" (Brown 2005, 53). Such a politics of representation, as I argue in this book's conclusion, could emerge out of the democratic recognition of a growing ambivalence among many LGBT-identified people about the value and consequences of the movement's emphasis, since the 1990s, on making out in the mainstream.

### Mainstreaming

The idea of mainstreaming emerged in the 1990s as a useful shorthand to describe what many scholars and critics saw as the LGBT movement's increasingly single-minded pursuit of inclusion within dominant institutions such as marriage, the military, the capitalist market, organized politics, churches, media, and the corporate world. Of course, this tendency of gay and lesbian people to seek inclusion was nothing new: as historian John D'Emilio (2000, 37–8) writes, the gay and lesbian movement has, over the entire course of its history, opposed "those who pursued mainstream methods of lobbying, education, and negotiation" against "those who urged more militant, confrontational tactics" and "those whose work gave priority to opening up mainstream institutions to gays and lesbians" against "those who valued the building of almost 'nationalist' communities." Over time, D'Emilio (2000, 38) claims, these opposing tendencies have resulted not in two polarized factions but in a "more densely organized community" that has, at various historical moments, shown itself "capable of a variety of alignments" (D'Emilio 2012, 91). Understood from this historical vantage point, mainstreaming is helpful as a way to describe the specificity of the direction taken by the national organizations of the gay and lesbian movement since the 1990s and as a heuristic device with which to investigate the relative weight of opposing historical tendencies in the movement's recent history.

Notably, mainstreaming describes a tendency and not a fait accompli, which is to say, as political scientist David Morton Rayside (1998, 3) writes, it "co-exists with other strands of activism more wary of or antagonistic to that mainstream" and can "never wholly coopt" the gay and lesbian movement because "a movement is always more than a single organization, a single set of political networks, or a uniform strategy." "One strategy," he insists, "can as easily provoke as supplant others," and each strategy "depends on the others," which leads him to conclude that, although mainstreaming strategies have grown in importance, the gay and lesbian movement is still best understood as a "field of action, encompassing an enormous range of cultural, social, and political work" (3).

Although I agree with Rayside that mainstreaming is best conceptualized as operating within a field of action made up of conflicting forces, I want to guard against making it appear as just one tendency competing with others on an even playing field. Strategies do not simply co-exist; they are enabled or constrained by the power relations that structure the fields of action in which they are deployed. In thinking of the social movement field in this way, I am influenced by the work of French sociologist Pierre Bourdieu (1971, 161), for whom a field consists of the force relations among various "constituting agents or systems of agents" in a given sector of human activity. A field is like a game, with its own rules and conditions of entry, in which social agents compete with one another for the forms of capital that the game makes available to them. Agents' ability to succeed in a given field depends on the type and amount of capital (which can be economic, but also social, cultural, political, symbolic, etc.) with which they are endowed. The more capital an agent possesses, the more dominant its field position, and the better its chances to make the field function to its advantage. That dominance is never absolute, however, as dominant agents must contend with more or less dominated agents who also want to advance their positions (Bourdieu and Wacquant 1992, 102).

By understanding field relations in this way, we can explain mainstreaming's dominance in the gay and lesbian movement in terms of the ability of certain strategies (and not others) to attract forms of capital with which dominant institutions are endowed. As queer theorist Lauren Berlant (1997) suggests, strategies focused on mainstream inclusion came into prominence because they were suited to the hegemonic social formation that arose with Reagan and continued through the Clinton years. In this ideologically neoliberal and socially conservative context, mainstreaming strategies such as "gay marriage, critically-motivated acts of commodity consumption, and identity-based investment zones" function as "tactics for survival from within capitalist culture," and "are said to make marginalized social groups more central, more legitimate and powerful in capitalist society" (Berlant 1997, 9).

In basing its appeals on notions of respectability, professionalism, integration, inclusion, cooperation, engagement, acceptance, and finding common ground with the dominant culture, mainstreaming promotes the seductive fantasy that gays and lesbians could assimilate seamlessly into liberal society (Goldstein 2002), be given "a place at the table" (Bawer 1994), and be seen as "virtually normal" (Sullivan 1996). Relative to the long history of gays and lesbians being ignored; excluded; erased; or represented as little more than perverts, social deviants, or sinners, the appeal of such a fantasy, however partially realized, is not hard to see. But what are the costs of investing in mainstreaming at the expense of building a wider and more inclusive movement whose advances are not limited to those for whom respectability is afforded (and affordable)?

For Vaid (1995) and other critics of mainstreaming, strategies that seek equality on the basis of respectability do little to disrupt the cultural underpinnings of the exclusions that movement actors seek to rectify; the social enfranchisement of those who already enjoy the most (relative) privilege depends on the continued exclusion of those who enjoy the least. Moreover, as cultural critic Michael Warner (1999) points out, making homosexuality respectable requires representational strategies that attempt to divorce gay identity from the shame of gay sex. These strategies, he argues, are ultimately inauthentic, disingenuous, and out of step with the world the large organizations of the movement claim to represent, and therefore can only function as a "temporary pretense" until such time as the movement is able and willing to reengage with the politics of sexual shame (1999, 33–4, 40).

Using concepts initially developed by sociologist Erving Goffman, Warner (1999, 43) further theorizes that lesbian and gay politics have always existed in the tension between the "stigmaphile" space of the stigmatized among themselves, and the "stigmaphobe" world of those who aspire to normality. On one end of the spectrum are the sex radicals whom Warner champions as advocates of dignity in shame. On the other end are the mainstream political organizations that base their appeals on the repudiation of sex. The two poles, however, are not equal: "Political groups that mediate between queers and normals find that power lies almost exclusively on the normal side. The more you are willing to articulate political issues in a way that plays to a normal audience, the more success you are likely to have" (44). This tendency of wealth and power to accrue on the stigmaphobe side of Goffman's equation helps to explain why mainstreaming took on such force in the 1990s and resulted in an unmistakable power shift. The gay and lesbian movement, Warner concludes, has become "dominated by a small group of national organizations" and "an equally small group of media celebrities" who are "connected to a network of big-money politics that revolves around publicity consultants and campaign professionals and litigators" (67). These "new conditions of movement politics," he concludes, "have vastly heightened the tensions that have simmered in the movement since the Mattachine Society, increasing the tendency to present the movement in terms oriented to the dominant culture" (67).

In *The Twilight of Equality*, Duggan (2003) connects the structural shift in movement politics that Warner diagnoses to the politics and rhetorical strategies of the post-Reagan neoliberal world order that has vastly exacerbated the disparities between those at opposite ends of the world's economic food chain. Duggan terms the "new neoliberal sexual politics" of the 1990s *the new homonormativity ... a politics that does not contest dominant heteronormative assumptions and institutions, but*

upholds, and sustains them, while promising the possibility of a demo-
bilized gay constituency and a privatized, depoliticized gay culture an-
chored in domesticity and consumption" (50). To seek equality in this
context is to attempt to accommodate oneself to the mainstream imagined by the discourse of neoliberalism, which consists of little more
than "access to the institutions of domestic privacy, the 'free' market,
and patriotism" (50–1).

This book is aligned politically with the queer critique of mainstreaming advanced by Vaid, Warner, Duggan, and others, but my analysis does not uphold a view of GLAAD as nothing more than a lapdog to
the media industries or a slave to the legitimationist strategies of gay conservatives. As such, it challenges not only homonormativity as practised
by GLAAD but also the overdetermined theoretical abstractions of queer
radicals. As sociologist Steven Seidman (2002, 6) argues in *Beyond the
Closet*: "If champions of mainstreaming accept too quickly the virtues of
assimilating into America as it is, some critics on the left too easily sur-
render to a romanticism that imagines America as fundamentally repres-
sive and gays as potential revolutionaries." A critical understanding
of the politics of mainstreaming requires avoiding the replication of a
false dichotomy between assimilation and liberation and using theoretical frameworks that can account for the dialectical push and pull between
the opposing tendencies and power relations that historically propelled
– and continue to propel – the movement. Mainstreaming may be the
dominant strategy of the large organizations of the gay and lesbian movement since the 1990s, but crucial debates rage underneath the surface,
including within these same organizations. Mainstreaming may be largely
illusory and fail to deliver its promised fantasy of full integration (Vaid
1995), but it has a social force, including that of occasionally producing
resistance to its own terms. Mainstreaming may be inauthentic (Warner
1999) and may debase left-progressive ideals (Duggan 2003; Warner
1999), but it does not merely reproduce the dominant power structure;
it also shifts it in ways that need to be better understood. As sociologists
Amy Hequembourg and Jorge Arditi (1999, 668, 675) argue, the emphasis on sameness in an assimilationist strategy like mainstreaming has the
potential to "subvert the very civic order it allegedly embraces" by introducing "ambiguity" into "the very notion of the same."

Critics of mainstreaming have, for admittedly polemical reasons, underestimated the extent to which residual and emergent ideological formations that run counter to (or alongside) mainstreaming persist within the movement. If we are to build a more progressive LGBT movement on the basis of what exists, as we must, the moment is ripe to develop our understanding of how we got here and what queer possibilities might lay ahead. As I encountered it, GLAAD's media activism formed a contested field in which variously powerful social actors – some of whom, to varying degrees, opposed mainstreaming – competed for economic, cultural, and social resources. Media activism as it existed in 2000–01 did not seamlessly reproduce the cultural and economic logics of mainstreaming. It was a field in which social actors struggled on a daily basis and in a variety of institutional settings to reconcile the conflicting demands of personal, organizational, and movement politics; economic pressures; and their desire to maintain and improve their authority and that of the organization(s) they served. The outcomes of these struggles often corresponded to those the mainstreaming critique might have predicted, but the roads that led to and branched out from them were full of cracks and fissures that also contained seeds of queer possibility. The future development of a new politics of sexual representation beyond mainstreaming necessitates living accounts of the actual practice of gay and lesbian politics and representation, cracks and all.

## Defamation, Representation, and Cultural Production

Media activists and scholars in LGBTQ media studies approach questions of representation from vastly different angles. Whereas activists tend to adopt what they see as pragmatic, common-sense definitions of positive versus negative images, scholars influenced by post-structuralist intellectual traditions emphasize the complex, subjective, indeterminate, and polysemic nature of images understood as elements in a broader politics of representation. GLAAD's approach to representation was initially developed on the basis of an expansion of the legal concept of defamation that encompassed an extra-legal "cultural advocacy" dimension oriented to fighting defamation by other means. Although this approach has rallied many gays and lesbians who feel angered or misrepresented by media, it has also tended to reproduce value-laden assumptions about the social consequences of ostensibly positive versus negative images. The scholarly "politics of representation" approach, in contrast, challenges us to adopt more complex perspectives on the power of images to shape social attitudes than a positive images framework can sustain.

In strictly legal terms, the concept of defamation refers to false and derogatory public statements, made orally or in writing, which can be shown to have harmed an individual's reputation (Wilson 2006, 1363). Because defamation law has evolved to protect individual reputations, and the First Amendment to the US Constitution protects freedom of speech, there are few legal avenues in the United States to combat hate speech or defamation directed at groups rather than individuals, leaving organizations like GLAAD and the Jewish Anti-Defamation League, after which GLAAD was initially modelled, to fight defamation by non-legal means.

In a 1992 article published in a law journal, Craig Davidson, GLAAD's first executive director, and his partner, Michael Valentini (both lawyers), propose that GLAAD's anti-defamation work could be understood as a form of cultural advocacy, which they define as "a group of activities including media reform ... that has the common goal of full integration of the lesbian and gay community into 'mainstream' society (i.e. non-gay and non-lesbian) through strategies that generally do not involve the legal or legislative process" (Davidson and Valentini 1992, 103). On the basis of this cultural definition of GLAAD's mission, objectives, and strategies, they define defamation as encompassing "five basic categories": "(1) vicious slander; (2) reliance on stereotypes; (3) casual prejudice; (4) deference to the prejudice of others; and (5) invisibility" (111).

Using the definitions in Davidson and Valentini (1992), the GLAAD employee handbook that was in use in 2000–01 defined the first type of defamation, vicious slander, as "raw prejudice against the lesbian, gay, bisexual and transgender community," and gave as an example the claim that homosexuals "recruit children" in lieu of reproducing. The next category, negative stereotypes, encompassed everything from "making lesbian/gay characters psychotic, homicidal, suicidal, pedophilic, or sin-ful," to representing "only the most flamboyant … giving the impression that all lesbians and/or gay men are into leather or drag," to depicting LGBT "relationships as unstable." Casual prejudice referred to the "sometimes unconsciously damaging" impromptu remarks of "celebrities and opinion makers" who use terms like "avowed homosexual" or include "homosexuality in a laundry list of social ills." Deference to homophobia encompassed allowing homophobia to go unchallenged, perhaps out of an "ill-considered concern for a 'balance' of views." Finally, invisibility was the "failure to cover stories that vitally affect" the LGBT community, the "absence of positive … characters in film or on television," erasing the historical "contributions of lesbians and gay men" throughout history, and the "absence of [LGBT] parenting in the media."

What is striking about these efforts to define defamation is the presumption, especially evident in the categories of negative stereotypes and invisibility, that it is possible to clearly distinguish between positive and negative representations and that the effects of representations, thus categorized, can be anticipated with certainty. As Davidson and Valentini (1992, 107) see it: "Common sense supports the notion that public attitudes … can be changed for the better by a long-term strategy which discourages negative portrayals and promotes fair, accurate and positive portrayals of lesbians and gays in the media." But can common sense be relied upon to determine which portrayals count as negative and which should be celebrated as fair, accurate, and positive? In 1992, for example, GLAAD famously protested the film *Basic Instinct* for its portrayal of lesbian and bisexual women as ice-pick-wielding man-killers, a representation that many lesbian and bisexual women found campy, enjoyable, and empowering, even as others worried about how such negative images might impact public perception.[8]

The key point is that, for Davidson and many of GLAAD's early leaders, being against defamation meant being for images of gays and lesbians that corresponded to what the presumably heterosexual mainstream would most readily embrace and find least objectionable. How gays and lesbians themselves might feel about these representations was largely beside the point. This approach to fighting defamation was, by Davidson and Valentini's own account, influenced by an essay, "Waging Peace," published in the December 1984 issue of the New York-based gay and lesbian magazine *Christopher Street*. In it, Harvard-trained psychologists Marshall K. Kirk and Hunter Madsen (the latter writing under the pseudonym "Erastes Pill") argue that the future success of the gay and lesbian movement depended on employing sophisticated public relations and advertising techniques to "soften the social attitudes of the mainstream" and remedy against the public perception of gays as "alien, loathsome, and contrary" (1984, 34, 36). To achieve these objectives, they argue that the movement needed to foreground respectable community members, downplay sexual imagery, cast gays and lesbians as victims in need of protection, embrace "accepted standards of law and justice," and make strategic use of celebrity endorsements. The centrepiece of their strategy was a proposed publicity campaign designed to get straight audiences to identify with gays and lesbians. "To this end," Kirk and Madsen (1984, 38) write, "the persons featured in the public campaign should be decent and upright, appealing and admirable by straight standards, completely unexceptionable in appearance: in a word, they should be indistinguishable from the straights we would like to reach." In their 1989 book, *After the Ball*, Kirk and Madsen express the same idea in more vehement terms, making explicit what they had earlier only implied: "Fringe" gay and lesbian groups, they write, "ought to have the tact to withdraw voluntarily from public appearance" because they "fatally compromise the rest of us ... especially when the rest of us are working our butts off to convince straights that, in all respects other than what we like to do in bed, we're exactly like folks" (Kirk and Madsen 1989, 146–7).

Davidson and Valentini were careful to distance GLAAD from the most controversial aspects of Kirk and Madsen's public relations strategy for the movement, but the focus on reaching mainstream audiences with positive images remained. On the one hand, Davidson and Valentini (1992, 128) state that "GLAAD rejects" Kirk and Madsen's argument that "fringe groups" should make themselves invisible, adding that "lesbian and gay diversity is a positive attribute in and of itself and that liberation only for the conventional is not liberation at all." On the other hand, they stress that "depictions of gays and lesbians have historically been heavily weighted against lesbians and gays, so merely showing accurate images would hardly counter or balance the years of defamation that have helped perpetuate the stigmatization of lesbians and gays" (127). "At this point in time," they insist, "accuracy about our community requires a dramatically different balance between positive and negative images than now exists ... so GLAAD should (and does) focus on promoting the positive" (127).

The aim of GLAAD's strategy was not to render anyone invisible, Davidson and Valentini insist, but to "discourage media obsession with the most unconventional parts of our community ... while ignoring the conventional parts" (128). In effect, they outline a strategy in the spirit of Kirk and Madsen's more radical plan for winning over the mainstream, but allow for the possibility that some images of unconventional gays and lesbians might be acceptable as long as they were balanced with images of more conventional community members (127). This subtle shift in perspective also reflects the outcome of early debates within GLAAD about whether to advocate for "fair, accurate and *positive*" images, or "fair, accurate and *inclusive*" ones (the latter formulation won out and was still in place in 2000–01). Even so, it was clear that the scales of fairness and accuracy in the inclusive formulation of GLAAD's mission statement tipped in favour of representations that would not offend white, middle-class, conventionally gendered, mainstream norms of respectable behaviour.

In contrast to mainstreaming activists, scholars in communication, media studies, and cultural studies who write about the politics of representation tend to reject a binary positive/negative images framework, even as they share the view that, as communications scholar Larry Gross (1994, 143) notes, "representation in the mediated 'reality' of our mass culture is in itself power." Media sociologist Suzanna Walters (2001, 28) further suggests that the problems media representation poses are especially salient for gays and lesbians who "can hide, be overlooked, be mistaken for heterosexual." "Thus," she argues, "issues of visibility and 'coming out' are centrally and inextricably linked to the process of acquiring civil rights, in a way I think quite different from other minority groups for whom *mis*representation has often been a more driving concern than simple *re*presentation." Where scholars diverge from mainstreaming activists is in recognizing the extent to which so-called positive images are not in and of themselves sufficient to bring about progressive social change. Visibility, whether positive or negative, guarantees nothing and signifies little until we ask who is made visible, by whom, for whom, and under what conditions.

As literary scholar Eric O. Clarke (1999, 86) argues in an article about the "limits of inclusion," it is erroneous to think of the public sphere as truly public when access to it is "mediated through value relations." He argues that the institutions responsible for the new visibility of gays and lesbians present "heroically bland" and "monochromatic" images as authentic, and in so doing conceal "how this inclusion is defined and on what terms it is granted" (84). Because access to the public sphere requires "sanitized representations" that exclude all that exceeds middle-class, heterosexual standards of propriety, it also requires "fundamental transformations in a group's self-identified interests" (86). Clarke's argument helps to explain Gross's (1994, 143) contention that "when groups or perspectives do attain visibility, the manner of that representation will itself reflect the biases and interests of those elites who define the public agenda." In sum, although there are indisputably important stakes for gays and lesbians in representation, the relationship between visibility and political enfranchisement is complicated, not least because disenfranchised groups do not control how images that depict them are produced and circulated.

Further complicating matters is that, as with *Basic Instinct*, representations can be meaningful in multiple ways. As film scholar Richard Dyer (1993, 2), writes: "People do not necessarily read negative images of themselves as negative." It follows that positive images will not always be read as positive; a classic example is the conservative deployment of the positive image of the affluent gay man to discredit the need for employment protections and civil rights. A more complicated perspective on representation, therefore, recognizes the extent to which meanings are enabled and constrained by the available cultural codes and conventions. To take this perspective is to recognize that representations may have effects (such as breeding prejudice and violence, or promoting tolerance and respect), but that these effects are highly variable, often unpredictable, context dependent, and difficult to measure.

The scholarly recognition of the complexity of how meanings are made, circulated, and interpreted exists in a difficult tension with activists' pragmatic need to draw political lines in the sand. As independent scholar

Jeffrey Escoffier (1995, 22–3) explains, activists are concerned with producing knowledge to create solidarity, whereas academics are concerned
with producing knowledge their peers will recognize as intellectually legitimate. This tension is evident in the work of one of GLAAD's founders,
film scholar and activist Vito Russo. Russo's (1987) pioneering study of
Hollywood cinema, *The Celluloid Closet*, documents the history of Hollywood's depiction of gays and lesbians as psychopathic, suicidal, self-
loathing, and/or as objects of contempt or ridicule. According to queer
film scholar Ellis Hanson (1999, 7), the value of typological studies like
Russo's (among which also stands Parker Tyler's 1972 *Screening the
Sexes*) was to elicit "a mood of political resistance to mainstream cine-
matic representations that are thought to reinforce homophobia" by appealing to "the rage of the community that is offended by what it sees as
an insult." However, Hanson points out, the only question asked by such
criticism, "does it offend me?" is entirely unconcerned with aesthetics
and the complexities of cinema viewership, pleasure, and desire (8). Related calls for more "realistic" images of gays and lesbians raise further
questions: "What is the truth of homosexuality? Whose experience is
genuine and whose is merely a stereotype? Why valorize verisimilitude
over fantasy in works of art? ... Does the reality of gay people's lives necessarily make for good cinema?" (8). Hanson concludes that those who
call for truthful representations of gay and lesbian people are not really
interested in truth or in more complex, psychologically deep, or artisti-
cally rich depictions, but in affirmation by the dominant society, which
he calls a "disguised plea for idealization and fantasy" (11).

According to Berlant and Warner (1998), such affirmation can only
come from representations of gays and lesbians that conform to narrow
cultural norms regulating intimate relationships, coupling, kinship, and
community. US culture, they write, has come to associate citizenship
with the private realm of intimacy, imagined as "the only (fantasy) zone
in which a future might be thought and willed, the only (imaginary)
place where good citizens might be produced away from the confusing
and unsettling distractions and contradictions of capitalism and politics" (553). The problem for queers is that the private realm of intimacy
– and the very definitions of what constitute legitimate intimate relationships – is overdetermined by naturalized heterocentric discourses.
To attain legitimacy, therefore, is to conform to heterosexual norms that

permeate "almost every aspect of the forms and arrangements of social life" (554).

In assessing the limitations of visibility politics as practised by GLAAD, we are confronted with a paradox. Is there any way around the fact that advocating for positive or inclusive images produces new kinds of exclusions and perpetuates the very structures of power that these depictions were meant to redress? One proposed solution has been for queer cultural producers located in independent media culture to call for positive images of a different, more diverse kind. But as Hanson writes about the edited collection *Queer Looks*, which features writing by some of the most influential queer artists and filmmakers of the 1990s, "instead of positive images of lesbians and gay men as bourgeois ladies and gentlemen, many of these writers call for positive images of lesbians and gay men as queer subjects with impeccable multicultural credentials" (10). For Hanson, this queer approach, as invaluable and important as it may be for opening up new modalities of representation, can be just as prescriptive and moralistic as the mainstreaming strategy it opposes.

If ostensibly positive images are too constraining and more inclusive images made by LGBT people may produce new exclusions, what avenues might exist for a transformational politics of representation? This type of dilemma is well summed-up by Hall (1996, 444), who writes about black filmic representation in Britain that "films are not necessarily good because black people make them" or "by virtue of the fact that they deal with the black experience." Hall's approach to the politics of representation in "New Ethnicities" is to recognize that differences of gender, race, class, and sexuality, among others, exist within all social groups and that to speak of blacks, or members of any other marginalized group, as though they all shared the same interests is to do "epistemic violence" (quoting Spivak) to the differences between group members (Hall 1996, 444). To recognize such differences is to assert the need for new critical approaches that point us in the direction of "the politics of the end of the essential ... subject," which is characterized by "a continuously contingent, unguaranteed, political argument and debate: a critical politics, a politics of criticism" (444–5). Instead of opposing negative representations with ostensibly positive ones, thereby substituting one fictional unity for another, an alternative politics of representation, Hall argues, would "work with and through difference" to continuously expand the range of languages that are available to describe the varied experiences of marginalized groups within a given social formation (444). My hope is that this book will contribute to the development of such a politics of representation by documenting the lived experiences of activists caught in the tension between the pragmatic need to draw clear distinctions between positive and negative images and the scholarly interest in advocating for a "politics of criticism" that renders such distinctions permanently unclear.

If a new politics of representation can be devised, it must begin with a detailed understanding of the actual conditions in which activists operate. With this focus on praxis in mind, I have modelled this study after the growing body of work known as the ethnography of cultural production, which explores the practices, subjectivities, and institutional contexts of cultural producers. Collectively, ethnographic studies of cultural production – by Espinosa (1982), D'Acci (1994), Dornfeld (1998), Radway (1997), Gamson (1998), Grindstaff (2002), Henderson (1995, 1999, 2013), Hesmondhalgh and Baker (2011), Banks (2009), and Mayer (2011), among others – emphasize the collective nature of all cultural production, its embeddedness in economic and political processes, the importance of the social organization of work and professional routines, the key influence of cultural producers' constructions of audiences, and the extent to which they are constantly called upon to resolve conflicting institutional demands and personal ambivalences about the cultural texts they produce. Media activists, I found, work under conditions and constraints that resemble those found in other fields of cultural production, and compete with other cultural producers for many of the same symbolic and economic resources.

Media activism as practised by GLAAD in 2000–01 had a great deal in common with occupations that have been studied under the rubric of "cultural intermediaries," a concept first proposed by Bourdieu to encompass the range of knowledge-based and service-oriented occupations in contemporary capitalism that (often invisibly) mediate between production and consumption via "the production and transformation of meanings" (Edwards and Hodges 2011, 5). As Maguire and Matthews (2014, 2) explain, cultural intermediaries mediate "how goods (or services, practices, people) are perceived and engaged with by others," are further "defined by their claims to professional expertise in taste and value within specific cultural fields," and "are differentiated by their locations within commodity chains (vis-à-vis the actors and stages of cultural production they negotiate with and between, and the goods that they mediate." From this perspective, GLAAD can be productively understood as mediating between media and social movement fields by influencing how images of gays and lesbians were produced by media companies and received by audiences. As the most powerful cultural advocacy organization of the movement, GLAAD possessed a unique ability to shape the destinies of gay and lesbian representations in the media marketplace.

Others who have written about the politics of sexual representation have focused on the textual or ideological properties of the representations themselves, on how audiences make sense of them, or on the macroeconomic conditions that give rise to (or limit) them. This book goes behind the scenes to examine GLAAD's important role in shaping how gay and lesbian people were represented and its relationships to the other agents who had personal, institutional, economic, and/or political stakes in that representation of sexual minorities. These agents included other LGBT movement activists, entertainment industry producers, mainstream journalists, LGBT journalists, other national movement organizations, celebrities, politicians, wealthy donors to gay and lesbian organizations, media executives, marketing professionals, media scholars, corporate donors, GLAAD's membership, the LGBT community writ large, LGBT artists and independent media producers, and anti-gay conservative groups, among others. Given the complexity of this field of cultural production and its multiplicity of actors, what room for manoeuvre, if any, might exist for GLAAD to engage in a politics of representation more attuned to the concerns raised by scholars in communication, media studies, and cultural studies? I return to this question in the conclusion.

## Community, Visibility, and Diversity

When I began this study, very little scholarly work about LGBT media activism in general, or GLAAD in particular, had been published, and few of the existing ethnographic or otherwise empirically based studies explored the broader intersections among the contemporary LGBT movement, culture, media, and politics. Scholarly work about GLAAD remains scarce, but a good number of studies make use of sociological and anthropological methods to provide a more grounded assessment of the current state of the LGBT movement. Taken as a whole, these empirical studies, which explore related themes of community, visibility, and diversity, add a great deal of nuance to earlier, more theoretically driven (and polemical) critiques of LGBT movement mainstreaming.

The pioneering study of media activism is sociologist Kathryn Montgomery's (1989) *Target: Prime Time*, which documents how activists in the 1970s and 1980s pressured television networks to change how they represented various minorities and social issues. Although she does not exclusively focus on gay and lesbian media activism, Montgomery suggests that the efforts of gay and lesbian organizations in the 1970s were particularly successful and became the model for other minority groups to follow. I discuss this history at the beginning of chapter 1, and also draw on other historical accounts of gay and lesbian media activism and GLAAD from Clendinen and Nagourney (1999), Gross (2001), Capsuto (2000), and others.

A few people who have worked for GLAAD have published article-length studies about their experiences and perspectives. Davidson and Valentini (1992), discussed above, portray GLAAD's early history and founding philosophy. A number of GLAAD staffers also describe their work on specific projects in contributions to an edited collection, which explores how media advocacy groups attempt to influence communication policy (Suman and Rossman 2000). Kristen Schilt (2004), who was a doctoral student in sociology and an intern at GLAAD's Los Angeles office during my fieldwork, published an ethnographic account of her experiences. Finally, media studies scholar Van Cagle (2007, 157), GLAAD's former director of research and analysis, published an article reflecting on the tensions he encountered while launching GLAAD's short-lived Center for the Study of Media and Society, which was to become a think tank devoted to "practical research" about LGBTQ media issues.

In this study of GLAAD, I gather together the pieces of its history that have been published elsewhere and expand the scope of the few studies that have usefully analyzed specific aspects of its programmatic work. In focusing on understanding GLAAD's role in the mainstreaming of the LGBT movement, I also add to a number of recently published books that have begun the difficult and important work of interrogating the consequences of how movement organizations at the local, regional, and national levels have adapted to the realities of a neoliberal world (although not all of the books invoke the framework of neoliberalism to make sense of the dynamics they describe, the analysis of contemporary capitalism is never very far in the background). Among the notable characteristics of these studies, which this book also shares, is a willingness to take on internal debates over strategies and tactics; reflect on where mainstreaming strategies have led the LGBT movement; question the meaning and value of celebrated concepts like community, visibility, and diversity; and propose new conceptual frameworks to help chart alternatives to the status quo.

Miranda Joseph's (2002) *Against the Romance of Community* is an ethnographic study of queer arts organizations in San Francisco that aims to contest queer activists' tendency to view community as an unquestioned good and small, non-profit organizations as opposed to, outside of, or complementary to (but separate from) capitalism. Joseph posits that the way in which capitalism positions subjects as alienated workers and individualized consumers leaves unfulfilled persistent human desires to engage in collective action and form communities on the basis of shared identities. Insofar as communities and non-profit organizations help to fill this "subjectivity gap at the heart of the capitalist project" (90–1), she argues, they "function as a hegemonic apparatus, articulating the desire for community with a desire for capitalism" (73). In other words, Joseph contends, non-profits help to produce and gather into communities the subjects to whom capitalism is addressed.

That markets, movements, and identities constitute one another is an insight shared by scholars Alexandra Chasin, Arlene Dávila, and Katherine Sender, who explore different facets of the interactions among markets, marketing professionals, movement organizations, consumers, and brands. In her 2002 book *Selling Out*, Chasin examines the extent to which gay and lesbian movement organizations and the gay and lesbian market have become interdependent since the 1990s, leading to the "constitution and consolidation" of gay and lesbian identities "in the marketplace," and to reshaping the priorities of the LGBT movement in ways she considers "inimical to progressive political change" (24). Similarly, Dávila (2001, 2), in her study of Hispanic marketing, explores how "commercial representations may shape people's cultural identities as well as affect notions of belonging and cultural citizenship in public life." As individuals come to think of themselves primarily as consumers and groups become constituted as markets, "matters of equality, social rights, and wellbeing" (xxiii) tend to fade from view, only to be replaced by the notion that the needs of distinct populations are "best met by the market and by more carefully targeted offers" (xxxiv).

Chasin argues that the power of marketing is such that consumption has become the primary means by which LGBT people construct identities and feel connected to the movement, a situation that tends to reinforce class divisions by heightening the power and influence of the wealthiest community members. As market dynamics increasingly take hold of the movement, they influence its priorities by channelling money away from controversial issues, favouring larger organizations, creating a need for leaders from corporate backgrounds, shifting accountability toward corporate funders, and homogenizing the differences between gay and lesbian people via marketing practices that assume "group unity on the basis of sexuality" (Chasin 2000, 44). "Identity-based movement and market activity," Chasin concludes, "ultimately promote sameness, leaving difference vulnerable to appropriation and leaving it in place as grounds for inequality" (244).

Sender (2005, 236) adds nuance to the view that gay and lesbian marketing produces only sameness by pointing out that "gay marketing is troubling not because it is assimilationist but because it promotes particular kinds of distinction," constructing gayness as different from the mainstream "within dominant conventions of an essentialized sexuality marked by privilege and good taste." Still, not unlike Chasin, she argues that gay consumers are overwhelmingly constructed as affluent, tasteful, and trendsetting, not to mention male and white, which tends to reinforce existing exclusions and inequalities even as it opens the door to new kinds of positively valued, but highly limited and limiting, mainstream visibility and inclusion.

In *Out in the Country*, her ethnographic study of LGBT-identified youth in rural US settings, Mary L. Gray (2009) takes a closer look at some of the unintended consequences of the visibility politics pursued by the large national organizations of the LGBT movement. She suggests that mainstream visibility strategies are complicit in a binary logic whereby visibility requires an invisible other. "A politics of visibility," she writes, "needs the rural (or some *otherness*, some *place*) languishing in its shadow to sustain its status as an unquestionable achievement" (9). She argues that the organizational models of the large national movement organizations are "tailor-made for and from the population densities; capital; and systems of gender, sexual, class, and racial privilege that converge in cities," a state of affairs that leaves rural youth "with a shortfall of LGBT-identifying people and dollars" (30). And to the extent that the large organizations of the LGBT movement recognize the need to welcome others, they must grapple with how to do so "without excluding those with the purchase power to keep these organizations going" (175), a situation that tends to leave LGBT youth in rural settings ignored or underserved.

In two recent ethnographic studies, anthropologist David Valentine (2007) and sociologist Jane Ward (2008) suggest that, to the extent the organizations of the LGBT movement have found ways to welcome others, they have tended to do so on the basis of a corporate, neoliberal model of diversity. Valentine examines the emergence in the 1990s of the concept "transgender" as a new category from which to conduct political action. He provides evidence that – in the midst of movement mainstreaming – transgender issues and identities were incorporated into a reconfigured LGBT movement, but notes that this was accomplished "through the mode of inclusion, rooted in a model of diversity," which he argues did little to disrupt the assumptions that structure participation in movement organizations (201). The diversity model, he argues, operates by augmenting "the central concerns of the [dominant] group" rather than by challenging "the boundaries of groups themselves" (200).

The relationship between corporate diversity discourses and queer politics, as practised by a number of Los Angeles-based LGBT organizations, is the central theme of Ward's (2008) *Respectably Queer*. Ward finds that even though many LGBT organizations have become more diverse in terms of race and gender since the 1990s, they have done so largely to "garner funding and legitimacy, or to get a competitive edge in an increasingly diversity-interested, neoliberal world" (132). In such a climate, she argues, diversity initiatives "can function to stifle forms of difference that are not easily professionalized, funded, or used for other institutional or financial gains," and lead movement organizations to value "professionalism, attention to public image/respectability, and the pursuit of financial prosperity" above all else (132–3). Despite the dominance of what she terms "diversity culture," Ward also finds that instrumental views of diversity were often contested from within organizations and sometimes gave way to the assertion of "defiant diversities" characterized by a refusal to conform to the codes that govern respectable mainstream diversity politics (137).

Scholarly work that analyzes the limitations of LGBT movement mainstreaming in a neoliberal age also provides an important empirical basis from which to imagine alternatives – as this book will do. As the gains of mainstreaming come to fruition across the United States (marriage equality, the repeal of the Defense of Marriage Act and Don't Ask, Don't Tell, heightened visibility, etc.), so have the signs of queer opposition to mainstreaming multiplied. Such an environment in movement politics suggests that the time is ripe for scholars of LGBT culture and politics to reflect on how we got here and engage in – and think with – the debates that are happening on the ground. The existence of such debates should not be seen as a threat to movement effectiveness, as sociologist Amin Ghaziani (2008) argues in his study of the controversies surrounding the LGBT movement's four marches on Washington. We must, he writes, get past the notion that infighting within movements indicates "social disorganization" and move toward the view that it "can be generative by allowing activists to muse on ... the *state of the movement*" (2008, 5). *Making Out in the Mainstream*, like the other studies discussed in this section, interrogates the LGBT movement's fraught relationships to neoliberal capitalism in light of the latter's demonstrated effectiveness in colonizing the common sense of our era (Hall 2011, 728) and appropriating of some of the central organizing principles of traditional LGBT movement politics: community, visibility, and diversity.

## The Road Map

The efforts of GLAAD's leaders to maintain GLAAD's dominant position in LGBT media activism form the arc of this book as I tell the story of how they built an organization oriented to the inclusion of gays and lesbians, had reason to think for a time that they had reached the mainstream, and were awakened from their dream by would-be usurpers who forced them to change their ways. Even though the tale may not end happily for all, it demonstrates the ongoing vitality of a movement that cannot remain content with mainstreaming's unevenly distributed rewards.

In chapter 1, I provide a historical narrative of GLAAD's evolution from a local grassroots effort begun by New York-based activists responding to hostile media coverage about AIDS, to a chapter-based structure with national coordination, to an increasingly centralized national organization headed up by former corporate executives oriented to the mainstreaming of the LGBT movement. I argue that this trajectory toward ever-greater institutionalization and incorporation was not natural, but evolved out of earlier media activism and debates in the gay and lesbian movement. GLAAD's rise as a national organization, I show, was marked by power struggles over the scope and definition of its central mission and disagreements over strategies and tactics. What emerges from my account is a gradual narrowing of the field of political possibilities, as the organization's more radical elements were pushed aside over time in favour of a vision oriented to mainstream visibility; institutional growth; insider tactics; avoiding controversial stances; and building relationships with powerful corporate executives, large donors, and corporate funders.

In chapter 2, the first of three chapters to draw on my ethnographic fieldwork, I analyze how GLAAD's leaders, many of whom had come from the corporate world, saw themselves as the vanguard of a new kind of media activism oriented to mainstream inclusion and access to decision-makers. I focus on the conditions that allowed them to think they were uniquely suited to engage with media professionals and mainstream culture without confrontation. High-profile activities like the Media Awards, which provided GLAAD with the bulk of its funding, and the redesign of GLAAD's visual identity, signalled the organization's adoption of a model of diversity aligned with the marketing needs of its corporate donors.

In chapter 3, I give an account of the public campaign to oppose the homophobic rhetoric of Dr Laura Schlessinger, a radio talk show host whose afternoon television show, produced by Paramount Television during the 2000–01 season, was successfully derailed by GLAAD and other gay and lesbian media activists who organized under the banner Stop-DrLaura.com. My analysis of the campaign highlights the contrast between GLAAD's initially conciliatory approach to the campaign versus StopDrLaura.com's confrontational tactics, which included holding Internet-coordinated street protests and pressuring advertisers and local affiliates. Rather than view the campaign too simplistically as the triumph of outsiders over insiders, as I argue the gay and lesbian press tended to do, I frame its success as a contest over cultural authority in the field of gay and lesbian media activism that exposed some of the strategic limits of mainstreaming and ultimately forced GLAAD to adopt the more aggressive strategies and tactics of its more confrontational counterpart.

In chapter 4, I progress from chapter 3 in analyzing how GLAAD's leaders grappled with the difficulties of reconciling mainstreaming strategies with their obligation to represent the wishes and interests of diverse LGBT constituencies. I focus on two especially difficult cases, Showtime's *Queer as Folk* and Eminem's *The Marshall Mathers LP*, which pitted GLAAD against media companies with which it had enjoyed especially close relationships. In contrast to StopDrLaura.com, disagreements over mainstreaming strategies and tactics in these cases emerged not from the outside, but from within GLAAD itself. These internal contestations amounted to a robust challenge to the failures of sexual and racial representation inherent in GLAAD's approach to mainstreaming, even as the outcomes in both cases reinforced the overriding importance for GLAAD of maintaining good relationships with media companies.

Finally, in the conclusion, I come to a summative assessment of what my fieldwork uncovered about the value and limitations of GLAAD's mainstreaming approach to fighting defamation. I suggest that the future development of a new, more inclusive, responsive, and effective politics of representation must take account of the structuring conditions of media activism. The key to developing such a cultural politics might be for activists to better recognize the limits of neoliberalism's ambivalent embrace of (some) LGBT people. Activists, I suggest, might exercise their limited autonomy differently to embrace neoliberalism more ambivalently by working both with and against what current conditions make available to them.

## CHAPTER I

# Rags to Riches: GLAAD's Rise to the National Stage

I open this chapter with a brief history of gay and lesbian media activism before GLAAD, and then document how GLAAD grew from a New York-based grassroots organization to the preeminent cultural advocacy organization of the US LGBT movement. My narrative of the development of media activism in the movement is necessarily partial, and I shape it to highlight a number of themes that recur in subsequent chapters: debates over the movement's strategic and philosophical orientations; questions about the value of different representational strategies; the choice between confrontation or engagement with dominant institutions; centralized top-down leadership versus local autonomy; self-promotion and visibility versus service to the community; movement-based versus corporate leadership; the diversity of staff and leadership; and how best to strike the balance between autonomous programmatic priorities and donors' interests. Against a tendency in some institutional discourses to narrate the history of movement organizations as a natural evolution toward institutionalization and mainstreaming, my account of GLAAD's development stresses that these outcomes were the result of struggles engaged in by unevenly positioned actors. In sum, I argue, GLAAD's orientation to mainstreaming is the outcome of struggles fought and won on the basis of prior battles fought and won by social agents who possessed the necessary capital to succeed in a corporate-dominated media environment.

## Media Activism before GLAAD

Homosexuals have long been preoccupied with visibility and its consequences. As George Chauncey (1994, 105) notes in his landmark study
of the social history of gay men in New York City, many middle-class
men of the early twentieth century blamed mainstream society's anti-
gay hostility on the "fairies" who refused to "abide by straight middle-
class conventions of decorum in their dress and style." The conflict
between more and less conventional members of the homosexual world
also figures prominently in historian John D'Emilio's (2012) account of
the 1951 founding of the Mattachine Society, the first organization in
the United States to advocate for the rights of homosexuals. Calling itself a "homophile" organization, the Mattachine Society was begun by
Communist Party members and other leftists who saw a need to develop
a homosexual group consciousness by encouraging them to view themselves as an oppressed minority, free themselves of internalized self-
hatred, and form a positive view of their subculture against the prevailing construction of homosexuality as sin, sickness, and crime (58).

As McCarthy-era anti-communism rose to a fever pitch, the ambi-
tious program laid out by the Mattachine founders was soon replaced
by a more moderate agenda. The new leaders of the Mattachine Society
repudiated its founders and moved aggressively to rid themselves of the
stigma of communist affiliation (or the appearance thereof). The men
who took over in 1953 sought to overcome society's prejudices through
"education, policy reform, and help for individual homosexuals" (Marotta
1981, 11). They affirmed the view that homosexuals were no different
from heterosexuals and that the best strategy for gaining acceptance was
to conform to the norms of straight society.

A more militant branch of the homophile movement, led by Franklin
Kameny, emerged in Washington, DC, in the early 1960s. Kameny had
been employed by the US government but was fired as the result of an
FBI anti-gay witch-hunt. He understood from his observations of the
civil rights movement that visible protest strategies like picket lines
would eventually attract media attention and help publicize the homosexual plight. Indeed, as the decade progressed, the growing visibility
and assertiveness of homosexuals led to groundbreaking articles in such
publications as *Life* and *Time*. Media historian Edward Alwood (1996,

57) notes that although much of this coverage was dismissive or even hostile, each new major article was greeted with some excitement in the fledgling gay and lesbian press. The prejudicial language of the period, however, also gave rise to criticism from gay and lesbian journalists and editors with knowledge of journalistic conventions (Streitmatter 1995, 70). The movement had begun to reflect on its relationship to mainstream media, and it would not be long before activists would start to demand that media alter their treatment of gays and lesbians.

The Stonewall riots of June 1969 were the catalyst of important changes in the relationship between gays and lesbians and mainstream US culture. In their wake, hundreds of thousands of people came out to friends, family, and co-workers and demanded sexual freedom. They built social institutions like bars and community centres, formed associations, joined picket lines, and organized the movement's first mass marches. Many of those who spoke the revolutionary language of the New Left joined the first large political organization to arise in the aftermath of Stonewall, the Gay Liberation Front (GLF). As John Loughery (1998, 324) writes, the GLF "saw itself not as a civil rights or protest organization but as a loose association of men and women at odds with racism, sexism, militarism, and the consumer culture as well as homophobia." And although its meetings were often raucous and even chaotic, the "GLF was capable of concrete, practical 'actions' when they were called for" (324).

In September 1969, the GLF conducted "the first gay picket line of the post-Stonewall era," which successfully lobbied a New York weekly newspaper, the *Village Voice*, to allow the use of the words "gay" and "homosexual" in its classified ads section (Clendinen 1999, 45). Larry Gross (2001, 42) states that this action was "a milestone of lesbian and gay media activism: it was a sign of the new militancy of a gay movement that was taking its demands directly to the media, making them targets of protest along with politicians, psychiatrists, and preachers." At around the same time, the *Los Angeles Times* was among the first targets of the GLF in that city (Alwood 1996, 94–5).

Writer Steven Capsuto (2000, 59–60) claims that the movement's early "revolutionary" elements had relatively little interest in the mainstream media, which it tended to dismiss as a mouthpiece of the establishment. Toby Marotta (1981, 138) offers a more nuanced appraisal, distinguishing among "reformers," "revolutionaries," and "radicals" in the GLF. GLF reformers, among them Marty Robinson and Jim Owles (who were later involved in GLAAD's early days), pioneered the tactic of "zapping," which involved infiltrating public gatherings and noisily confronting politicians in the presence of media (Marotta 1981, 137). Although GLF revolutionaries were wary of Robinson and Owles's willingness to get involved in the "system," they saw value in the potential of zaps to raise gay and lesbian political consciousness (138). Radicals, in contrast, argued that any engagement with the political machinery of the establishment "would inhibit the spread of liberated consciousness" because it necessarily involved the "pursuit of traditional political recognition and reward" (139).

The GLF soon fell apart as a result of the difficulty of maintaining a sense of cohesion within a group that combined so many different agendas and espoused "structurelessness" as an organizational ideal (Marotta 1981, 140). Along with a few other men who had been active in the GLF, Robinson and Owles founded the Gay Activists Alliance (GAA) in late 1969. Marotta (1981, 143) recounts that, wanting to clearly distinguish themselves from what they saw as the political hodgepodge of the GLF, the activists were quick to devise a focused statement of "reformist gay liberationist ideals." While the GAA abandoned the goal of dismantling oppressive structures, confronting dominant institutions remained central to its political philosophy.

The GAA quickly asserted itself with a series of high profile zaps, many of which targeted media. In perhaps the most famous such action, GAA members staged a protest in the offices of *Harper's*, which in September 1970 had printed an article by Joseph Epstein that characterized homosexuality as "anathema" and homosexuals as "cursed." Epstein wrote that, if he could, he "would wish homosexuality off the face of the earth," and that nothing any of his four sons could do would make him "sadder than if any of them were to become homosexual" (quoted in Teal 1971, 267). GAA members, more used to dealing with politicians than with media, debated their response. The more "culturally oriented" among them argued that the GAA needed to develop new tactics to deal with "institutions popularly perceived as nonpolitical" and to "make an impression not only on *Harper's* but on the whole literary establishment, and to win the support of homosexuals, liberals, and others sensitive about freedom of the press" (Marotta 1981, 182).

Peter Fisher, a graduate student in political science at Columbia University, headed the committee assigned to elaborating the GAA's response. He advocated that the GAA find ways to influence media without appearing to want to impose its views. The committee began by sending *Harper's* a letter listing its grievances and asking that the magazine print a mutually acceptable rebuttal. When *Harper's* refused, Fisher circulated a letter among fellow activists that called for stronger action: "We need tactics that will bring pressure to bear on them. We've learned how to embarrass politicians in public; we've got to learn how to embarrass TV stations, publishing houses, and the like" (Marotta 1981, 183).

On the morning of 27 October 1970, in a protest strategy inspired by similar tactics used in the women's movement, some forty GAA activists showed up at the *Harper's* offices and set up a table with coffee and donuts while another group placed leaflets on every desk in the company. According to a GAA activist interviewed in one of the earliest books about the post-Stonewall movement, "as people came in to work, we walked up to them, offered a handshake, introduced ourselves, saying, 'Good morning, I'm a homosexual. We're here to protest the Epstein article. Would you like some coffee?'" (Teal 1971, 267–8). Fisher, this activist said, "had carefully planned and explained the tone he wanted the day's action to strike: civilized, intelligent, educational, consciousness-raising, hospitable – no demands, no threats, no damage to offices or files" (269).

Media, warned in advance of the action, showed up in appreciable numbers. Three television stations covered the events, and a radio station broadcast a heated exchange between Midge Decter, an editor at *Harper's*, and Arthur Evans, the GAA's president, which demonstrated the extent to which the GAA was willing to employ confrontation in the service of its reformist objectives. The GAA would continue to make media activism an important focus of activity, which soon led to national exposure on *The Dick Cavett Show*, a well-attended protest of the *New York Daily News*, and a first-ever meeting between representatives of the gay and lesbian movement and an editor at the *New York Times*.

Those early successes prompted the GAA's changing leadership to attempt to institutionalize the organization's media activism. Ronald Gold was a former reporter for the Hollywood trade publication *Variety* who became the head of the GAA's media committee in early 1973. He and the GAA's new president, Dr Bruce Voeller, began to write letters to all three television networks asking to meet with their standards and practices departments, which function as internal censors that set and enforce policies concerning what can or cannot be said or shown on television. They also serve a public relations function by handling complaints and, as was increasingly the case by the early 1970s, meeting with advocacy organizations.

Media activism in the gay and lesbian movement to this point had often been creative and effective, but also "scattershot and uncoordinated" (Capsuto 2000, 94). Some at the GAA, Gold and Voeller chief among them, believed it was time for the movement to assert its presence on the national stage. As early as May 1973, the GAA began to take steps in this direction by running ads in national gay periodicals asking readers in all parts of the United States to send complaints about negative media coverage to its office in New York. Meanwhile, Voeller proposed to restructure the GAA by moving toward a more institutional model. The organization's more radical elements reacted to these proposals with hostility, and it soon became clear that if Voeller was going to head an organization with national ambitions, he would have to do it under different auspices (Marotta 1981, 320). Faced with the threat of censure for authorizing a demonstration that the membership had not yet voted on, Voeller quit the GAA in early October 1973 (Clendinen and Nagourney 1999, 190).

Along with Gold, reform-minded former GAA members, and others handpicked from among his circle of friends and professional acquaintances, Voeller founded the National Gay Task Force (NGTF) at the end of 1973. The NGTF was to be a national organization explicitly devoted to coordinating the entire movement from the top down (Clendinen and Nagourney 1999, 195–6). Guided by a liberal reform philosophy, the NGTF would argue that gays and lesbians were not so different from the mainstream; it would press for anti-discrimination legislation in Congress and try to convince corporations to change their anti-gay employment practices; it would try to coordinate local activist groups; and it would seek to improve the representation of gays and lesbians in mainstream media (192). Accomplishing these objectives would require the involvement of a class of people who had heretofore not been very visible or active in the movement: professionals with the skills, connections, and wealth needed to deal with mainstream institutions on their own terms.

Of particular value to the newly nationalized movement, argued Gold, were professionals like himself with public relations and media skills: "The whole gay movement is public relations," he stated in a NGTF newsletter. "For me, the 'political' things we do ... are simply [public relations] tools ... to create a climate in which everybody can come out" (quoted in Clendinen and Nagourney 1999, 192). Gold's formulation inverted how liberationists tended to think about the relationship between political action and coming out. For liberationists, coming out had been a tactic of political consciousness-raising, a necessary first step in a process of confronting and eventually dismantling oppressive social institutions. For Gold, in contrast, creating a climate in which everyone could come out was the goal of politics, a formulation that anticipated mainstreaming. Gold no longer wanted to radically transform institutions so much as open up new spaces of inclusion within them. He saw public relations and increased media visibility as the means to this end.

Gold was put in charge of the NGTF's media activist efforts, and, in accordance with his reformist outlook, sought improvements within the standards and practices framework media companies had elaborated. As Kathryn Montgomery (1989, 54) explains, television networks restructured themselves in the early 1970s in response to pressures exerted by new social movements. Standards and practices departments were created so "criticism could be channeled into a manageable form" and networks "could keep track of which groups were most active, and what their reactions had been to content." These departments were also responsible for ensuring "the programming which was distributed to affiliates across the country and in which advertisers placed their commercials was safe," i.e., not so controversial as to cause problems.

It was to the networks' advantage to recognize only one organization for each political constituency with which they had dealings. The chosen organizations were then rewarded with some measure of access and influence in exchange for helping to contain potentially controversial situations. Groups that were unable or unwilling to "adapt their strategies to fit the network system" faced losing their access and influence and "were generally replaced by more moderate organizations" (Montgomery 1989, 55). As Gross (2001, 50) explains, playing by the rules of the networks' containment strategy limited what activists could expect from television, insofar as the prevalent logic of broadcasting for a mass audience in the network era meant that producers were not "looking to please gay and lesbian people; they [were] merely trying to avoid arguing with them afterwards."

Nevertheless, the few portrayals the NGTF helped to bring about within the standards and practices framework were a welcome change from the overtly hostile and pathologizing representations of gays and lesbians scattered about the televisual landscape in the early 1970s. Gay and lesbian media activism of the kind Gold and the NGTF practised had a lot to do with these changes, but so did an evolving cultural and political climate in which dominant institutions were struggling to adapt to the upheavals of the sixties and early seventies. As activists were about to find out, that climate was about to take a dramatic turn for the worse with the anti-homosexual crusade begun by Florida citrus queen Anita Bryant in 1978. That same year, the Briggs Initiative in California nearly succeeded in making it illegal for gay men and lesbians to hold teaching jobs in public schools. On 27 November 1978, former County Supervisor Dan White burst into the San Francisco City Hall and killed both George Moscone, the mayor, and Harvey Milk, by far the most famous gay politician in the United States. The following year, the first-ever March on Washington gathered over 100,000 gays and lesbians but received minimal media coverage. With the advent of the AIDS crisis in the early 1980s, the NGTF largely abandoned its media activist efforts to focus on more pressing issues. The gay and lesbian movement would only regain its media activist voice with the founding of GLAAD in 1985.

## GLAAD Enters the Scene

Decades of relative media invisibility for gays and lesbians came to a dramatic end in the summer of 1985 when AIDS became a major news story with the revelation that actor Rock Hudson was suffering from the disease. One evening that fall, a small group of gay friends – many of them writers, activists, or academics – were gathered in the New York City apartment of writer Allen Barnett. The occasion was a party, but the mood was gloomy: AIDS was exacting a vicious toll on friends and acquaintances, and, to make matters worse, the *New York Post* had taken to publishing incendiary attacks on gay men. The *Post*, a conservative tabloid owned by media mogul Rupert Murdoch, had referred to bathhouses as "AIDS dens" and described gay men as "desperate ... without families ... without real friends" (quoted in Alwood 1996, 235). In an editorial, the *Post* had gone so far as to characterize "AIDS as fitting punishment for homosexual behavior," thus making explicit the flip side of the "innocent victim" trope that prevailed in media (Gross 2001, 105). Some in media were even calling for people with AIDS to be quarantined and/or tattooed (Gross 2001, 104; Schiavi 2011, 237). Was it not time, the men in Barnett's apartment wondered, for the gay and lesbian movement to have its own version of the Jewish Anti-Defamation League?

The organization that was to become GLAAD was founded on 30 October 1985 by a group of eight men gathered at the offices of the New York State Council for the Arts: writers Barnett and Darrell Yates Rist, film scholar Vito Russo, Latin Americanist writer and translator Gregory Kolovakos, veteran GAA activists Robinson, Owles, and Arnie Kantrowitz, as well as *New York Native* editor Barry Adkins. Within a few more meetings, they had recruited a few more people to join the new organization, among them former GAA activist Hal Offen, gay music critic Bruce Michael-Gelbert, author Jewelle Gomez, who worked with Kolovakos at the New York State Council on the Arts, and writer and editor Marcia Pally, a friend and colleague of Rist's.

The as-yet-unnamed organization called a community meeting by distributing leaflets on street corners in Greenwich Village. "AIDS is being used by both the government and the media to erode the basic rights for which we have struggled these past 15 years and more," the leaflets read. "Sensationalized accounts of gay activities, blatant scare tactics and outright misreporting of facts have produced an unnecessary panic and a new fear of gays in the minds of millions of our neighbors. Fight AIDS, not gays!" (Clendinen and Nagourney 1999, 524–5). This organizing effort was successful beyond the activists' wildest expectations: on the evening of 14 November 1985, an estimated 500 to 700 people showed up at the Metropolitan-Duane Methodist Church on the corner of Seventh Avenue and Thirteenth Street.

In the speech Russo gave to that night's gathering, he characterized the divisive bathhouse debate as a "smokescreen for what's really going on, which is that the AIDS epidemic is being used by right-wing fanatics and yellow journalists to create a witchhunt mentality" (quoted in Gross 2001, 105). Rist spoke with equal passion: "Tonight is the final notice to the bigots! ... Many of us had to live a lie too long. But in these years since Stonewall brought us out, we have learned the truth about ourselves, and it is good. We will not go back: not to closets, nor to shame, nor to fear, not to celibacy, not to letting heterosexual lies about us rule our lives ... In the name of all of our friends who have died and in the name of us who are still alive, we are putting out the warning: no more lies!" (quoted in Clendinen and Nagourney 1999, 525). Gomez, the only person of colour and one of only three women among the early organizers, also spoke and emphasized the need to "take responsibility for what is being said about us ... for our attitudes ... for our images" (Gross 2001, 105).

The meeting confirmed that many members of the New York City gay and lesbian community were ready to take action. Dozens signed up as volunteers and joined committees. One of these committees would monitor media coverage of gays and lesbians, one created a phone tree able to mobilize hundreds of people in a matter of hours, and yet another, called the Swift and Terrible Retribution Committee, would conceive and execute direct action protests in the spirit of the old GAA zaps under the direction of veteran activists Robinson and Owles. The committee chairs and founders formed a steering committee (later a board) to oversee the organization's activities. At the outset, they decided to call themselves the Gay and Lesbian Anti-Defamation League, but it was not long before the Anti-Defamation League of B'nai B'rith took notice and threatened to take legal action for copyright infringement.

Wanting to avoid a potentially costly and distracting fight, the founders settled on another name: the Gay and Lesbian Alliance Against Defamation (GLAAD).

GLAAD's first major action was held on 1 December 1985, and took direct aim at the *New York Post*. Some 500 to 700 people gathered on a cold and wet Sunday afternoon on the fringes of Lower Manhattan, where the *Post*'s offices were located. Brandishing yellow rags to symbolize what they saw as the paper's yellow journalism, they chanted slogans like "Close the *Post*, not the Baths" (Clendinen and Nagourney 1999, 526). The demonstration mobilized hundreds of New Yorkers, garnered substantial media coverage, and led to a meeting with the *Post*'s editors. Within the next year, GLAAD had also coordinated protests of the infamous Supreme Court *Bowers v. Hardwick* decision that eliminated the right to sexual privacy, rallied against the LaRouche initiative to quarantine people with AIDS, and activated its phone tree to protest articles in the *Post* and the *Wall Street Journal*.

GLAAD's founders, like those of the GAA before them, employed militant tactics in the service of reformist objectives. They devised actions that at once appealed to those oriented toward street activism, others more interested in cooperating with established institutions, and still others interested in both as a matter of strategy. Gomez, in an interview with me, recalled telling a reporter that GLAAD's goal in organizing protests was to "put the *New York Post* out of business at the very least and at best make the *New York Times* tremble." While this might have been the organization's public position, she told me that no one actually wanted to shut down the newspaper or even thought doing so possible. The position was designed to rally the community, warn other media, and ultimately "get the *Post* suits to meet with GLAAD representatives and to get them to agree to put a damper on the kind of language they used around AIDS."

In the interviews that I conducted with them, both Gomez and Kantrowitz singled out the same three individuals as the people most responsible for elaborating GLAAD's founding vision: Kolovakos, Rist, and Russo. They were, in the words of Gomez, "engendering visionaries" who "created a very strong core ... helped to balance each other out ... and really kept each other on an even keel because they were so different." The linchpin in this regard was GLAAD's first board chair,

Kolovakos, whom Kantrowitz named the "guiding light" of the fledgling organization. Gomez, who once wrote a poem calling her seven-
year friendship with him "Like a marriage / the better part of marriage,"
described blond, blue-eyed Kolovakos as a Princeton graduate from a
middle-class background who understood skin and class privilege and
"felt insistent that GLAAD start out as having gender and racial parity"
(Gomez 1995, 38–41). She remembered him as someone who "could be
this very upper crust privileged person, certainly externally, but who
could also hold these radical viewpoints and progressive ideas about
change and actually be activist about them." Kolovakos, she said, understood that "you needed to have a big picture so that you saw how
your movement related to other movements, nationally, locally, and in-
ternationally. And perhaps that was because he was an internationalist,
he was a translator, he was committed to Latin American literature.
But for whatever reason, he did have a big picture." This broad perspective, Gomez emphasized, gave him a unique ability to mediate
among diverse viewpoints and personalities, which "was a very big deal
for starting an organization."

Kolovakos had been diagnosed with AIDS, and in the summer of
1986 he began to feel too ill to continue with his work at GLAAD and
retreated to a house in upstate New York. He officially resigned as chair
of the board in September of that year. Many of the early board members were also gone by this point, including Russo, who left after six
months, Kantrowitz, Offen, Owles, and Gelbert. Some, like Kantrowitz
and later Gomez, left because they were eager to refocus their energies
on other aspects of their lives. Others left for more explicitly political or
ideological reasons that foreshadowed battles to come. In his letter of
resignation, Gelbert wrote: "I am sorry more of our meeting time has
not been devoted to discussion of GLAAD's goal and ideology, to iron-
ing out misunderstandings and disagreements. It has been dishearten-
ing to me, for example, to hear some of my colleagues here resent being
asked to approve plans formulated by [GLAAD's direct action arm] Terrible Retribution; express certainty that that committee's actions will
'embarrass' GLAAD; and attempt to invalidate the contributions of all
who sought in GLAAD a militant organization." According to his biographer, Russo was also uncomfortable with the direction GLAAD was
taking under Kolovakos, who "seemed to want another NGTF, complete

with governing body, mailing list, and notable absence of democracy among the membership" (Schiavi 2011, 240). With tensions simmering, the departures of so many of the original board members left a leadership void that was soon filled with a power struggle between former friends.

By September 1986, Rist had stepped in to run GLAAD's day-to-day operations and been replaced in the role of acting chair by Pally, whom he had brought into the organization. Pally, who had activist experience as a feminist anti-censorship advocate, recalled in an interview with me that Rist threw his support behind board member Rosemary Kuropat's proposal to launch a major advertising campaign aimed at demystifying homosexuality: "He and [Kuropat] came in with this plan to impose – to railroad, I guess people felt – and the board just said no! And he just gave an ultimatum and said do it my way, or do *this* my way, or I'm going to leave." The initiative, Pally told me, would have consumed all of GLAAD's limited resources at a time when it was only beginning to devise fundraising strategies and had survived largely on donations from board members. Pally said she tried to remain neutral, but recognized that the proposed campaign placed Rist at loggerheads with board members who saw in GLAAD an opportunity to build an institution. One such individual was Christopher Paine, a lawyer who joined GLAAD shortly before the *Post* rally, and who oversaw the process of formally incorporating GLAAD as a non-profit organization.

Paine's institutional outlook did not sit well with the more radical and militant Rist, whom Pally described as short-tempered, flamboyant, and charismatic. Gomez offered a similar characterization: "Darrel was a firebrand ... He was so passionate and explosive. And of course, that was what I found so compelling about him: that he was really not interested in being polite ... that he knew how to use his voice to get attention and that his anger was really quite deep. According to Pally, Rist "wanted to be setting the guiding vision of the organization – those were his words – to have a guiding, fatherly or avuncular role in the organization." When the board vote on the campaign proposal did not go as he wanted, Pally recalled, Rist stormed out of the meeting. He resigned from the board in October 1986.

The aftermath played out in the pages of the *Philadelphia Gay News* and the *New York Native* between late December 1986 and February 1987 as Rist lashed out at GLAAD and Pally and accused the board of having become more oriented to institution building than to militant action. In a letter to the *Native* published on 19 January 1987, Rist wrote that GLAAD had become symptomatic of the gay movement's tendency to appoint leaders "who busy themselves ... with politely demurring in order to buy the approval of straights" instead of engaging in "radically unapologetic actions."[1] The response letter by the remaining thirteen GLAAD board members, which was published alongside Rist's in the same issue of the *Native*, emphasized that the organization's lower visibility since the *Post* protest "does not constitute abandonment of the group's goals to respond to and correct media distortion and misrepresentation about gay men and lesbians." It went on to state: "There are ways to influence media coverage of the gay community and not all of them involve colorful pickets and demonstrations, however important those may be." GLAAD, the board members pointed out, was beginning to have success in arranging meetings with media professionals, and although this strategy "may not seem sufficiently 'radical'" to its critics, "opening up such dialogues with print and broadcast executives will be crucial in rectifying the coverage of gay men and lesbians in both news and entertainment venues."

Aside from the personality conflicts that inevitably occur in organizational work, the public skirmishes between Rist and the remaining board members reveal the extent to which GLAAD's institutional discourse had, by early 1987, shifted in favour of insider strategies. What had begun as a militant grassroots organization founded with the help of veteran GAA activists had quickly become something more institutionalized and oriented to gaining access to media companies. This occurred not as a natural evolution away from direct action, as GLAAD's first executive director would later claim, but as the result of internal struggles over the organization's philosophy and mission that resulted in the gradual expulsion of activists who did not believe in mainstreaming as the most effective way to promote social and cultural change.

## The Institution Builder

In just over one year's time, GLAAD had experienced dramatic leadership changes and had begun to position itself as the gay and lesbian movement's principal media advocacy organization. Many board members believed it was now important to devote more time and resources to fundraising so the organization could support a paid staff. But they were confronted with a catch-22: without paid staff to fundraise full-time, the organization could not afford to have paid staff. Craig Davidson, a board member and a graduate of Harvard Law School, came forward with a solution. He would abandon his Wall Street corporate law practice to become GLAAD's first full-time, and initially unpaid, executive director. His partner, Michael Valentini, also a lawyer, had agreed to support him during the transition.

According to former board chair Jeffrey Sosnick, the idea of hiring a full-time executive director was not universally well received. Sosnick had been a GLAAD volunteer who, ascending from the ranks of the phone tree committee, had been invited to join the board in mid-1986 and had succeeded Pally as chair in early 1987. In an interview, Sosnick told me that Davidson's candidacy spawned two factions. On one side were people who said: "Why do we need staff, why do we need an office, why do we need money? We're doing good stuff now, why do anything else?" On the other side were people who saw in hiring Davidson "a stepping stone to something that ... the founding members envision[ed], which would ultimately be this national organization" and "the possibility that we can in fact move our agenda forward by not only being reactive but being proactive as well." Being proactive, for Sosnick and like-minded board members, meant providing ongoing education and resources to media professionals, something for which having paid professional staff was an absolute necessity. After a heated public meeting at the New York gay and lesbian community centre, the board voted to hire Davidson, after which, Sosnick said, "a number of people departed the organization. Some stuck around, but there were a number who felt that this was something they just didn't want to be a part of."

By mid-1987, Davidson had become GLAAD's first executive director and soon hired an assistant, Karin Schwartz. He set out on the difficult task of building an institution by raising money for the organization and expanding its membership. Within three years, GLAAD had mushroomed from 500 to 5,000 members and its annual budget had grown to nearly $500,000. It is indicative of Davidson's zeal for institution building that, unlike other leaders of the gay and lesbian movement of this period, he was willing to entertain the possibility of accepting money from the Coors Brewing Company. Following years of controversy and boycotts resulting from its anti-gay, anti-union, and racist practices in the 1970s, as well as a documented pattern of funding ultraconservative organizations, Coors had begun to reform its internal policies and rehabilitate its image. Although GLAAD then ultimately did not accept its contributions, Davidson, along with a few other gay and lesbian community leaders, met with company representatives in 1988 and wrote in a subsequent letter to a Coors corporate communications manager that "if we think creatively, we all may be able to work together to the mutual benefit of the Company and our community."

Pally remembers Davidson as someone who could balance "the need for respectability against the need to be a thorn in the side of the status quo." Davidson, she suggested, was philosophically aligned with many of the more militant individuals within GLAAD, but presented a moderate public face to the world: "Craig came from the corporate law world, could put on a suit and knew a lot of rich people. On the other hand, most of the time he hung out in a T-shirt and jeans, was finished with the corporate world, and had very sharp politics so he … knew exactly where the activist types were coming from and had a vocabulary to talk to them." Davidson was also aware that the media activist efforts of the 1970s had fallen by the wayside with the advent of AIDS and the right-wing backlash against the gains of the gay and lesbian movement. In a scholarly article about GLAAD that he co-wrote with Valentini, Davidson stated: "The rise and fall of television reform organizations over just a few years in the 1970s tells a cautionary tale" (Davidson and Valentini 1992, 110). Determined not to allow this fate to befall GLAAD, he adopted a cautious approach to issues that might have compromised the organization's ability to fundraise. For example, in a June 1990 memo to the GLAAD/NY board about outing closeted public figures who actively worked against the interests of the gay and lesbian community, Davidson argued: "While we can't put ourselves in a position of dancing to the tune of our donors, we must nonetheless accept that outing is a controversial issue likely to polarize our donors (not to mention our members)." The board voted seven to two in favour of not having a position on the issue.

The same cautious approach was evident in the article Davidson co-wrote with Valentini. Designed to win allies in the legal community, the article emphasized GLAAD's moderate, cooperative approach to cultural advocacy and downplayed the need for confrontational strategies. Davidson and Valentini (1992, 103) defined GLAAD's cultural advocacy as: "A group of activities including media reform, education and curriculum reform, and religious reform that has the common goal of full integration of the lesbian and gay community into 'mainstream' society (i.e., non-gay and non-lesbian) through strategies that generally do not involve the legal or legislative processes." The three strategies of media reform they outlined did not involve anything more confrontational than letter-writing: (1) mobilizing the gay and lesbian community to respond to positive and negative portrayals through letter-writing campaigns; (2) educating media professionals through letters, meetings, style guides, and seminars; and (3) promoting gay and lesbian visibility, including in reference works and textbooks. As for more militant, confrontational tactics, they wrote: "GLAAD also supports the media-related work of other activist groups, including those more oriented toward direct action" (108).

They acknowledged that questions about GLAAD's priorities and emphases with regard to its mission, strategies, and tactics had divided its early leadership. They went on to claim that, with the advent of the AIDS Coalition to Unleash Power (ACT UP) in 1987, "much of the energy of GLAAD members who were more oriented to direct action and more motivated by AIDS issues shifted to ACT UP and away from GLAAD's direct action arm, the Swift and Terrible Retribution Committee" (106). The passive construction of this passage suggests that an organizational shift away from direct action had simply occurred as a matter of course, and that struggles over strategy were a thing of the past. However, this shift is better understood as the result of an active struggle between the few remaining militants oriented toward direct action and others who favoured a more moderate, cooperative approach.

In her interview with me, Pally recalled tensions between Davidson and a board member by the name of Michael Stolbach: "Craig had one vision of balancing street action and organization-building, but his balance was not Michael's balance. So the two of them would go at it at board meetings and outside of board meetings." According to Pally, Davidson eventually grew tired of conflict with Stolbach and began working behind the scenes to have the rest of the board vote him out. Stolbach found out about the planned ouster and, in response, delivered to the board a presentation that Pally described as "steady" and "persuasive," in which he argued that a vote to exclude him from the board could not possibly be based on the substance of his work. The only reasons board members could have to vote him out, Stolbach insisted, were either personal or based on discomfort with his style of activism. In the end, Pally recounted, Davidson admitted that the issue really had been Stolbach's confrontational style. That, Pally said, "opened ... another way for them to deal with their differences."

Davidson strongly believed that the key to GLAAD's long-term survival would be its evolution into a truly national media advocacy organization. Toward the end of his term, he worked tirelessly to lay the groundwork for that idea. He met with activists in cities across the United States interested in forming GLAAD chapters. Chapters began to emerge in Los Angeles, and then in San Francisco, and eventually in such cities as Atlanta, Chicago, Dallas, San Diego, and Kansas City. By the time Davidson left the post of executive director in September 1990, it was possible to imagine that GLAAD might evolve into a hybrid structure combining local activist efforts under a national umbrella. In a memo dated 20 February 1990, Davidson told chapter representatives: "I do think that we need some kind of national organization if GLAAD is going to play in the same league with *Time* magazine, the American Family Association, the ADL and others. So, it seems to me that our challenge is to conceive and implement a structure that is simultaneously personal, grass-roots and flexible on the one hand and professional, national and powerful on the other." He went on to reassure local activists that such a hybrid model could be compatible with "GLAAD's grassroots origins and with local autonomy." The national GLAAD, he wrote, "can be quite professional (with staff, major funding, etc.) while local GLAADs can, if they wish, stay quite volunteer-based."

Davidson died on 31 August 1991 of complications from AIDS. He was one of many important figures in GLAAD's history to die of the disease; of the eight men who were present at GLAAD's founding meeting, only two, Kantrowitz and Adkins, were still alive when I ended my fieldwork. Russo died in 1990, Kolovakos in 1992, and Rist in 1993. If these last three men were the visionaries who brought GLAAD into the world, Davidson was largely responsible for turning their vision, or at least a version of it, into an institutional reality. He was the architect of GLAAD's ambitions on the national stage.

## GLAAD/LA

In 1988, gay and lesbian activists in California organized a march on Sacramento to demand equal rights and better AIDS funding from the state legislature. Richard Jennings, an entertainment lawyer based in Los Angeles, was among the participants. While reading the newspaper coverage about the protest, Jennings was struck by a quote from then-assemblyman Art Agnos. Agnos, well-known for his support of the gay and lesbian community, described an editorial cartoon in which a literal fairy could be seen leading him by the nose. He went on to lament that no gay and lesbian activists had responded to the offensive cartoon. In a videotaped interview recorded in 1993 (archived in GLAAD's Los Angeles office), Jennings said:

> That hit me like a ton of bricks. The fact that here's one of our biggest if not only major supporter in the State legislature feeling that this is a community that doesn't speak up for itself when it is defamed in the media. I started thinking about all the instances I was aware of where I'd seen negative editorials about gays and lesbians. I knew from my experience with other media watch organizations – I'd been involved with the NAACP many years before, I know about the ADL's good work in immediately responding to defamatory kinds of things about the Jewish community, and I realized that we needed something in this community that, on an ongoing basis, monitored and addressed the ways in which gays and lesbians were being defamed every day.

Back in Los Angeles, Jennings began to meet with friends in the legal profession to think about ways to improve the media representation of gays and lesbians. At a time when the courts were packed with Reagan appointees, if the movement hoped to make any gains with state or federal legislators, they believed, it would first have to change the culture at large.

In July 1988, Jennings received an invitation to a cocktail party at the home of his friends, lawyers Richard Llewellyn and Chris Caldwell. They informed him that Davidson would also be attending. Jennings had heard rumours of GLAAD's existence in New York and was curious to hear what Davidson had to say. In an interview with me, Jennings said that he came away from the party impressed by Davidson and inspired to emulate him: "He came out of a corporate law firm environment and took the risk of making very little money and being a full-time activist. I thought, if he could do it – and he's a pretty sharp guy – maybe I could do it too." Along with attorney Dean Hansell, Judge Rand Schrader, and Schrader's partner David Bohnett, Jennings left the party determined to begin a Los Angeles GLAAD chapter.

Jennings held a meeting to which he invited attorneys Carol Anderson, Karen Lash, and Carmichael Smith-Low, among others. They established basic principles that would guide the GLAAD/LA chapter's early evolution. First, they resolved not to form an organization until they had successfully conducted outreach to women and people of colour. In support of these outreach efforts, they set aside some seats on the board of directors for representatives of Latino/a, African American, Asian American, and women's organizations. The group incorporated itself as GLAAD/LA in October 1988. By November, it had formed a board of directors, begun to publish a newsletter, and held regular committee meetings. But as Hansell recalled in an unpublished article he wrote about GLAAD/LA's history, which he shared with me when we met in 2000, "the use of representatives from other organizations on GLAAD's board created an unforeseen problem later ... More than one of these representatives began to become extremely active on the GLAAD board at the expense of his or her involvement with their own host group." The early GLAAD/LA board may have reflected some of the gender and ethnic variance within the Los Angeles gay and lesbian community, but it did so in a manner that created tensions with other organizations.

It was not long before GLAAD/LA meetings began to involve media professionals like Deborah Bergman, a *Los Angeles Times* editor, and Jehan Agrama, who had recently left the helm of her family's international film distribution business. In GLAAD/LA's fifth anniversary newsletter, Jennings recalled an early meeting held in Hansell's home in which the group discussed tactics to respond to defamatory editorials that had aired on a local CBS television station: "The sophisticated level of discussion that night about the relative effectiveness of various tactics, including weighing the needs and concerns of journalists and media organizations, set the tone for the high level of brainstorming and tactical thinking that GLAAD/LA has tried to pursue ever since." By taking the "needs and concerns of journalists and media organizations" into consideration, GLAAD/LA hoped to quickly establish a reputation as a legitimate and professional media advocacy organization.

A major turning point in this regard was the first national media controversy in which GLAAD was involved. During a CBS year-end news special in 1989, *60 Minutes* commentator Andy Rooney had said: "There was some recognition in 1989 of the fact that many of the ills which kill us are self-induced. Too much alcohol. Too much food, drugs, homosexual unions, cigarettes. They're all known to lead quite often to premature death" (quoted in Gross 2001, 106). GLAAD/NY requested and obtained a meeting with CBS executives. Meanwhile the two most important GLAAD chapters, Los Angeles and New York, began a coordinated letter-writing campaign encouraging their members to complain to CBS. Shortly before the scheduled meeting with CBS, Rooney wrote a letter to the gay and lesbian news magazine, the *Advocate*, which followed up by interviewing Rooney. The resulting article attributed racist comments to him, further fuelling the controversy and leading CBS to suspend him for three months, though he was reinstated after just a few weeks. Through media insiders in Los Angeles, GLAAD found out about the suspension before it was announced and immediately arranged for on-camera interviews with high-profile media, including CNN. The exposure gave GLAAD national prominence for the first time and landed the Los Angeles chapter on a sectional front page of the *Los Angeles Times*. As Jennings described it in the 1993 videotaped interview: "It was the first story in a national newspaper about GLAAD and the work we were doing. The *LA Times* is widely read by people in the entertainment industry and certain people in the media and all of that made it a lot easier for us to start getting in the door with the TV stations." Thanks to the Rooney controversy, media professionals began to perceive GLAAD as a legitimate player. Suddenly, local media outlets that had previously refused to meet with GLAAD were returning phone calls and accepting meetings with activists.

Agrama, who along with Jennings was co-president of GLAAD/LA at this stage, recalled in an interview with me that she and Jennings deliberately put forward a conservative image during their meetings with local media managers. "We probably looked like missionaries," Agrama quipped, describing how she would wear lipstick and put on a skirt suit to match Jennings's lawyerly suit and tie. "They would look at us," she said, "and here we were, you know, 'gay' and 'lesbian' is coming out of our mouths, all this homosexual rhetoric is coming out of our mouths and they're looking at us. It was very intentional, it was a jamming." According to Agrama, the meetings often led to heartfelt discussions: "It really felt like we were educating people."

With GLAAD/LA beginning to make inroads with media professionals, Jennings decided the time was ripe to follow Davidson's example and become the chapter's first executive director, a position he assumed in July 1990. His first priority was to fundraise on a large scale to complement the yard sales and other small-scale efforts that had constituted most of GLAAD/LA's fundraising to that point. Although the chapter was not yet in a position to hire support staff, it did benefit from Agrama's full-time involvement, as she was financially independent and had been running GLAAD/LA's daily operations out of her home. Agrama told me that her full-time devotion to the organization arose from the fact that, after leaving the family business, she had "wanted to do something a little more socially redeeming than just making deals." Although she had been living with a female partner for many years, she had little sense of belonging to a gay and lesbian community and she saw GLAAD as "a good way to get involved in this community that I knew nothing about." The organization, she said, "felt like a perfect marriage" because it allowed her to be "more out" and use the skills she had acquired in the entertainment industry.

Peter M. Nardi, a sociologist based at Pitzer College, took over from Jennings as co-president in November 1990. By then, GLAAD/LA's grassroots element had grown significantly. The monthly membership meetings, which included lively panel discussions on such topics as outing, lesbian representation, and GLAAD's relationships with the Anti-Defamation League and the National Association for the Advancement of Colored People, had spilled out of Hansell's living room to fill the meeting hall of Temple Beth Chayim Chadashim on West Pico Boulevard. GLAAD members who wanted to get more involved could take part in media monitoring and response, outreach, or finance committees, and/or seek election to the board via a general membership vote. GLAAD/LA also published a Media Watch column in three Los Angeles gay and lesbian publications and coordinated a speaker's bureau.

GLAAD/LA leadership began to think that it was urgent to find ways to reach the big movie studios and television networks. Recent films like *Darkman, Men at Work, Wild at Heart, House Party*, and *Bird on a Wire*, they felt, had employed terms of contempt or offensive stereotypes of effeminate gay men and gay villains. GLAAD/LA was also aware of at least three films in development, including *Basic Instinct*, that promised to deliver more of the same. In television, meanwhile, the number of recurring gay and lesbian characters had declined in the 1990–91 season relative to the previous one. GLAAD/LA's leaders were also aware that Hollywood studios were taking more and more heat from the religious right, which was increasingly framing its battles in terms of a "culture war" founded on "the idea that a national consensus had given way to a de facto civil war over irreconcilable value systems" (Becker 2006, 2).[2]

After discussing a range of possible tactics, GLAAD/LA leaders opted to place full-page ads in entertainment industry trade publications, one directed at movie studios and another at television networks. The first ad appeared in *Daily Variety* on 25 September 1990 to coincide with the release of the previous weekend's box office figures. Titled "Hollywood Images Fuel Gay/Lesbian Bashing," the ad posed the question: "With all due respect for freedom of expression, isn't it time Hollywood used that freedom to depict lesbians and gay men in a more realistic and responsible way?" The second ad, published in the *Hollywood Reporter* on 3 October 1990 (on the day the television ratings came out), asked, "Where Are the Lesbian and Gay Characters this Season?"

In addition to generating stories in the *Los Angeles Times*, local television and radio stations, wire services, CNN Headline News, and E!, the ads prompted Los Angeles councilman Michael Woo, whose electoral district encompassed the lots of many movie studios, to call the GLAAD/LA office and offer his assistance in brokering meetings with studio representatives. As a result of that support, in early 1991, Jennings held what the GLAAD/LA newsletter called an "informational meeting" in Woo's office with representatives from three studios: Disney, Sony/Columbia, and MCA/Universal. Previous to that point, GLAAD/LA had only met with the studios twice: once with Universal about *Darkman*, and once with *Basic Instinct* director Paul Verhoeven.

In February 1991, GLAAD/LA moved its operations to a small office on Sunset Boulevard and La Brea and, in April, organized its first Media Awards. The first such dinner, held in New York City the previous year, had been hosted by Phil Donahue and Marlo Thomas and attended by Mayor David Dinkins. It had been a modest financial success for GLAAD/NY, and the GLAAD/LA chapter leaders, particularly Jennings and Agrama, were convinced that the formula had the potential to be even more successful in Los Angeles. A similar awards show, hosted by a group of media industry professionals called the Alliance for Gay and Lesbian Artists, had enjoyed a good run between 1981 and 1988 but had since ended. According to Capsuto (2000, 175), the alliance's leaders had "redirected their energy into AIDS organizations," which had left the field open for GLAAD/LA to host its own awards show.

Some within the GLAAD/LA ranks had reservations about the Media Awards because they knew of other organizations that had folded as a result of taking risks for which they were not yet ready. In my interview with her, Agrama summed up this position, which was not hers, as: "We don't have money for postage and you're telling me we're going to do an awards show?" Will Halm, a board member who co-chaired the first Media Awards in Los Angeles, told me in an interview that the fear of failure prompted the organizers to joke that "we wanted to have [the dinner] at a Ramada Inn, some motel, in a small banquet room and serve hot dogs and potato chips because we were afraid this would bankrupt us!" Instead of giving in to those fears, Agrama said, GLAAD/LA "really bit the bullet" and rented a small ballroom at the Beverly Hilton.

The first GLAAD Media Awards in Los Angeles was organized entirely by inexperienced volunteers who had full-time jobs. Besides the sheer volume of work – from advertising, to sending out invitations, to producing the show, to arranging table seating – the biggest challenge was convincing celebrities to attend. Much of this task fell to Agrama, who had the industry contacts, personality, confidence, and persistence under pressure needed for the job and the means to devote herself to it full-time. Agrama told me she must have sent out 300 invitations to celebrities in the first year, each of which she followed up with calls and more calls. Most celebrities, she said, would not give her a firm answer.

She was eventually able to line up Judith Light, star of the sitcom *Who's the Boss*, John Lithgow, who presented an award to actor Bruce Davison for his role in *Longtime Companion*, actress Helen Shaver, one of two leads in the pioneering lesbian film *Desert Hearts*, and Amanda Donohoe, whose character on the television drama *L.A. Law* had recently been revealed to be bisexual.

According to an article in the GLAAD/LA newsletter, the most moving part of the evening was a speech by writer Paul Monette, who received an award named after his late lover, casting director Stephen F. Kolzak. Standing before a crowd of over 500 people, Monette described Kolzak as "the queerest man I've ever met," adding that he had been openly gay and openly HIV-positive at a time when most gays and lesbians in Hollywood were deeply closeted. "We're in an Inquisition ... a cultural McCarthyism that would see us dead," Monette declared. "How many times do we have to lay these prizes on people's graves? You tell me that, then you go out and be queer and fabulous."

Some activists in GLAAD/LA were concerned that the Media Awards might come off as elitist and be beyond the financial reach of many in the community. According to an interview I conducted with Nardi, however, most felt that the high price of admission was acceptable as long as GLAAD also did things that were accessible to people with lower income levels. Hansell told me that the Media Awards, although not within everyone's reach, were necessary as a way of "reaching out to some of the different institutions and people we felt we needed to reach out to." That such reaching out also constituted fundraising and event segregation by class was something most GLAAD/LA members could live with.

In financial terms, the first Media Awards in Los Angeles were a modest success. Hansell recalled that they made a profit of about $7,000. For the leaders of the fledgling organization, however, the event was a huge confidence boost and a promising indication of things to come. Sylvia Rhue, who was a GLAAD/LA board member, told me in an interview that, although she herself could barely afford to attend the event at the time, the "feeling in the room was that we were all dressed up and it was like we had arrived. We were surprised that stars showed up ... It really felt like we've grown up and we've arrived." The following year, the awards moved out of the small ballroom into the biggest room the Beverly Hilton had to offer. The year after that, the event left the Hilton altogether to take up residence in the Century Plaza Hotel, the largest venue of its kind in Los Angeles. As Agrama told me, "The rate of growth of this organization," largely fuelled by the Media Awards, "was monumental."

The remarkable early success of the Media Awards reflected changes that were beginning to take place in Hollywood. In the summer of 1991, Jennings attended the first-ever Hollywood fundraiser for the National Gay and Lesbian Task Force, where he had the opportunity to meet Barry Diller, then head of the Fox Television network. To Jennings's surprise, Diller called the GLAAD/LA office shortly after the fundraiser. He told Jennings that he had recently seen a program on Fox that reported on widespread AIDS-phobia in the entertainment industry and announced his intention to set up a new organization to address the problem. Diller felt that whatever organization was created would have to address homophobia alongside AIDS. Would GLAAD be interested in contributing its expertise? Said Jennings in the 1993 videotaped interview: "I couldn't believe what I was hearing. To have the support of the head of a major studio and network was not something that was in our dreams at that point."

Jennings met with Diller, MCA/Universal chairman Sid Sheinberg, and Motion Picture Association of America president Jack Valenti on 19 September 1991. By October, Diller and Sheinberg had put up the money to create an organization devoted to combating AIDS-phobia and homophobia in the entertainment industry. In January 1992, Jennings was hired away from GLAAD to become the executive director of the new organization, named Hollywood Supports. Its objectives were to provide sensitivity training about AIDS and homophobia, encourage reform of discriminatory employment practices affecting gays and lesbians and people with HIV, and assist the industry in educating the public about AIDS and gay and lesbian issues. A year later, almost every major film studio and television network had adopted a non-discrimination policy for gay, lesbian, and HIV-positive staff based on model policies developed by Hollywood Supports. By the end of 1993, over 400 seminars about AIDS and/or homophobia had reached thousands of media professionals.

## GLAAD/USA

Back in January 1989, during a tour of US cities intended to drum up support for new GLAAD chapters, GLAAD/NY executive director Davidson had met with interested activists in San Francisco. The resulting chapter, GLAAD/San Francisco Bay Area (SFBA), began operations a few months later. By 1994, GLAAD chapters had formed in Washington, DC, Kansas City, San Diego, Chicago, Denver, Atlanta, and Dallas.

The first meeting to discuss setting up a national structure for GLAAD's chapters occurred in November 1989 in Washington, DC, and resulted in the adoption of guidelines concerning the composition of an interim national steering committee conceived as a precursor to a national board of directors. Each chapter, the delegates decided, would send two representatives to national planning meetings: one male and one female, at least one of whom had to be a person of colour.

The second meeting of the steering committee, hosted by GLAAD/LA in October 1990, led to the creation of a national body called GLAAD/USA. The delegates adopted the following mission statement: "[GLAAD/USA] is a diverse group dedicated to confronting public expressions of homophobia or heterosexism, and to promoting the fullest possible understanding of the breadth and diversity of our lives." They also outlined a series of potential responsibilities for the committee, including developing a governing structure, overseeing national programs, coordinating national fundraising efforts, building coalitions with other groups, developing national communications capabilities, and coordinating the formation of new chapters.

GLAAD/USA meetings, which were held quarterly, turned out to be extremely contentious. In an unpublished 1996 article about GLAAD's history, Hansell recalls they were "consumed with lengthy disagreements about chapter autonomy, voting rights of various chapters, the format for a national structure, and the representation of women and people of colour." The chapters were in various stages of development, with memberships that in 1991 ranged from just five in Atlanta to 7,000 in New York, different conceptions of the rights and obligation of members and chapters, vast disparities in fundraising ability, and conflicting opinions about how best to achieve gender and racial/ethnic parity on an eventual national board of directors. GLAAD/NY, the original and largest chapter in terms of membership and budget, held the rights to the GLAAD name and required that other chapters sign agreements outlining the conditions under which it could be used. Therefore, any plan to form a national GLAAD would necessarily have to be approved by New York.

The transcript of a GLAAD/USA meeting held in San Francisco in September 1991 provides insight into the difficulty of finding common ground. Two core issues emerged from the meeting: (1) What would be the roles and responsibilities of the national governing body? (2) What would be the composition and structure of the board?

On the first question, the delegates debated the extent to which a national board would set policies that chapters would then be obligated to follow. Would it administer national programs, or would it support and help coordinate local chapters' programs? Would it fundraise, or be financed by the chapters? Would it function exclusively as a way for the chapters to communicate with one another, or would it also issue external communications on issues of national importance? As the discussion progressed, it became clear that the representatives from GLAAD/NY were unwilling to give up on the idea of chapter – i.e., their own – autonomy. They saw a limited role for GLAAD's national component, which they conceived as a "communication link" between chapters with a role in coordinating national "activations" (like letter-writing campaigns) and the nominations process for the Media Awards. They proposed that the national organization be financed through a percentage of membership dues charged by each chapter and that it not be empowered to speak on behalf of the whole organization. The GLAAD/LA representatives, in contrast, proposed a national board that could "speak with one voice" on major issues and engage in fundraising and public relations activities. GLAAD/SFBA representatives, meanwhile, imagined a national body whose role would be limited to engaging in national fundraising efforts in support of local chapter development.

On the second question, discussions centred on whether and how to build gender and racial parity requirements into the structure of a national board of directors. On this point, the Los Angeles and San Francisco delegates felt strongly that the board composition should continue the parity guidelines adopted with regards to the GLAAD/USA interim steering committee: each chapter would be represented by one man and one woman, one of whom had to be a person of colour. This left the question of what to do about the discrepancies between chapters in terms of size and budgets. Should each chapter have equal representation on the board? Would at-large members, i.e., board members not affiliated with any chapter, be permitted? Los Angeles delegates to the steering committee argued in favour of a weighted voting system in which each chapter would be assigned a certain number of votes based on the size of its membership. A chapter that was unable to fulfill parity requirements would see its votes reduced by 50 per cent – a penalty that New York's representatives strongly opposed. The Atlanta delegates stated that their leadership was split on the question of parity, while Denver's representatives had reservations about the weighted voting system, which they felt would favour the coasts and move the organization toward a divisive regionalism that would force the smaller chapters to align themselves with one another against Los Angeles and/or New York.

In the end, of the six chapters represented at the San Francisco meeting (New York, Los Angeles, San Francisco, Washington, DC, Dallas, and Denver), four voted to adopt the parity policy and two abstained. The adoption of the policy meant that, once the national board was formed, a chapter could only be represented by a white man (a demographic that formed the majority of active GLAAD members) if its other representative was a woman of colour. As for the other issues brought up at the meeting, a weak consensus emerged around the lowest common denominator functions of an eventual GLAAD national entity: interchapter communications, resource sharing, chapter certification/ decertification, chapter development, and the internal production and dissemination of informational materials intended for the various chapters. Chapter representatives could not agree on whether or how the national body would set policy, design and implement programs, or maintain a national media profile.

By the spring of 1993, it was clear that the GLAAD/USA process was mired in conflict and was unlikely to lead to a unified organization. The Los Angeles chapter, with its large and dynamic volunteer base, proximity to Hollywood, and growing (Media Awards-fuelled) budget and membership, had by then become the second dominant pole of the organization. Ellen Carton, who succeeded Davidson as the executive director of GLAAD/NY, initiated a plan to bring the New York and Los

Angeles chapters closer together. Peggy Brady, an attorney who had been recruited to represent the New York chapter on the GLAAD/USA steering committee, supported her in this endeavour. Brady and Carton approached their Los Angeles counterparts, and as Jennings explained in an interview with me, found that the GLAAD/LA board was receptive to their ideas. GLAAD leaders on both coasts, he said, "saw that the organization couldn't grow much anymore as a city-based entity, that it had to become national to go to the next level."

The Los Angeles and New York delegations met secretly in advance of a GLAAD/USA meeting in the spring of 1993 to discuss the possibility of creating a national organization out of the merger of the two chapters. The first hurdle, they recognized, was that they needed to establish a basic level of trust before they could engage in productive discussions. As Halm told me: "At that point, everyone in LA hated everyone in New York." "Really," he emphasized, "there was no trust whatsoever." The chapter delegations came up with the idea of bringing the entire boards of both cities together for a weekend retreat in Los Angeles in August 1993. An organizational consultant named Debra Johnson, whom Jennings said he selected because she "was really good at motivating people and getting people to see their commonalities," facilitated the retreat. Through a series of group-building exercises, Jennings told me, members of the Los Angeles board came to realize that "the New York people were not these heartless, arrogant money people, that they really were people like them." The retreat, he asserted, was "pivotal" because it "cut through years and years of jealousy and animosity and resentment."

After the retreat, the New York board developed a proposal to merge GLAAD's Los Angeles and New York chapters. Under this plan, other chapters that met certain conditions would be folded into the national organization. The proposal was adopted at a January 1994 meeting of GLAAD/USA as the basis for continued negotiations, but there remained many difficult issues for the two boards to work out: Where would the merged organization's headquarters be situated? Who would run it? What would be its governance? What autonomy, if any, would the two founding chapters retain? Would there be other chapters and, if so, what role would they play? What efforts, if any, would be made to achieve gender and racial parity? The two boards appointed representatives to a "restructuring committee," composed of negotiators from the two chapters: Brady and Rick Hutcheson from New York and Halm and Jennings from Los Angeles.

Over the course of the seven months that followed the January 1994 GLAAD/USA meeting, the restructuring committee met frequently to work out a specific merger agreement. The question of where to locate the national headquarters soon emerged as the major stumbling block as the issue was debated, postponed, and debated again with no resolution in sight. The two negotiating teams eventually agreed on a set of criteria to be used in determining which city would get the headquarters, including "size and impact of the media market, abilities to impact media, types of media work, fundraising ability, volunteer pool, the number of other national organizations located in the area, public perception and other specific resources that may be peculiar to either Los Angeles or New York." A special meeting was held in New York on the weekend of 4–5 June 1994 to come to a final determination. Each negotiating team brought in two "media experts" to make their respective cases. GLAAD/NY argued for New York's importance as a news media centre and site of corporate media decision-making. GLAAD/LA countered with arguments about Hollywood's overarching cultural influence. Unsurprisingly, the discussion failed to sway either side of the debate. Finally, during dinner one night that weekend, Halm, who told me the story, turned to Brady and said: "Let's just have two headquarters. I don't care if it makes sense or not ... I mean, at least we can move on, at least we can move on."

The merger of GLAAD/NY and GLAAD/LA was announced in August 1994. There would be one executive director whose time would be split between the two cities. The Los Angeles board, renamed the Los Angeles Council, would continue to administer local programs. The plan called for the national board to be made up of thirty members: eight from Los Angeles, eight from New York, two from San Francisco, some at large, and one from each of the chapters that agreed to merge with the new national organization. Each board member would be required to "give or get" $10,000 annually. Setting aside the gender and racial parity requirements originally devised by GLAAD/USA, the restructuring plan listed "diversity" (as to gender, ethnicity, physical ability, and age) among board member selection criteria, alongside experience with non-profit organizations, "media literacy," and geographic provenance. Brady and Halm were selected as GLAAD's first national co-presidents and charged with overseeing the transition process.

## Nationalization

The merger of GLAAD's New York and Los Angeles chapters initiated a challenging two-year transition period in which the newly national organization struggled to find a workable structure, define its functions, staff its offices, resolve old (and some new) conflicts, and assert itself on the national stage. Among the crucial decisions requiring immediate attention was who to hire as the organization's first executive director.

In the June 1995 edition of the (newly national) GLAAD newsletter, Los Angeles-based attorney and board member David Huebner, who had replaced Halm as national co-chair, reported that efforts to create an infrastructure for the national organization were proceeding "surprisingly well." He wrote that financial systems had been put in place, payroll and accounting functions had been centralized, computers had been upgraded, and work had begun on linking the New York and Los Angeles offices through a computer network.

Behind the scenes, however, a battle had erupted between Los Angeles and New York board members over who would become the merged organization's first executive director. As Los Angeles-based board member Michael Keegan explained in an interview with me, the fight almost killed the merger: "You had one person favoured by New York. You had one person favoured by LA. You had all the LA people supporting the LA person. You had all the New York people supporting William Waybourn, and you had the non-New York and -LA people split down the middle. It was really bad."

Waybourn, a white gay man who was then in his late forties, was the candidate most highly recommended by the two corporate headhunting firms GLAAD hired to help with the executive director search (a search process said by one ex-GLAAD employee to have cost upwards of $30,000). Waybourn had extensive corporate managerial experience and was the founder and executive director of the Gay and Lesbian Victory Fund, an organization devoted to contributing campaign funds to gay and lesbian political candidates. In contrast, the candidate favoured by the

Los Angeles board members was younger, African American, and active in a variety of gay and lesbian, AIDS, and people of colour organizations.

In the end, and by the narrowest of margins, the GLAAD board voted to hire Waybourn, a decision made even more complicated by the fact that he would only accept the position on the condition that his management firm, Window, be the titular head of the organization and that he be named "managing director." According to a 1995 report submitted by GLAAD to one of its funders, Window was an offshoot of the Widmeyer Group, a management, media relations, and public affairs consultancy. Its aim was to "satisfy rising market demands for professional services within the expanding gay community." "This market," the report went on to state, "is vastly underserved by mainstream organizations, thus providing a most opportune time for the launch of such an endeavor."

Waybourn's focus on quickly professionalizing GLAAD led to a number of highly publicized and controversial firings. The pre-merger New York office under Carton's leadership had two people of colour in high-level positions: Cathay Che, an Asian American lesbian, and Donald Suggs, an African American gay man. In the Los Angeles office, Latina activist Nancy Perez was program coordinator. Waybourn fired all three. As Showtime Networks executive and national board member Gene Falk told me in an interview, "we got rid of some of the people" with "traditional activist agendas" who "wanted to fight racism and sexism and all sorts of other things." The focus, he said, was clearly on centralizing power in the organization in order to build an organization. Perez negotiated a severance package that forbade her from discussing her dismissal. Che and Suggs, in contrast, were unable to come to an agreement with GLAAD and released an open letter to "all concerned community members" in which they charged that they had been driven out because their commitment to serving a diverse gay, lesbian, bisexual, and transgender constituency was incompatible with the direction in which Waybourn was taking the merged organization. In the new GLAAD, they wrote, "the goal of making the organization more inclusive has taken a backseat to making the organization more 'mainstream' and more powerful." The firings, they pointed out, left only one person of colour working for GLAAD and on the board of directors. The sole remaining person of colour on staff, a Filipino American gay man named Loren Javier, "has no history of activism in the people of color community," Suggs and Che wrote, and "is responsible for sending out GLAAD's message, not for shaping it" (Javier was then working in a technical capacity to develop GLAAD's email capabilities).

For Jennings and others who would have preferred GLAAD to strike a different balance between the sometimes-competing demands of professionalization and activism, Waybourn was, in Jennings's words to me, the "hatchet man" come to "sacrifice" the organization's more "radical" elements. For others, the staff changes represented an unfortunate but necessary step along the way to building a viable institution. Meanwhile, elsewhere in the organization, a similar battle was being fought on a different front as chapter volunteers waited to see what role, if any, they would be called upon to play in the national GLAAD.

Back in August 1993, following the retreat of the Los Angeles and New York boards, GLAAD/USA had hired a full-time staff person dedicated to national organizing and helping to establish new chapters. The chapter leaders chose seasoned activist Donna Red Wing, who was then the executive director of the Lesbian Community Project in Portland, Oregon. With the merger officially in place, Red Wing was given a mandate to develop a "regionalization plan." She travelled extensively to the various chapters to assess their strengths, weaknesses, and members' needs and expectations. She began to draft a working model of the relationship between the national GLAAD office and the local chapters and, in the May 1995 edition of the GLAAD national newsletter, wrote the following rallying cry: "GLAAD is the cutting edge of the movement ... We are a presence in the backyard of our adversaries. We have thousands of GLAAD members and supporters acting as our eyes and ears, monitoring and responding to their local media outlets and sending to the national media outlets letters with Postmarks from places like Versailles, MO, Normal, IL, Palm Bay, FL, and Salem, OR. We are truly beginning to realize our possibilities and we are becoming a national grassroots organization." The notion of a national grassroots organization expressed the hopeful vision that GLAAD, whose local chapters had been built from the ground up, might avoid some of the pitfalls of centralization and retain a strong and active grassroots, thereby creating something unique among national movement organizations.

In the fall of 1995, Jason Heffner, an activist who had been involved in ACT UP, was hired as the director of organizational development and given the task of creating a structure to govern the relationships between

GLAAD and its chapters. He developed a "growth plan" with Red Wing that laid out a "new model for an organization which is national in scope and authority yet grassroots in orientation." The plan argued that "a tightly integrated, efficient operational structure" would facilitate "grassroots programming" by freeing local chapters from administrative, financial, and fundraising obligations. Larger chapters would become GLAAD media centres with local paid staff, while smaller ones would be designated as unstaffed GLAAD outlets. The plan also called for local groups of volunteers to be organized into Monitor and Response Project Teams. While programmatic decisions would become the sole responsibility of the national GLAAD, chapters designated as media centres could, if they wished, retain a consultative body called a Program Steering Committee made up of local activists.

In early 1996, Heffner and Red Wing proposed a summit of chapter representatives to be held in Portland. The idea was to present the restructuring plan in its entirety, get input from the chapters, and convince representatives to sign on to the project and participate in its implementation. Of particular concern to the national leaders was the incorporation of GLAAD/SFBA, the chapter with the largest volunteer and membership bases, largest budget, and most highly developed local programs.

As had already been clear under the old structure of GLAAD/USA, GLAAD/SFBA had priorities that were substantially different from those that animated members in New York and Los Angeles. The minutes of a 1992 SFBA board meeting, for example, suggest that its leaders were more oriented to improving the media literacy of the LGBT community than to engaging with corporate media on its own terms. GLAAD's goal, one board member argued, "is doing the work of media analysis, not to get covered on the news per se." GLAAD, she said, should not emphasize conflict in order to obtain media coverage or speak as though it represented the whole gay and lesbian community. The organization, she argued, does not need to accept the terms by which issues are debated in media: "We need to advance and enlarge the debate."

The GLAAD/SFBA's different orientation also came to light in the context of a poster campaign organized by GLAAD in mid-1995. The Images Campaign featured family portraits of gay or lesbian couples of various ages and from diverse racial and ethnic backgrounds, some with children. The largest of the portraits featured professional bodybuilders Rod and Bob Jackson-Paris, the gay couple poster boys du jour. Over the portraits, the following heading appeared: "Family. It's All Relative." In a memo to Che (prior to her dismissal), GLAAD/SFBA board secretary Bonnie Haley wrote:

> Our GLAAD chapter will not be participating in the campaign ... Whatever formative research might have been done around this scheme certainly glossed over the insidious consequences that can arise from such strained efforts at "positive" portrayals ... Additionally, we must point out that the selected families all are well within conformist notions of monogamous, two-person relationships. There is still some work to be done, especially by the queer communities, in the area of sexual liberation before we can blithely move on to sexual assimilation. The content of this campaign will, in fact, be received as an insult to many multi-partner families that live happily in the Bay Area. The bottom line is: We didn't become activists to defend the status quo. Of course, we nevertheless wish you the very best of luck in your project.

Contributions like the above earned the SFBA chapter a reputation for being, in Keegan's words, "really out there," something he told me helped to bring the Los Angeles and New York chapters closer together at the start of the merger process.

The unconventional views of some SFBA board members caused concern among many national staffers and on the national board. For several months, the chapter had been disseminating a weekly GLAAD MediAlert column written by media scholar and SFBA co-chair Al Kielwasser, whose tone was often sharply critical of media companies and celebrities. With the national office now in place, some national leaders began to see the column as a potential liability. In a memo to Waybourn, interim news media director Chiqui Cartagena wrote that she was "deeply concerned about GLAAD/SFBA," whose media alerts and press releases "are opinionated and sensational, which is exactly what we don't want." Of particular concern to Cartagena was an item Kielwasser had written in which he had accused syndicated gossip columnist Liz Smith "of being a two-faced closeted lesbian." Cartagena wrote: "Hello – did they [GLAAD/SFBA] wonder if that would affect our relationship with her!!!!!" In response, Waybourn sent Kielwasser a cease and desist letter and ordered the chapter to refrain from speaking out on national issues.

The growing rift between GLAAD/SFBA and GLAAD lent added urgency to the chapter integration process. In a January 1996 memo to national co-chairs Huebner and Brady, Waybourn proposed a strategy "of containment and benign neglect" for "dealing with SFBA." The idea was to do nothing more that might antagonize the chapter in the coming months, get as many of the other chapters as possible to agree to the restructuring, and ultimately present GLAAD/SFBA with an ultimatum: either join as a GLAAD media centre or operate under a different name.

Meanwhile, in a memo to Waybourn, Heffner described the Portland summit, in which GLAAD/SFBA did not participate, as an "unqualified success." "We built a team that is committed to implementing and nurturing the plan," he wrote. By paying for participants' travel costs to the summit, the national office had been able to ensure the participation of only those chapter representatives it deemed cooperative. Shortly after the summit, GLAAD's national board formally approved the chapter integration plan. The SFBA chapter now had a choice to make: to join the national organization or go it alone.

On 14 April 1996, the seven-member SFBA board of directors voted unanimously to reject GLAAD's chapter integration plan. About three weeks later, on 2 May 1996, a four-member quorum of the same board voted to accept it. It is unclear what occurred between the two votes to convince the four board members to change their positions, but in a MediAlert distributed online, Kielwasser alleged a classic case of divide and conquer. Between 14 April and 2 May 1996, he charged, secret meetings had been held between national GLAAD representatives and the four SFBA board members. The 2 May meeting, Kielwasser wrote, "was really a covert action, which observed none of the criteria for public accountability." The national office, he claimed, had "finally succeeded in its hostile effort to shut down the outspoken San Francisco Bay Area Chapter."

The votes in other cities were not nearly so contentious: chapters in Kansas City, Atlanta, and Washington, DC, voted in favour of the merger and became GLAAD media centres. Others, like Dallas and Chicago, were deemed insufficiently developed to warrant a GLAAD office presence and became unstaffed GLAAD outlets. Now fully integrated, nationalized, and restructured, GLAAD was ready to enter a new stage, initiated by Waybourn's departure and the highly consequential 1996 hiring of Chastity Bono (daughter of Sonny and Cher) as entertainment media director. Waybourn, who had been mandated with orchestrating the national transition, was nearing the end of his two-year term as managing director. According to a board member I interviewed, he had performed well in his first year, but "after that, at the very least, William lost interest and let things drift." As a result, the board co-chairs wound up spending much of their time running the organization, which was beginning to experience serious financial difficulties.

## "A Hint of Activism around the Edges"

The board began a national search for a new executive director. There were three finalists, one of whom pulled out at the last minute. Of the remaining two, one was an experienced community activist who had been the executive director of LGBT community organizations and had extensive fundraising experience. The other, Joan Garry, was a media executive at Showtime who had started her career at MTV (both Viacom properties). Garry had almost no fundraising experience or history of involvement in LGBT activism. On the other hand, she possessed highly developed financial, communication, and managerial skills and knowledge about the inner workings of large media companies. She also had relevant expertise in "new business development," which involves drawing up operational plans for the start-up ventures of media companies looking to expand into new areas.

A former board member told me that Garry's lack of activist credentials was not generally perceived as a liability:

> Given where we were ... the skill in building an institution was primary, followed very closely by communication skills and the general sense was that because activism is not genetic, that if you found somebody who could manage people, who understood people and could communicate with people, you could build the

activist piece even if it took a little bit of time ... and there was a hint of activism around the edges, just a hint of it that most people thought could be cultivated successfully given the bundle of other skills.

The GLAAD board, which had been bitterly divided during the last executive director search, was virtually unanimous in choosing Garry, who began work in June 1997 at an organization that was a few weeks away from falling short on payroll.

In an interview, Garry recalled that GLAAD's financial situation was so bad that she and GLAAD finance director Kerry Mitcham "basically lived together" for the first three weeks of her tenure as executive director. By her first board meeting on 7 July 1997, she and Mitcham had completely recast the budget that had been approved nine months earlier. Garry then invited GLAAD's auditors, from Leslie Accountancy, to participate in the board meeting to make clear "how bad this thing is." As Garry told me: "I want[ed] them to know that it's not just my problem, it's their problem too and the implicit message being, where *were* you guys ... I also had a pretty good sense at that point of ... how I would cut back on expenses and people I would lay off [if obligated to do so] ... I was really clear that I had no interest in doing that; that I did not want to be tainted as an executive director who came in and had to chop heads and that I expected that we would all work together to do whatever it took to make sure that that didn't have to happen." In her report, Garry spelled out what she meant by doing whatever it took to get GLAAD back on a sound financial footing: "We must build a strong major donor program, and all of our collective energies must be dedicated there." In the meantime, she convinced a few board members to make short-term loans to the organization in order to avoid lay-offs.

Garry saw a need to analyze GLAAD's programmatic work in relation to its development objectives and ordered a complete audit of GLAAD's programs, a task that fell to Heffner, who had been named senior director of programs. Heffner's areas of responsibility included the full range of GLAAD's programmatic activities: both those oriented to serving and reflecting LGBT community interests – like media training seminars and volunteer monitor and response committees – and communications and public relations activities directed at mainstream audiences and media professionals. Garry made clear her sense that fundraising objectives would best be served by activities geared toward the latter two audiences. GLAAD's priorities, she wrote in a report to the board, should be to "develop new relationships with senior entertainment executives," "cultivate resources throughout the industry," "capitalize on [GLAAD's] visibility," and "market GLAAD as an organization." In addition, she stressed, "we need to identify several programs which will be compelling for a major donor and will lead to high level multi-year commitments."

After the July board meeting, Garry and development staffer Julie Anderson set out to sell GLAAD's renewed mission to targeted wealthy individuals like *Frasier* producer David Lee, who agreed to double his annual commitment to GLAAD from $25,000 to $50,000. Garry's recollection was that, upon her arrival, the organization had collected only about $13,000 in major gifts for 1997. By the end of the year, she told me, major gift revenue had increased to about $325,000 and the total number of major donors had increased to 148, or 60 per cent more than in 1996. This major donor drive occurred a few weeks after two important media events: Ellen DeGeneres's much-publicized coming out on the cover of *Time* magazine, which had coincided with the coming out of her character on the TV show *Ellen*; and the murder of fashion designer Gianni Versace by Andrew Cunanan, who had been dubbed a "gay serial killer" in media after committing five murders in three months. Both occurrences had contributed to GLAAD's media visibility, as the organization celebrated the historical coming out of a major television star and her fictional alter ego and vigorously objected to the sensationalistic media practice of linking a murderer's sexual orientation to his crimes. Garry told me: "The good fortune about [the heightened visibility] was that we were actually then able to make those donors feel really good about their connection, that the organization did start to get some visibility and then we had hooked them."

Alongside this major donor drive, Garry initiated a complete overhaul of GLAAD's visual identity (see chapter 2). If the first year of her tenure was focused on rebranding the organization and stabilizing its financial situation, the second year was a period of restructuring and seeking greater visibility. Garry promoted Heffner to deputy director, placing him in charge of overseeing programs and day-to-day operations, which freed her to focus on fundraising, analyzing operational needs, and recruiting staff in key positions. The most important position to fill, according to internal documents from late 1997 and early 1998, was that of the director of communications, an area in which Garry saw the need to make "an aggressive push."

The momentum Garry was hoping to build in communications would have to wait, however, to deal with the crisis brought about by Bono's comments concerning *Ellen*'s direction after the coming out episode. On 8 March 1998, *Variety* quoted Bono as saying that *Ellen* "is so gay it's excluding a large part of our society." "It's one thing to have a gay lead character," she continued, "but it's another when every episode deals with pretty specific gay issues." The statement proved controversial at a time when DeGeneres was pleading with ABC not to drop her show, which had been struggling both creatively and in the ratings. As cultural studies scholar Jennifer Reed (2007, 16) explains, after the coming out episode the show's writers suddenly "had to deal with Ellen as a lesbian" and struggled with the limited possibilities for "lesbians caught in realist texts." Genre-bound narrative forms like sitcoms, she argues, are structured by taken-for-granted heterosexual norms (in connection to dating, family, and friendships, for example), so there was little for Ellen to do that would not alienate a heterosexist audience. And where DeGeneres might have expected GLAAD to help in her quest to open up new lesbian subject positions in conventional narrative spaces, what she got instead was a public lecture about the need to be more "realistic." Bono told *Variety*: "This is network primetime. When a show treats gay issues over and over again, it becomes 'a gay show,' and the average viewer says, 'Hey, I'm not gay – I'm not going to watch it.'" In the wake of these statements, Garry said that she "cut a deal" that allowed Bono to leave GLAAD a few weeks later and tell media that the decision had been entirely her own. "I could have fired Chastity right on the spot," she told me, "but I really was always conscious of the fact that I came in from corporate America and I didn't want to be read as the person who just insensitively dismissed people."

Bono's departure forced GLAAD to seek out a new entertainment media director. The search announcement resulted in some sixty-five applications, many of them from highly qualified individuals from the private sector. Meanwhile, as it was reviewing these applications, GLAAD hired Jennifer Einhorn as its new director of communication. A former music journalist who had worked for social justice, arts, and women's health organizations, Einhorn brought a mix of activist and professional credentials to GLAAD. According to Garry's report to the board in May 1998, Einhorn was given the task of creating "two significant media opportunities" in the coming year and of giving GLAAD a voice in the same-sex marriage debate, which was beginning to heat up on its way to becoming the defining issue for the gay and lesbian movement.[3]

In September 1998, GLAAD announced the hiring of Scott Seomin, who had spent years as *Entertainment Tonight*'s director of media relations, to the post of entertainment media director. Garry told me in an interview that Seomin's arrival "was absolutely a watershed" because it "completely changed our ability to garner visibility." Like Bono, Seomin was a known quantity in the insular world of Hollywood power brokers and, Garry said, could "get meetings we couldn't have gotten before." Together, first Bono and then Seomin provided GLAAD with the social capital the organization needed to further position itself as a legitimate entertainment industry player. The perceived value of this newfound access was in part responsible for the extent to which GLAAD's programmatic work emphasized entertainment media during my fieldwork in 2000–01, to the relative exclusion of news media.

According to the minutes of the first board meeting he attended in September 1998, Seomin saw his role primarily in terms of emphasizing GLAAD as a resource to media professionals. GLAAD, he told board members, is "not an angry group" and his efforts would be focused on meeting "with editors of major trade publications, news directors at local TV stations and development people from the networks." The minutes go on to describe how, in response to Seomin's statement that GLAAD was not an angry group, Falk, himself a corporate media executive, "noted that many [GLAAD] staffers have become media insiders" but that GLAAD "is still about activism." "The dual role of insider and critic is a hard thing to balance and we need to be aware of that," Falk pointed out. Ironically, Falk, who told me he had for years been considered one of the most moderate and "insider" voices on the GLAAD board, now found himself defending a more militant perspective on media activism than Seomin appeared willing to entertain.

One of Seomin's first challenges was to deal with the fallout from the controversial decision to accept a donation in the amount of

$110,000 from the Coors Brewing Company in 1998, which made GLAAD the first large organization of the gay movement to accept money from the company. As mentioned above, Coors had long sought to dismantle a boycott against it begun in 1974 by labour unions and successfully taken up by the gay and lesbian community, especially in California, where Harvey Milk had once led the charge against the company. As an article in *Salon* reported, the instigators of the boycott accused Coors of "spying on its workers and discriminating against a variety of minorities, including gays, blacks and Latinos."[4] The most infamous accusation levelled at Coors was that, in the 1970s, it had screened prospective employees and investigated current employees using polygraph testing. According to affidavits, sworn testimony before the Senate, and media reports, Coors polygraph operators "routinely asked questions about one's sex life, such as whether one was married, single, or divorced, had single or multiple sex partners, frequency of sexual activity," as well as questions about political views (Bellant 1991, 66).

Beginning in the 1980s, in a bid to reform its public image, Coors was among the first large American companies to add sexual orientation to its non-discrimination policy and, in 1995, among the first to offer domestic partnership benefits to its employees.[5] Then, in the late 1990s, Coors hired Mary Cheney, future vice president Dick Cheney's openly lesbian daughter, as its manager of lesbian and gay corporate relations. Meanwhile, Coors family members continued to funnel millions of dollars annually to ultraconservative, anti-gay organizations like the Free Congress Foundation, largely through interests controlled by the Coors family, such as the Castle Rock Foundation.[6] On the one hand, Coors – the company – had become "one of the most gay-friendly companies in the country," in the words of David Smith, the former communications director for the Human Rights Campaign.[7] On the other hand, millions of dollars of Coors-family-controlled profits still ended up in the hands of ultraconservative, gay-bashing organizations. To put things in perspective, Coors company contributions to gay and lesbian organizations between 1990 and 2000 – presumably including the $110,000 donated to GLAAD – totalled about $500,000, or an average of about $50,000 per year.[8]

GLAAD's strategy in dealing with LGBT community reactions to the grant was to distinguish between Coors the company on the one hand, and Coors the family and Coors-controlled foundations on the other hand. However, as the author of a Coors family biography argues, since the family owns all voting stock in the Coors Brewing Company (and therefore controls its board), "the company and the family are one," making distinctions between them spurious at best.[9] Despite the force of the arguments against taking Coors money, GLAAD's leaders were convinced that it was time to end the boycott and moved to limit the damage to its interests. The minutes of a November 1998 executive committee meeting stated: "Seomin is working behind the scenes to kill many negative stories." In other words, GLAAD's leaders used the organization's influence with media to muffle debate on an issue of importance to many LGBT activists.

Meanwhile, Garry continued to insist that GLAAD needed to make an "aggressive push" in communications. In her report to the board in July 1998, Garry listed "GLAAD Visibility" as one of her top goals for 1999: "We can defer this no longer. We must dedicate the necessary resources to ensure that we are getting covered in the press, both gay and straight. We also need to increase visibility of our staff in all our locations through speaking engagements and other opportunities we create. It's time." But Einhorn saw it differently. In her report to the same July 1998 board meeting, she espoused another philosophy regarding the visibility of the organization: "We are an organization which exists to serve a community, not ourselves. Sounds clique-ish, but given the climate that national lgbt organizations are finding ourselves in, the more we demonstrate this temperament, the better. Mind you, we're not cutting off our noses, or selling ourselves short. Its [sic] just that, as many of our staff here say (and I firmly believe), we know when we've succeeded when the story is balanced, the community is present on the page and GLAAD is not, and of course, the journalist feels as though they were helped."

Einhorn's comments to the board referred to the work of staffer Cathy Renna, who started as the manager of GLAAD's Washington, DC, office and had been promoted to the post of director of community relations. Soon after taking up the job, Renna flew out to Laramie, Wyoming, to support local activists dealing with the groundswell of

media attention caused by the appalling murder of twenty-one-year-old
Matthew Shepard in October 1998. Renna's own report to the board
stated: "I was able to become ground zero for the media … provide
background information, frame the issue, and provide spokespeople
from the LGBTA [a University of Wyoming student group] and friends
of Matthew's." Renna's talent for framing issues is evident in her report,
which stated that her work in Laramie was "GLAAD's most visible work
in 1998." In contrast, Einhorn emphasized that Renna had flown out to
Wyoming "without any fanfare, without a release."

By the end of January 1999, Einhorn "submitted her resignation,"
according to the minutes of an executive committee meeting, as the result "of an ongoing conversation" and of "her recognition that communications needed the kind of support that she did not want to focus
on (daily management)." However complicated Einhorn's reasons for
leaving may have been, it is clear that she was not the right person to
lead the "aggressive push" in communications that Garry had in mind.
For that, Garry would turn to Einhorn's replacement as director of communications, Steve Spurgeon, who began at GLAAD in July 1999. Spurgeon had most recently been the communications director for Nissan
America and a senior vice president at Fleishman-Hillard, one of the
largest public relations firms in the world.

Upon his arrival, Spurgeon set out to overhaul GLAAD's publications'
purpose, content, production schedules, and distribution. Noting in his
first report to the board that GLAAD's publications had been sporadic
and lacked a "'family' look," Spurgeon emphasized the need for the organization to build its brand identity and figure out better ways to communicate with donors, members, and media professionals. Among his
other top priorities was to design a "profile-building plan for our Executive Director, which is needed to reinforce GLAAD's national media
stature as well as for fund development identification."

After two years of Garry's leadership, with its financial situation dramatically improved, the rebranding process completed, and Seomin and
Spurgeon hired along with additional support staff in communications,
GLAAD was ready to move in new directions. Garry engaged the board
in a process of strategic planning that culminated in September 1999
with the adoption of a three-year plan (see chapter 2), followed in November 1999 by a major organizational restructuring. According to the

minutes of an executive committee call, Garry sent out a memo to staff explaining that "a change in structure was necessary" to help GLAAD "focus more on external concerns and appearances involving GLAAD in the media." Accordingly, she moved Renna from community relations to director of regional media and divided the organization into three teams, each headed by a deputy director who would also form part of the management team: (1) programs and operations, led by Dilia Loe, who had moved up from managing GLAAD's Atlanta office; (2) communications, led by Spurgeon; and (3) development, led by Anderson. Whereas GLAAD's programs function previously included both activities oriented toward the LGBT community (such as providing media training to local activists) and external communications activities (such as assisting media professionals and increasing GLAAD's visibility), the new structure separated out, and therefore emphasized, the external communications function. Community-oriented programs, in contrast, were lumped together with other things, like operations, that cost money rather than raised it.

As for Heffner, who had been deputy director in the early part of Garry's tenure, the November 1999 restructuring left him in charge of a new research and analysis program and nothing else. By the summer of 2000, he had left the organization. In an interview I conducted with him in March 2000, Heffner said he felt that he had no choice but to leave GLAAD because the restructuring had made him powerless and the organization was no longer accountable to a grassroots constituency. Apart from Loe, he said, there was no one left in a senior position with an activist background. GLAAD had become, in his estimation, nothing more than a "gay PR firm." From Garry's perspective, Heffner "had very strong ideas" about what GLAAD should focus on, and his "community background" with ACT UP, among other organizations, "was an important complement" to her own strengths. Heffner, she told me in an interview, was "somebody who was about where we were going next, somebody about vision and about 'let's do this now,'" but his vision did not accord with Garry's immediate priorities. By the end of Heffner's time at GLAAD, he and Garry were only speaking through their lawyers.[10]

Heffner's fate in a restructured GLAAD illustrates the argument I have made throughout this chapter, namely that the organization's trajectory from grassroots mobilization to an institutional model oriented to main-

streaming was neither natural nor inevitable, but the outcome of decisions made by agents who, at key moments, had the power to exclude
those whose perspectives did not accord with their own. As I describe in
the next chapter, GLAAD's leaders as I encountered them in 2000–01 had
largely given up on confrontational activism and were oriented to insider
strategies. They had good reason to feel as though their moment had
arrived; until, that is, the repressed began to make its inevitable return.

## CHAPTER 2

# "We Want In": The Politics of Access and Inclusion

In this, the first of three ethnographic chapters at the heart of this book, I examine the cultural and economic conditions that enabled GLAAD's leaders to see themselves as the vanguard of a new brand of media activism oriented to access to decision-makers and the inclusion of LGBT people within mainstream institutions. As I first encountered them, GLAAD's leaders appeared confident that they – and their values, skills, and approaches – were exactly what the LGBT movement needed at that point in history. They found support for this belief in an article they commissioned from historian John D'Emilio, which provided the backdrop for the strategic plan GLAAD adopted in September 1999.

In "Cycles of Change, Questions of Strategy: The Gay and Lesbian Movement after Fifty Years," D'Emilio (2000) distinguishes between three "core outlooks" that have characterized different phases of the gay and lesbian movement's evolution. The first of these, "give us a hearing," describes efforts in the 1950s and 1960s to counter prevailing conceptions of homosexuality as a sin, crime, or illness. The second, "here we are," encapsulates the movement's emphasis on visibility and community-building in the 1970s and 1980s. D'Emilio argues that the third and current core outlook, "we want in," is oriented to the "full inclusion of homosexuals in the core institutions of "American society" (49), a strategy predicated on winning support from the heterosexual majority.

In the essay's conclusion, D'Emilio states that his characterization of the movement's emphasis on integration within mainstream institutions is "meant to be descriptive rather than prescriptive" (50). Ignoring this caveat, the strategic document GLAAD adopted in September 1999 was striking for the way it rhetorically positioned D'Emilio as a mainstreaming-sanctioning authority, someone whose illustrious credentials somehow helped to guarantee that history was on the organization's side as it envisioned its strategic direction for the next three years. GLAAD's strategy, the board of directors mandated, would focus on "all that is explicit and implicit in the phrase 'we want in.'"

In support of this strategy, the plan outlined three "strategic imperatives." The first, "Engage Constructively," emphasized dialogue, persuasion, influence, education, and "common ground" when dealing with media institutions, but added that confrontation might still be used "when necessary." The second, "Maximize Impact," suggested that GLAAD's leaders understood that further organizational growth was intimately connected to its mainstream media visibility. To maximize impact, therefore, meant to prioritize activities with the greatest potential for "reach and efficacy" and for developing new revenue streams. The third, "Harness the Power of Diversity," asserted an intention to "define ourselves broadly and openly," "seek out and incorporate diverse life experiences, talents, expertise, ideas and opinions," and "work to knit these together into a whole which is greater than the sum of its parts."

In this chapter, I analyze key examples of how GLAAD's strategic plan was put into practice. First, I employ a mix of archival, observational, and interview data to describe how GLAAD's leaders saw themselves (and their backgrounds, motivations, values, and attitudes) in relation to the media professionals they wanted to engage. Second, I narrate my experiences as a participant observer at the various Media Awards ceremonies I attended during my fieldwork. I also analyze how the Media Awards portrayed GLAAD to media professionals, major donors, and mainstream audiences as the catalyst of great changes in how media represent LGBT people. Finally, I employ a mixture of interview and archival data, as well as textual analysis, to discuss GLAAD's rebranding, which I argue expressed a vision of "state-managerial" diversity aligned with the marketing objectives of its corporate donors, Absolut Vodka chief among them. Together, these three sections sketch a portrait of the core values that animated GLAAD's leaders as they implemented a strategy based on access to media producers and inclusion within mainstream institutions, and constructed themselves as the historical agents best able to realize their vision of full LGBT integration into mainstream US society.

## Engage Constructively

Here, through an examination of the self-narratives of GLAAD's leaders and their backgrounds, expressed motivations, and attitudes, I describe what they saw as the movement's history and their unique contribution to it. GLAAD's newly branded activists, I argue, steeped in a media professional habitus that valued insider status above all, produced the organization in their own "respectable" image and that of the institutions from whence they came. As a result, traditional activist strategies like direct action came to be minimized in favour of the imperative to engage constructively, wherein being constructive signified avoiding confrontation whenever possible. Even so, an unresolved tension between their roles as both corporate/media professionals and LGBT activists lingered in the background.

I first met Joan Garry, GLAAD's executive director from 1997 to 2005, on 2 February 2000. I had set off at five in the morning to catch the New York City train in Berlin, Connecticut, about an hour's drive from my home in Northampton, Massachusetts. As the train pulled in to Manhattan, the sky overhead was tinged with citrus hues of pink, yellow, and orange as rays of sunlight pierced through the clouds and cast sharp sheets of light over large expanses of the city, making it appear strangely new to me. I had made this voyage before, but only as a tourist; on that day, I was a participant observer encountering my field site for the first time.

From Penn Station, I made my way to GLAAD, which was located in a dingy industrial building in Chelsea. The building had no lobby to speak of, only a narrow entranceway with painted concrete floors, banged up metal doors, and an old freight elevator that I rode up to the fifth floor to find the GLAAD office, which could not have been much larger than a tennis court. GLAAD's deputy director, Jason Heffner, who had been my first contact with the organization and helped with the process of negotiating entrée, welcomed me. My meeting with Garry was scheduled for that afternoon, so Heffner was kind enough to provide me with a three-ring binder full of archival materials he had gathered from GLAAD's storage locker. I sat down in the cluttered conference room and began rifling through the documents: the articles of incorporation, the first set of bylaws, and minutes from early GLAAD meetings.

Garry arrived for our meeting twenty minutes late from a hair appointment. I had been speaking with Heffner in his office, and Garry popped in to see us, apologized for the delay, and invited me to sit down with her. Garry as I encountered her was a petite woman with medium-length brown hair and a charismatic countenance that amply compensated for what she lacked in stature. She had a disarming way with humour, and a folksy gift for putting people at ease. Her first words to me were: "I hope you're not going to grill me on anything today." I responded: "Actually, I was hoping you weren't going to grill me!" She told me how pleased she was that I was conducting a study of the organization and expressed how valuable she thought an outsider's perspective would be.

Asked how I had come to be interested in GLAAD, I explained that I was a doctoral student in communication and had long been interested in the relationships between activism and media. Born in Ottawa, Ontario, I had spent the early 1990s in Montreal at a time when segments of the local LGBT community had been experiencing conflicts with the local police. I had witnessed how the community had rallied and organized in response to police harassment, leading to the creation of Montreal's Pride festival, Divers/Cité, which had grown by leaps and bounds over a few years to become one of the largest in North America. In the process, I said, the community's relationship to local media had also been transformed as Divers/Cité came to be seen as an important summer festival alongside such mainstream events as the Montreal Jazz Festival and the Just for Laughs comedy festival.

My master's thesis at McGill University explored how the formation of a gay village in Montreal had contributed to the emergence of a shared sense of identity and community and helped to transcend conflicts in gay politics over language and Quebec independence. The gay village, I argued, is a paradoxical space that both reinforces and counters the exclusions wrought by the dominant culture. The symbolic exclusion of gays and lesbians is made material in gay space, even as that space provides a basis from which to revalue gay difference as integral to the city's economic and cultural life. As such, I came to see the gay village as enacting a compromise with the dominant culture whereby gay difference is simultaneously set apart from and incorporated within the mosaic of the city's cultural mainstream. This incorporation, however, comes at the cost of reinforcing other exclusions based on class, age, gender, and race as some differences, especially those that best lend themselves to commodification, came to be valued above others. Thus, I argued, the relative inclusion of some is predicated on the further marginalization (both material and symbolic) of those who occupy less central positions in the cultural economy of sexual differences.

As I was finishing my master's thesis, I yearned for the kind of methodological training that might allow me to render in more concrete terms how space, identity, community, cultural practices, and politics manifest themselves in lived experience. I resolved to pursue my academic training at the University of Massachusetts, Amherst, where I would have the opportunity to study ethnographic methods alongside cultural studies and queer theory. When the time came to propose a topic for my dissertation, I went in search of a field site that would allow me to put what I had learned into practice. It was right around this time that Chastity Bono, who GLAAD had recently hired as its first entertainment media director, gave a talk at my university. Heffner, whose weekend home was not far from my university, accompanied her.

Bono's talk struck me as steeped in the kind of positive images framework that I had been taught to critique in my doctoral coursework, an impression that led me to wonder if the same framework could be said to guide GLAAD's activism as a whole. I spent the next few weeks mapping out a project that would explore how GLAAD went about deciding between good and bad representations of LGBT people. Meanwhile, I sought out opportunities to meet with Heffner, a task made easier by the close-knit nature of small-town gay life. Heffner showed up at a friend's Christmas party and I was able to pitch my idea for an ethnographic study of GLAAD. He responded with interest, and some weeks later I was able to meet with him and, with his help, eventually gain entrée into the organization.

In telling Garry about the circumstances that had led me to GLAAD, I spoke of how all of the necessary elements had come together in short succession to make it possible for me to embark on this project. "The stars were in alignment," Garry responded, as indeed I felt they had been. In retrospect, I have come to understand that the timing of my request to study GLAAD was fortunate because I arrived when many people in the organization had reason to feel as though it had the wind in its sails, and comparatively fewer reasons to feel threatened by an outsider. Like the media professionals the organization regularly dealt with I, too, could be engaged constructively.

Shortly after I arrived at GLAAD, I obtained a written copy of a speech Garry had given to the gay and lesbian employee group of Bell Atlantic. The speech connected Garry's personal narrative as a mother and former media executive to a story about the evolution of the gay and lesbian movement. She described herself as someone from a corporate background who, until she came to GLAAD, "did not consider [herself] political at all." "My activism was all about my family," she said. As a partnered lesbian with kids living in the New Jersey suburbs, Garry claimed, she brought a unique ability to put herself "in the other guys' shoes."

Garry went on to describe her sense of how GLAAD had evolved: "Things have changed in fifteen years. We've made solid progress culturally ... And as a result of that progress, GLAAD's strategies have changed. Today I see our work is largely ... about building relationships and much about education." In a key section of the speech, she invited her audience of corporate managers and executives to "revisit the images we conjure up when we consider the word 'activist.'" Activism, she said, is no longer just the "direct action methods" that "helped create a picture for America of a gay rights activist." Referring to the early years at GLAAD, she stated, "back then, no one was paying any attention, and the only strategy that made any sense was of the 'in your face' variety," a mode of activism she compared to banging on the door. "Their job," she said, "was simply to be heard and to do what they could ... to get that door open." The new professional activism, by contrast, was about building relationships and educating corporate decision-makers. The ground of advocacy, she implied, had shifted away from the unruliness of the street and been replaced by the efficiency of the boardroom. The speech positioned GLAAD as the vanguard of this new brand of activism.

That Garry's perspective on the evolution of activism was widely shared at GLAAD can be illustrated with three short examples. In an interview I conducted with him, GLAAD board member and Showtime Networks executive Gene Falk summed up the strategic value of access-based strategies in this way: "It's so much better to not have to fight the fights." Similarly, GLAAD communications director Steve Spurgeon told me that during his job interview, one interviewer said that it would be difficult to picture him "chained to the fence in front of the *New York Times*." Spurgeon told me he answered: "Why would I chain myself when I can just call them up for a meeting?" Another high-level GLAAD staffer referred to people in the movement who still believed in militant direct action as "good activists for ten years ago." Such references to traditional activists on the part of GLAAD staffers were sometimes followed by phrases like "God love them!" or "Bless their hearts!" Why protest in the streets when you can simply walk through the corporate door, briefcase in hand, and hold polite discussions in well-appointed boardrooms?

As I began to research GLAAD's history, however, I came to feel that this view of direct action as part of the past tended to minimize its value and central importance for GLAAD's founders. At one point in her speech, Garry went so far as to say that the "folks who founded GLAAD back in 1985 probably did not consider themselves activists either but rather just a group of writers fed up with how the *New York Post* was covering the AIDS epidemic." Such talk would, no doubt, have come as a surprise to the many GLAAD founders, Arnie Kantrowitz among them, who had cut their teeth in the militant Gay Activists Alliance in the early 1970s. In an interview I conducted with him in his Staten Island office, Kantrowitz, a professor of English literature, told me that when he introduced himself to Garry at a GLAAD function toward the beginning of her tenure, she responded with an "uh-huh" that betrayed a complete lack of recognition. "I felt very nice about that," Kantrowitz continued, chuckling under his breath. Then, he adopted the campy tone of voice of a matriarch in a soap opera confronting a character with amnesia: "But Joan!" he squealed with visible delight, "You're my daughter!"

I too had been struck by how little new entrants to GLAAD (by which I mean top-level staff and board directors recently recruited from the private sector) seemed to know about the history of gay and lesbian media activism or even about GLAAD's own organizational history. An early GLAAD board member, Jewelle Gomez, told me about an otherwise pleasant encounter with a new board member who she said displayed no interest whatsoever in learning about the organization's early days. Scott Seomin, the director of entertainment media, had no idea that a one-man organization called the Gay Media Task Force had performed duties virtually identical to his in the mid- to late-1970s. Addressing college students in the fall of 2000, Spurgeon stated that GLAAD had existed for "ten to twelve years," as though its 1985 founding was so far in the past that the date could only be approximated.

Equally striking to me was the extent to which GLAAD's leaders appeared invested in foregrounding gay and lesbian identities that were, in all respects apart from sexual orientation, congruent with mainstream norms and values; an observation consistent with Michael Warner's (1999) contention in *The Trouble with Normal* that, over the years, movement leaders have learned that the quickest route to power and acceptance is to repudiate sex, i.e., to attempt to distance gay and lesbian identity from sexual practice.

A 2003 op-ed by Garry in *USA Today*, perhaps the most mainstream of newspapers, is emblematic of Warner's account of movement leaders' attempts to separate respectable gay and lesbian identities from shameful sex. Garry begins with a confession seemingly designed to provoke her readers into identifying with her: "I get uncomfortable talking about sex. As a good Irish-Catholic girl, public discussions of that most private of associations bring out the prude in me." Then she casually informs the reader that she is, perhaps just like them, a parent of "school-age kids." When her kids "bring it [sex] up" she assures her audience, "we don't talk about the mechanics, but about love, family, respect, safety, honesty and responsibility." "Being gay," Garry tells her presumably heterosexual audience, is less about "what someone does in the bedroom" than it is about "common values" like love and family. It is "a state of being" and "not a sex act."[1]

In an earlier *USA Today* op-ed published in 2002, Garry took the strategy even further by almost disavowing that her leadership of one of the largest gay and lesbian organizations in the United States had anything to do with her lesbian identity. Writing about the coming out of actress and talk show host Rosie O'Donnell, Garry declared: "Rosie and I have a lot in common. We're both motivated more by our role as parents than as lesbians."[2] In privileging parenting over lesbian desire,

Garry constructed herself as a "postgay lesbian" whose "gay difference is swallowed into the norm" and who presents no challenge to the "all-encompassing force of the heterosexual contract" (Reed 2007, 21).

Warner's analysis of the cultural politics of respectability stresses that the strategy is ultimately untenable and exerts a high cost. It is untenable because it attempts to cover up what needs to be dismantled – the shame and stigma attached to minority sexual practices and identities – and thus leaves in place the cultural basis for the differential treatment accorded to sexual minorities. As Gayle Rubin (1993, 11) argues, Western societies have evolved sexual classifications that anchor cultural conceptions of sexual morality. Reproductive, monogamous, heterosexual sex is valued above all and is the standard by which sexual normalcy is measured. In this value system, gays and lesbians who conform most closely to the ideal of sexual normalcy (those in stable, long-term relationships, for example), are accorded a certain measure of respectability, while those who cannot or will not are consistently denied resources. To wage politics on the basis of respectability, therefore, damages the LGBT movement because respectability requires an "other" (deserving of stigma and shame) against which to define itself. The best that assertions of respectability can do is to help make life a bit easier for those who are willing and able to live by – or have the means to appear to live by – the rules, norms, and values of the majority heterosexual culture.

For these reasons, Warner (1999) laments the rise to prominence in the 1990s of movement leaders oriented toward respectability. The movement, in his view, became a victim of the success of earlier activists whose efforts to destigmatize homosexuality lowered the "threshold of defiance required for entry into the movement" (75–6). The movement's "new arrivals," he contends, "are less disposed to challenge the force of shame and stigma fully," often behave as though they believe the movement belongs to them, display a shocking ignorance of its history, or "dismiss that history as a stage of immaturity" (75). Under such conditions, he concludes, "the new respectability of lesbian and gay politics is not the movement's coming of age; it is, in effect, a takeover" (75).

Warner's critique of the movement's new leaders was familiar to GLAAD's leaders, to the extent that it accurately distilled the perspectives of many long-time activists with whom they interacted. I asked Spurgeon if he sometimes felt accused of being part of a movement takeover. He became visibly emotional and answered that he had found the "resentment and distrust" toward him "hurtful" and could not understand, echoing the famous words of Rodney King, why there could not be enough room for everyone to get along. "I can contribute something," he said, "I am here to be used." Spurgeon acknowledged his lack of prior involvement in the movement as a limitation, but pointed to his professional background in marketing and public relations as compensation.

Spurgeon told me that the movement now required people with a "sophisticated understanding of how the world works," which, in the context of our conversation, clearly referred to corporate experience like his own. He told me that he could not have taken the GLAAD job a few years prior to his appointment because, he said, he was not ready for the movement and the movement was not ready for him. Landing the job was a "fortuitous intersection of need and opportunity," he told me.

Elizabeth Birch, the former director of the Human Rights Campaign, expressed a similar sentiment when she told a reporter that in "the 1990s, there had to be a meeting of minds between raw activist spirit and the communications and marketing techniques that define a new voice for gay America ... It came together in the person of Elizabeth Birch" (quoted in Chasin 2000, 209). Apart from its breathtaking arrogance, this statement is symptomatic of a shift in the 1990s that allowed people like Birch and Spurgeon to feel like they were exactly what the movement needed at that point in history. The driving force for this shift, as Alexandra Chasin (2000) shows, was the construction of a gay and lesbian market, which considerably enhanced the value of LGBT organizations as sites of corporate philanthropy. That market development created pathways in both directions between corporations looking to expand their reach and movement organizations looking to secure additional resources. No wonder many new entrants to the movement felt like they had been anointed by history: "Imagine what you would have done if three years ago you woke up and found that someone had handed you the movement," Birch reportedly said. "I'll bet you would have made most of the decisions I've made" (quoted in Chasin 2000, 209).

Spurgeon saw himself as someone who brought to the movement knowledge about how to gain mainstream respect and acceptance, an expertise that, in an interview with me, he contrasted with an insular activism based on interacting with "cronies at [Boston gay and lesbian newspaper] *Bay Windows*." "I know how to market to America," he said, because he had spent many decades doing just that. This kind of expertise did not come cheaply, however. As highly skilled professionals from corporate backgrounds, he and other new entrants commanded some of the highest salaries in the LGBT non-profit sector.

Applying the market logic attached to their previous positions, new entrants tended to measure workers' value by the yardstick of what salaries they would fetch in the corporate world. Movement organizations, they reasoned, needed to offer competitive salaries if they were to attract the right kind of talent. In turn, these higher salaries reinforced the idea that GLAAD staff were professionals who provided resources to media companies rather than activists who opposed them, a shift that also provided a much better platform from which to raise money (as a kind of quid pro quo for services rendered). As GLAAD's annual budgets increased from year to year, so did the salaries of its top staffers. For example, Garry's total compensation in 1998 was $108,302. By 2003, she was making $228,250 per year, making her the highest paid executive director of any LGBT movement organization that year.[3]

Nonetheless, for those who came from the private sector, working for GLAAD represented a serious income loss. Spurgeon, who had at one point in his career held a top position at one of the largest public relations firms in the world, earned a salary in the low six figures. Seomin made $80,581 in 2001, a fraction of what he earned as a producer at *Entertainment Tonight*. In discussing his wages with me, Seomin made sure that I understood that he considered himself "well-paid," but also emphasized that working at GLAAD had meant sacrificing parts of the lifestyle to which he had grown accustomed. Similarly, on more than a few occasions I heard Spurgeon jokingly refer to the fact that since he had joined a non-profit organization, "the clothes that I had are the clothes that I have." The story may have dissimulated a deeper, less often acknowledged loss: during an ice-breaking exercise at a board meeting, Spurgeon shared that he had been disinherited by his father for taking a job in a gay and lesbian organization. New entrants to the movement may have benefited from a lower "threshold of defiance required for entry" into movement work, as Warner (1999) puts it, but this is not to say that they suffered no negative consequences as a result of it.

GLAAD staff from corporate backgrounds also found adjusting to the non-profit world personally difficult at times. As professionals from hierarchical corporate settings, they had come to expect a level of deference to their opinions that the more consensus-based traditions of movement work did not always grant them. Seomin, for example, told me of his frustration that his "professional opinion" was not always understood or respected. As a result, he said, he felt obliged to insulate himself from co-workers and activists in other organizations to get the "real work done": "It's either that or not get the work done because I'm pulling my hair out trying to be understood." Garry, he said, felt like a "soul-mate because she came from the for-profit world."

Despite identifying strongly as media professionals, Seomin, Garry, and Spurgeon all expressed ambivalence about their past corporate lives. During an interview in his office in Los Angeles, for example, Seomin told me that in spite of having landed his dream job at *Entertainment Tonight*, he found the experience of working in the television industry less than fulfilling. He described a conversation he once had with his therapist. "I've got everything I want," he said. "I have two houses, two cars, and I take every August at Martha's Vineyard with my friends ... what's missing?" His therapist answered: "I think it's about your work ... I mean, how many times can you interview Sharon Stone?" After this conversation, Seomin told me, he set out to find more meaningful work and soon heard that Bono had resigned from her position at GLAAD. Seomin said it was like "a light bulb" lit up over his head.

Garry also described her motivation for joining GLAAD as stemming from a desire to put her corporate skills to more progressive uses. During a board meeting, she talked about how she came out in 1980, met her partner in 1981, and was for years a "stay-at-home mom." In 1989, she successfully sued the state of New Jersey for the right to legally adopt her partner's children. The following year, she took a job at Showtime, where she stayed until she joined GLAAD in 1998. She told board members that her last role at Showtime was to promote such pay-per-view events as Mike Tyson's return to boxing after serving time for a rape conviction. As Garry put it: "I began to feel like I had more to offer." Her partner, also a media executive, was recruited to the GLAAD board around the same time as the search for a new executive director got underway. One day, Garry said, her partner turned to her and said: "They could really use someone like you." Garry thought it over and decided to apply because, she said, someone like her would "lend a refreshing voice to the community" by virtue of her stereotype-busting suburban lifestyle, complete with "picket fence, a minivan, and kids."

Spurgeon also cited dissatisfaction with his former corporate life as a major factor in his decision to work for a gay and lesbian organization. Introducing himself to a group of University of California students to whom he was giving a talk, which I attended and recorded, Spurgeon said:

> I've been in public relations for thirty years. Before that I was a school teacher. Most of my – in fact, all of my experience until about a year ago was in corporate environments, public relations, and agency work ... I worked at Fleishman-Hillard and Ketchum Communications for years and at Nissan North America where I was PR director. I have a master's in mass communications with an emphasis in broadcast journalism from Ohio State. [I] got involved in gay and lesbian work ... issues, probably about a year ago. I'd always been involved as a volunteer in some issues ... politically involved. But I decided to work in that area when I just couldn't stand my job any longer, and ... It wasn't that I disliked the job, it's just it ... when I turned fifty I decided, I think it would be nice if I did something I actually cared about and felt made a difference. I'm working awfully hard and frankly I don't really care what United Airlines's fourth quarter earnings are anymore. So I thought I'd put my efforts towards something I cared about.

The similarity of Spurgeon's narrative to those offered by Garry and Seomin complicates Warner's claims about the corporate "takeover" of the LGBT movement and points to the importance of understanding how working conditions in corporate contexts shape the subjectivities of private sector executives, managers, and professionals who make the switch to social movement work. New entrants to GLAAD from corporate settings hoped to gain personal fulfillment by engaging in socially redeeming work. In this sense, the profound transformations they may have caused within the movement were rooted not in a conscious attempt to take it over, but in a deeply felt need to put their skills to more pro-social uses and, in so doing, perhaps compensate for the alienation they had experienced in their corporate jobs. GLAAD provided them with a way to become involved in social change in a way that felt right, comfortable, and appropriate, and gave them a chance to apply their media-related professional skills. As some board members defined it, GLAAD stood for a brand of gay and lesbian activism with which they, as corporate insiders, could live.

David Steward, one of the board's co-chairs during my fieldwork, was exemplary of the complex motivations that drove GLAAD's leadership. According to a biographical sketch distributed to other board members, Steward's corporate expertise centred on "building or redeveloping" media brands. In 1997, he became the chief executive officer of TV Guide, which he described to other GLAAD board members as a "big job." He soon realized, however, that he was "working for [Rupert] Murdoch" and had "issues with that" because he "despise[d] him politically." His first contact with GLAAD was as a Media Awards table host, which he said was "a great thing to do with gay clients." This initial involvement stirred up guilt about "not doing something worthwhile." "I wanted my life to be not just about making money," he said. He became co-chair soon after joining the board, a quick rise that he attributed to his strategic planning experience.

Asked to talk about the events that had led him to get involved with GLAAD, he described coming out in college and joining Cornell Gay Liberation, not as an activist, he was quick to add, but to "organize disco parties." Like many gay men of his generation, he said, he was politicized by the AIDS crisis in the mid-eighties when his friends started to die; something he said got his "blood flowing." In 1988, angered by Republican inaction on AIDS, he voted Democratic for the first time and, in 1990, began to fundraise for Empire State Pride, a New York-based gay and lesbian political action committee. At around the same time, he began to summer in the Hamptons instead of Fire Island, which he said was indicative of having grown "more serious, more adult." Steward went on to describe his sense that the GLAAD board had evolved from being "made up of volunteer activist-picketers" to being "more professional." He contended that this orientation "better reflects the diversity of our community" and joked that the board was now made up of more "picketees than picketers," a transition he likened to GLAAD becoming more like an "adolescent," i.e., not quite yet adult but "in the midst of professionalizing."

Steward's narrative functioned to explain and justify (to himself and others) his newfound prominence in the movement: just as he had "grown up," so had GLAAD. He drew a parallel between his own personal and professional trajectory toward adulthood and GLAAD's development. In applying a personal/professional growth narrative to the organization's evolution, Steward implicitly labelled the more confrontational strategies of the past as similar to children acting out.

On more than one occasion, Steward expressed his discomfort with the word "activist" as a label to describe himself. "I'm not an activist," he said during a board meeting. "I always thought of myself as the inside guy." He explained that activism, to him, meant "making life unpleasant for other people," and recounted a conversation with Garry in which she had challenged him to "create a definition of the word activist that includes you." This way of approaching the activist-professional divide, he said, was "powerful to me" because he has "struggled to be an insider" all his life, but also "believes in organizational work." Being on GLAAD's board, he stated, was a way of being "associated with that word that doesn't make me feel uncomfortable." By redefining activism as an inside game that required the professional skills and values they already possessed, Steward and others from the corporate world were able to mitigate the cognitive dissonance that emerged from finding themselves at the helm of an activist organization. They had created a definition of activism whose core outlook, "we want in," not only included but also required them. No wonder, then, that they felt so good about their roles in GLAAD. As one long-time board member said to his colleagues: "Working with GLAAD makes me feel as good as you can feel about something you do."

In keeping with Warner's (1999, 75) contention that the LGBT movement leaders of the 1990s tended to "dismiss" earlier movement history "as a stage of immaturity," GLAAD's leaders constructed and institutionalized a historical narrative that justified their newfound prominence in the movement in terms of a progressive evolution away from confrontation with dominant institutions and toward a professionalization that mimicked their own personal and professional development as corporate high-achievers. To them, the "hostile takeover" of the movement that Warner writes about probably felt like a historically mandated handover: the ostensibly normal outcome of a process by which movements and organizations, like all well-adjusted children and teenagers, grow up to become pragmatic and reasonable adults.

This narrative, however, mistakenly takes a story of personal and professional growth and grafts it onto a teleological narrative of LGBT media activism. It forgets the extent to which the history of media activism has often involved both cooperation and confrontation with media companies, rather than the implied linear trajectory. Without the historical perspective needed to recognize LGBT visibility as an always/already precarious, negotiated, ambivalent, conditional, and revocable achievement, GLAAD's new entrants, by and large, tended to perceive the conditions that structured their possibilities for action as the culmination of a natural process that had put them in charge of leading the movement to new heights. Having internalized the limits and rewards of a media advocacy system designed by media companies to minimize confrontation and construct new markets (Pekurny 1977; Montgomery 1989), they saw themselves as ideally suited to the needs of a movement increasingly embedded within the machinery of corporate marketing. Their newfound positions, based in part on making a public case for their own professionalism and respectability, constituted, in a sense, a takeover of the movement, but one whose conditions were not of their making. Rather than to speak of a takeover, it is more accurate to state that GLAAD's leaders came to occupy positions created for them by the changing social relations, beginning in the 1990s, between LGBT people and market forces. To engage constructively, therefore, did not amount to a shift in political strategy relative to the past so much as a means of taking advantage of new opportunities to make out in the mainstream. Nowhere was this drive to capitalize on new opportunities more evident than in the investment made in the growth of the Media Awards.

## Maximize Impact: The GLAAD Media Awards

The annual GLAAD Media Awards, which honour "individuals and projects in the media and entertainment industries for their fair, accurate and inclusive representations," is given pride of place in GLAAD's 1999 strategic plan as "a unique and powerful way to constructively engage media professionals in the work we do." The awards also constitute a good example of how GLAAD's leaders put into practice the document's second strategic imperative: "Maximize Impact." It would be tempting to dismiss the awards as little more than a fundraising vehicle, but as scholar James F. English (2009, 7) argues in his book about literary prizes, awards are "fundamentally equivocal" in nature: they "cannot be understood strictly in terms of calculation and dealmaking: generosity, celebration, love, play, community, are as real a part of the cultural prize as are marketing strategy and self-promotion." Adopting this perspective can help us understand the centrality of the Media Awards to how GLAAD's leaders thought of themselves and of their organization. As Garry was fond of saying, the Media Awards were the organization's "most important program."

In this section, I give an ethnographic account of front- and backstage aspects of the Media Awards to provide a sense of their value for GLAAD, in both symbolic and economic terms. Much of my account is descriptive of events that I observed and in which I participated. I try to communicate something about the complexity of what is produced when marketing, fundraising, and organizational visibility objectives become intermingled with genuinely felt (if carefully engineered) experiences of generosity, celebration, love, play, and community.

The Media Awards gathered media executives, major donors, media professionals, and celebrities in New York, Los Angeles, San Francisco, and Washington, DC. I participated in and/or observed seven of the eight events held during my fieldwork. These ceremonies were a high-stakes affair for GLAAD because they accounted for a plurality of its annual income: as a whole, the events held in 2000 and 2001 cost over $2 million to produce, gathered some 10,000 people, and raised about $5 million, about $3 million of which came from corporate contributions. Altogether, these funds accounted for just under half of GLAAD's annual budgets for both years. Accordingly, a tremendous amount of time, money, and energy was poured into producing the shows. Four staff members were devoted to them almost full-time and, as Media Awards season rolled into high gear between early April and mid-June, almost every staff person and board member became involved in one way or another, joining a small army of volunteers and paid contractors in various aspects of production, logistics, fundraising, and public and media relations.

Nominations and voting for the Media Awards involved GLAAD volunteers, staff, and board members in a wide variety of roles. Special honorary awards were decided upon most straightforwardly: GLAAD board and staff members suggested potential honourees, the board deliberated, and a decision was made by a majority vote of the board.

Media content nominations, by contrast, arose from a complicated process involving a national nominations committee overseen by the board and administered by a communications staffer. The committee was made up of national nominations co-chairs appointed by the board and various volunteer subcommittees that monitored media content over the course of the year – a task that had become onerous with the rise in the quantity of LGBT images. Media producers were also encouraged to submit nominations for consideration.

In theory, anyone, anywhere in the United States with an interest in doing so could participate in the nominations process. In practice, participation was limited by the fact that most subcommittees met in person in a limited number of cities and were subject to cyclical variations in volunteer involvement. During my fieldwork, the most active subcommittees were both based in Los Angeles: the film and television subcommittee had about ten active members, while the Los Angeles theatre committee had thirty members and a waiting list, probably on account of the free tickets to which members were entitled. Other subcommittees, based in New York (responsible for advertising, daytime drama, newspapers, and magazines), Washington, DC (local theater), or on the Internet (comic books, comic strips, online journalism) were described in a staff report to the board as "functioning," a characterization that suggested low or inconsistent participation.

The national nominations chairs were responsible for developing a ballot proposal based on subcommittee recommendations. By early January, this preliminary ballot was sent to GLAAD board members, who had three days to voice objections or propose changes. In the absence of objections or changes, the ballot was distributed to qualified Media Awards voters: board members, national and local Media Awards co-chairs, national nominations co-chairs, nominations subcommittee members, and GLAAD staff. Subcommittee co-chairs and volunteers voted only in the content category to which they had been assigned. For the final vote, board members, board appointees, and GLAAD staff vastly outnumbered volunteers, despite claims made in GLAAD publications that the nomination and voting process was "volunteer-driven."

In cases where board members had raised objections or proposed that a nominee be added, the matter was referred to an arbitration committee (also controlled by the board leadership). For example, the arbitration process was used in 2001 to decide the fate of the John Schlessinger film *The Next Best Thing*, which starred Madonna and Rupert Everett as a straight woman and gay man who decide to raise a child born as the result of a drunken one-night stand. Though the movie was both a commercial and critical failure, some board members felt it deserved consideration in the category of "outstanding wide release film." This created some difficulties for GLAAD because not only had the (volunteer) nominations subcommittee not made the recommendation to nominate the film, but because it was widely acknowledged by staffers to be a terrible movie. The following excerpt from a mid-level GLAAD staff teleconference is paraphrased from my field notes:

> STAFFER 1: Uhh ... Do we need to talk about *The Next Best Thing*? [*laughter*] I mean, are we getting calls about it, what are we telling people? What is the community saying about it?
> STAFFER 2: Basically, what I'm hearing from the community ... [*pause*] ... is that the movie SUCKS! [*laughter*]
> STAFFER 1: It does, I saw it ... The problem is that you just don't believe anything in the movie. The acting is really bad ... Mind you, Madonna and Rupert Everett are all saying wonderful things in the interviews they're doing with the press.
> STAFFER 3: Ultimately, though, is this something we're going to have to deal with at next year's Media Awards? [*audible groans*]

The conversation reflects staff members' awareness that the nominations process involved considerations beyond the aesthetic and political qualities of individual texts. These mid-level staffers anticipated that the board might want to nominate the film and they would be charged with justifying the choice. Ultimately, the board did indeed decide to nominate the movie, along with *Best in Show*, *Billy Elliot* (which won), and *Wonder Boys*. *The Next Best Thing* may have been a terrible movie, but it was a terrible movie financed by Paramount, made by an illustrious and openly gay director, and starring Madonna and one of the best-known openly gay actors in Hollywood.[4]

According to the Media Awards program book distributed to attendees in 2000, GLAAD used the following criteria to evaluate media content: (1) fairness, accuracy, and inclusiveness; (2) prominence of LGBT content; (3) boldness, originality, and impact; and (4) overall quality. However, the instructions that accompanied the actual ballots distributed to voters stated: "All voting members are *urged* to take the [nominations] Criteria [*sic*] into consideration when casting their ballots" (emphasis mine) and "*must* read or watch all the nominees in their entirety in order to vote in any given category" (emphasis original). In other words, while the rules required that voters be familiar with the content of nominated materials, they merely encouraged them to consider the official criteria.

Among the official criteria, the perceived impact of a media text was a key determinant of whether or not it received an award. Given that mainstream audiences are generally thought to interpret and value texts differently from minority audiences, the question of what constitutes impact was a controversial one. While many LGBT volunteers of the nominations subcommittees tended to value texts for their originality and complexity, the voting patterns and discussions among GLAAD staff and board members suggested that perceived impact on heterosexual audiences was the most important criterion.

The question of impact is discussed in an archived 1997 draft for an op-ed written by then-GLAAD director of communications, Alan Klein, who appeared motivated by a desire to explain why more mainstream fare tends to prevail at the Media Awards. "The quality of the work is not the only criteria [*sic*] that the GLAAD Media Awards Nominations Committee volunteers measure," Klein wrote. "The ... nominations committees also examine the impact a work has on its audience. This criteria [*sic*] sometimes pits small and large circulation gay newspapers and magazines against mainstream consumer publications with readers that far outnumber those of lesbian and gay media. These larger and diverse audiences benefit greatly from gay- or lesbian-oriented stories they may have never been exposed to otherwise. The work's impact, then, may tip the scales in favor of a mainstream media submission."

A striking example of tipping the scales was the 2001 Media Award given to *The Broken Hearts Club*. The film, written and directed by television writer/producer Greg Berlanti, was nominated in the "Outstanding Film – Limited Release" category along with *Aimee & Jaguar*, *Before Night Falls*, and *Urbania*. Although *The Broken Hearts Club*, which is set in the gay enclave of West Hollywood, was among the films nominated by the film and television subcommittee, few volunteers had ranked it highly in comparison to the other nominees, all of which were critically successful art films.

*The Broken Hearts Club*, by contrast, was a rather mawkish portrayal of the romantic entanglements of a group of gay friends who re-evaluate the meaning and purpose of their lives after the death of a gay father figure played by John Mahoney, the actor who portrayed Kelsey Grammer's father on *Frasier*. Of the nominated films, Berlanti's had the broadest appeal because of an abundance of likeable characters, genre-bound plotlines, a familiar sitcom-like balance of humour and sentiment, and a neatly resolved moral message about thirty-something gay men who give up on their adolescent ways. In contrast to the dark and morally complex AIDS fable *Urbania*, which had strong support among nominations subcommittee members, *The Broken Hearts Club* played squarely into heterosexual norms of what it means to grow up. It was a film to which one might comfortably take one's mother.

Moreover, shortly before the vote that gave *The Broken Hearts Club* its Media Award, Berlanti made a $50,000 personal donation to GLAAD. Voters were not necessarily swayed by Berlanti's largesse, but the donation does raise the question of the extent to which the nomination and voting process – which gave the most weight to the very people most directly responsible for raising money for GLAAD – opened the door to a host of considerations other than those that were officially acknowledged.

The Media Awards were characterized by a tension between a publicly promoted dimension that emphasized volunteer involvement and aesthetic and political criteria for determining what constituted "good" or "impactful" representations of LGBT people on the one hand, and a disavowed dimension related to the fact that the Media Awards were first and foremost a fundraising vehicle designed to promote friendly relations with large media companies on the other. Maintaining the aura of prestige that made the Media Awards a successful fundraising vehicle required concealing their economic logic in favour of the claim that the voting was volunteer-driven and proceeded mainly on the basis of aesthetic and political criteria.

This economic dimension of the Media Awards also complicates the meaning of GLAAD's mission statement with regards to promoting "fair, accurate and inclusive" media representations. Notions of fairness, accuracy, and inclusiveness all assume a realist epistemology whereby representations are thought to have the capacity to show the world "as it really is," a realist framing of GLAAD's mission that allows the organization to align itself with the seemingly neutral values of journalistic "objectivity" and to appeal to media professionals' assumptions and values. However, as critics in cultural studies argue, there is no Archimedean standpoint outside of representation from which to assess images' fairness, accuracy, and inclusivity. By nature, representations constitute the reality they claim to represent (Hall 1997).

In practice, this means that far from reflecting an objective reality, representations become endowed with meanings, politics, and aesthetic value via discursive processes that implicate (and help to construct) the perspectives and interests of particular social agents at all stages of the production, dissemination, and reception of images. For an organization like GLAAD to claim a representation as fair, accurate, inclusive, or impactful, therefore, is to do so from particular standpoints. Thus, the realist epistemological framing of GLAAD's mission statement and of the Media Awards nominations criteria concealed the fact that what counted as fair, accurate, and inclusive tended to narrowly reflect the values, perspectives, tastes, and economic interests of an elite segment of the LGBT community with strong ties to media companies.

The process by which GLAAD determined the seating arrangements for the Media Awards was also governed by an economic logic. However, the protocol for making these decisions was complex: it involved not just economic considerations or the physical pieces of how to fit a set number of people, tables, and chairs into a particular room, but myriad other factors related to reputation, status, money, and professional and personal relationships. In 2000–01, all the Media Awards ceremonies were formal dinners held in hotel ballrooms, with the exception of Washington's, which was a stage show. Seating arrangements were among the last things to be decided before each event. A single change in the location of a table relative to the stage could have ripple effects throughout the seating chart.

I attended two seating meetings in 2001, one in New York and the other in Los Angeles. In both cases, specialized consultants had done much of the groundwork in advance. In New York, the meeting took place in a suite at the mid-town Hilton, where the New York Awards were held. In addition to the three consultants (all of them women), there were two GLAAD staffers present: Jason Burlingame, director of special events, and an assistant, Lane Brooks, manager of special events. Later, two more staffers would review the seating charts, each with an eye on their own constituencies: Julie Anderson, director of development, would ensure that corporate and foundation donors were appropriately seated, and Jeffrey Sosnick, director of annual giving, would do the same for individual major donors. As always, Garry, along with the board co-chairs, would have the final say.

Burlingame was responsible for determining priorities and Brooks helped with suggestions as needed. One consultant worked out the puzzle of where seats were still available and suggested possibilities when the rest of the group was stumped. Another consultant was assigned to clerical support: printing out materials, making phone calls, and finding information. The boss from the consultancy kept a certain distance from the nitty-gritty, but would sometimes offer to put Burlingame in touch with famous people or tell amusing anecdotes involving celebrities and seating difficulties she had solved in the past.

When I arrived at the Hilton, those gathered were already poring over a large diagram with numbered circles indicating the position of the tables. Names had been written on almost all the tables, indicating either a company or table host. The task now was to verify the seating plan and make changes where appropriate. Sosnick provided a list of major donors (people who contribute $2,500 and up annually), each of whom he ranked on the basis of their importance to the organization using a letter grade system ranging from A+ to C.[5] For the most part, table positions and rankings were determined by donation amounts, but other considerations also came into play: whether a donor was owed a favour, whether he or she had been helpful in ways besides giving money, how long he or she had been giving to GLAAD, and whether or not it was his or her "turn" to receive more favourable treatment. On some occasions, similarly ranked donors were assigned a better or worse table based on whether or not they had professional or personal connections to GLAAD board members or upper-level staff. On one occasion, the usual equation between giving and seating broke down completely: someone described as a "billionaire" who had only purchased two tickets at the minimum $350 level was given an excellent table on the assumption that this kind of preferential treatment might motivate him to give more to GLAAD in the future.

Seating assignments proceeded in the following order: first the corporate sponsors and award nominees, then the board co-chairs, other board members, major donors by rank, and high-level staff. Once these assignments were more or less in place, seats were found for those whose tickets were paid for by GLAAD, such as celebrities and a limited number of press, followed by the remaining unaffiliated individuals, who tended to be relegated to the back corners of the room along with low-level staff. When problems arose, board members and others with close ties to GLAAD were asked to move back slightly. In other cases, board members who had been particularly active and/or successful at fundraising were rewarded with better tables. A great deal of thought went into where to sit celebrities to maximize their impact. Burlingame pointed out that they should never be seated with journalists because celebrities "get upset when you do that." The best use of people like soap opera actress Susan Lucci, for example, was to make sure they were seated close to a "big corporate sponsor" because corporate people were "impressed by big stars." Brooks, agreeing with Burlingame, pointed out that representatives from a major clothing manufacturer were "dying for a big celebrity."

A few hours into the meeting, it became clear that the one thing that could not change in the equation was that both the Coors Brewing Company and Absolut Vodka, GLAAD's two largest corporate sponsors, had to be seated "centre first," meaning at the four tables closest to the stage in the centre of the room. Burlingame said he wished "we could seat this whole room right here" as he drew a square with his finger around the front centre stage area. "That would make our life easier," he said, notwithstanding the fact that such an arrangement, were it possible, would render the area meaningless as a signifier of status. He then reminded his colleagues that the slightest perception of having been cheated on seating could lead to embarrassing scenes like the one in the previous year when a well-known producer "threw a fit" over his table assignment. This led to talk about whether this producer should be mollified with a better table. "You don't reward bad behaviour," came the response from the head of the events consultancy.

## On with the Show

The 2000 GLAAD Media Awards in Los Angeles took place at the largest available venue of its kind, the Century Plaza Hotel, whose main ballroom can accommodate up to 2,000 people for dinner. Two days before the event, the Los Angeles-based GLAAD communications team – made up of Spurgeon, Seomin, and communications managers Nick Adams, Sean Lund, and Bob Findle – met with Burlingame to clarify roles and responsibilities on the day of the awards show.

The recurring theme of the meeting was the enviable but troublesome overabundance of celebrities, media crews, and corporate sponsors interested in attending the event. For example, E!, which already had two crews covering it for a one-hour special program, had asked for permission to add a third crew for a program Leeza Gibbons, formerly of *Entertainment Tonight*, was producing about gay Hollywood. Although GLAAD staffers were enthusiastic about the idea, they felt they needed to deny the request in order to keep control of the press line. Spurgeon said that media would sometimes try to catch celebrities away from the press line (and the approved background with GLAAD and corporate logos) to ask them questions unrelated to the event. The idea was to provide media with access to celebrities, but in a manner that kept the attention focused on GLAAD and its corporate sponsors. Spurgeon lamented that there were already some "questionable people" who had been approved, like *Taiwan Today* and small gay and lesbian publications. The question to keep in mind, Spurgeon said, was, "Who can serve us best?"

On the day of the event, I arrived at the Century Plaza a few hours in advance and Spurgeon offered to take me on a tour of the facilities. We began with the press line, a narrow area to the side of which a silent auction would take place.[6] Spurgeon explained that the press would be confined to a cordoned-off section about a hundred feet long by ten feet deep where risers had been set up to create three tiers and a de facto pecking order. Individual media representatives were assigned a position according to their perceived importance and the type of media outlet they represented. National media with the largest audiences were given top priority, while international media and LGBT outlets were relegated to the back of the line. Of the LGBT media in attendance, only national magazines the *Advocate* and *Out* were granted first-tier status.

As celebrities moved down the press corridor, they encountered the photographers from the Associated Press, *People*, and other print media photographers, followed by the television cameras and the print journalists. Spurgeon explained that, by convention, minor celebrities would arrive first to maximize their exposure, and the biggest stars, like Elizabeth Taylor and Sharon Stone, would not go through the press line at all. He expected an unprecedented number of media outlets to be represented: thirty-two television crews and fifty-six still photographers, not counting print media.

Spurgeon explained that GLAAD staff would be positioned at the end of the press corridor to intercept celebrities and invite them to take pictures with board members, corporate sponsors, and the Media Awards co-chairs. Beyond this area was a lounge where Absolut Vodka cocktails would be served. Spurgeon then took me to a backstage area where a room had been set up for volunteers to watch the proceedings on closed-circuit television and eat a boxed lunch (sandwiches and salads, soft drinks, and donated SlimFast bars). He referred to another room as the stationary pressroom, an area set up for journalists to photograph and interview celebrities who had just won an award or presented on stage. Seomin would be assigned to this area during the show. Only three photographers – one from the Associated Press, one from *People*, and one working for GLAAD – were permitted to take photos in the main ballroom during the event.

The backstage area also featured a lounge where media representatives could take a break, chat with colleagues, and eat the same meals given to volunteers. Across the hall, twenty tables were set up for dinner, along with two large screen projection televisions for paid guests who could not fit in the main ballroom because the event had been oversold as a result of a logistical glitch. Spurgeon first described it to me as the "overflow room," but later referred to it as the "angry room." The official designation on the sign outside the entrance was "Backstage Tables," as though those seated there would receive privileged access to goings-on.

Later that day, I attended the final production meeting, a harried affair that took place in the ballroom as volunteers were placing program books and promotional materials on the tables. Its purpose was to do a last run-through of all aspects of the show: where presenters would enter the stage, where they would stand or sit, which microphones they would use, what shots were needed (the event was professionally video-recorded), what the lighting scheme would be, how transitions would be made between segments, and whether any video clips would be shown. Much of the discussion centred on how to make the live stage show as telegenic as possible (despite the fact that the event was not broadcast). That the format of the show was modelled after other Hollywood awards shows was clear. At one point, someone raised the question of how presenters should behave when award recipients arrived on stage. The answer came without hesitation: they should be instructed to take two steps back, "like at the Oscars."

The production team consisted of eight men and three women, one of whom, Jehan Agrama, was the event co-chair in charge of production. Her manner was brusque, professional, and focused on the task, except when the situation called for humour. At one point, during a particularly tense part of the meeting, she reached for a large piece of bubble wrap that was concealed in her handbag. She popped just a few bubbles, pre-sumably careful to leave some for the rest of what was sure to be a nerve-wracking afternoon. Agrama ran the meeting with a firm hand: if discussions got carried away over relatively minor details, she pointed out that "we need to get through this. We're running out of time." Later in the evening, she could be seen wearing an elegant ball gown, having her picture taken with celebrities, and smiling as though she had not a care in the world.

The press line got underway at about six that evening, an hour before the official start of the event. As Spurgeon predicted, the first to make their way tended to be only moderately famous: local personali-ties, drag queens from the Los Angeles club circuit, and actors with sup-porting roles in lesser-known series. The press began to get excited when an actor from the MTV series *Undressed*, wearing a fringed, tan-coloured, leather outfit, started to make his way down the line. Photographers shouted things like "look over here" as intense bursts of light emanated from their cameras. Attendees in the adjacent room, where the silent auction was taking place, did not pay much attention. Later, as some of the more famous celebrities started to appear, a small crowd gathered behind the cordons to ogle the likes of Carrie Fisher, who walked through quickly, and ex-*Seinfeld* star Julia Louis-Dreyfus, who appeared to bask in the attention.

There was something seductive for me about the movement of celebrities down this bright and narrow corridor. Only a velvet rope separated us (the attendees) from them (some of the most recognizable faces in contemporary popular culture). With the level of access I had been granted, comparable on this occasion to that of a GLAAD board member or a high-level staffer, I was able to cross the last remaining divide into the restricted area at the back of the press line and feel as though I had reached some sort of Hollywood inner sanctum. At the risk of revealing too much about my enthusiasm for teen drama, I felt star-struck with the arrival, en masse, of the entire leading cast of *Dawson's Creek* (with the exception of Joshua Jackson). Their movement down the press line created a bottleneck that suddenly left Michelle Williams, who played my favourite character on the show, standing by herself right in front of me. I took this as an opportunity to have my picture taken with a bona fide celebrity. As though propelled by a mysterious force that instantly turned me into a blathering idiot, I approached Williams and blurted out: "Hey, you're Michelle *Wallace*! Could I take a picture with you?" Ever the academic, it seems, I had confused the young blonde starlet with the African American feminist cultural critic. I went on to tell Williams that, of all the celebrities that had come through the line, I was most excited to see the cast of *Dawson's Creek* (awkwardly implying that, despite the presence of much bigger stars, I myself was most impressed with the A-minus list). She was most gracious, and charmingly self-deprecating, in answering: "Always go for the cheesy ones, I guess."

As guests were seated in the ballroom, two large video projection screens on either side of the stage showed a stylized rolling list of the major sponsors of the event, including Absolut Vodka, the Coors Brewing Company, *Daily Variety*, and Gay.com. Other sponsors, whose visibility varied according to the amount contributed, included Jaguar North America, cigarette manufacturers Philip Morris, *People*, the anti-baldness drug Propecia,[7] a few financial institutions, and most major media companies. Brown & Williamson, makers of Lucky Strike cigarettes, had set up a smokers' lounge where hired female models handed out free cigarette packs literally by the armful.

The evening's program began with the event co-chairs' welcome, which described GLAAD's evolution "from a ragtag army with almost no resources and almost no power" to a "cultural movement." The media professionals honoured by the event were called "heroes" who "fought the battles and made the tough choices to produce the kind of work nominated" for the awards. Their efforts, along with those of media covering the event, were said to contribute to a process whereby "this community, working together, is going to take its rightful place in this world's culture."

After this formal introduction, Jay Leno appeared on stage to introduce a slickly produced video package. After a few garden-variety jokes about his aunt's belief that there are no Italian homosexuals, he declared: "These are a few of the images that define GLAAD's work." Leno was on stage for perhaps ninety seconds, but his presence contributed to the impression that the Media Awards are a top-tier celebrity event. The video montage opened with some generically uplifting piano music and black-and-white news footage of Marsha P. Johnson, the African American co-founder with Sylvia Rivera of the Stonewall-era Street Transvestite Action Revolution, who proclaimed: "Darling, I want my gay rights now!"

After a few humorous snippets ("These are the images that made us laugh"), the tone of the montage abruptly changed ("These are the images that made us cry") as the video cut to news footage of Diane Feinstein announcing the murders of Harvey Milk and San Francisco Mayor George Moscone, as well as images of people gathered around the AIDS Quilt. The video was built upon a series of emotionally charged oppositions – funny/sad, positive (Melissa Etheridge and her expectant partner on the cover of a major magazine), and negative (an excerpt from an anti-gay conservative propaganda video). By the time it ended, the audience had been bombarded with a quick succession of well-known faces clearly meant to elicit a range of disparate emotions: Ellen DeGeneres, Anita Bryant, Ronald Reagan, Bill Clinton, Matthew Shepard, Rock Hudson, Bette Midler, Sylvester, Elton John, Boy George, Madonna, Ru-Paul, George Michael, k.d. lang, and clips from *Soap*, *Dynasty*, *Xena: Warrior Princess*, *Teletubbies*, *Dawson's Creek*, *Oz*, *The Real World*, *Sex and the City*, and *Will and Grace*, among others. Excerpted movies included *The Boys in the Band*, *Mommie Dearest*, *South Park*, *Edge of Seventeen*, and *American Beauty*.

The basic proposition of the montage was made clear by an inter-title that said: "But it's more than entertainment," as the video cut to images from *Boys Don't Cry* that covered the emotional distance from romance to rape to murder in about eight seconds. This was followed by a second intertitle that stated, "It's the power to make change" as triumphant music swelled up and the video cut to news conference footage of James Dale, the clean-cut, all-American ex-Scout leader who had recently led a campaign against the anti-gay policies of the Boy Scouts of America. This proud beacon of change was then abruptly in-terrupted by right-wing radio talk-show host Dr Laura Schlessinger, who appeared disgusted and outraged: "Do I think we've become desensi-tized to immoral acts?" she sneered, after which an announcer's voice declared, "Dr Laura is coming to television." This was followed by a clip of a terrified-looking Homer Simpson screaming at the top of his lungs.

The final segment featured a live performance of Cher's dance an-them "Strong Enough" interspersed with cheerful and/or mildly sexy images from *Will and Grace*, *Oz*, *Edge of Seventeen*, *The Real World*, and *Sex and the City*. The last image, of Cher holding her fist in the air to the last note of the lyric "strong enough," echoed for a few seconds as "We're GLAAD to have helped" appeared on the screen. The video ended with the Media Awards logo and the caption "presented by Ab-solut Vodka."

I found the video to be very powerful, as I suspect many in atten-dance also did. It was expertly edited, fast-paced, and made impressive use of the emotionally charged oppositions that characterize LGBT peo-ple's historical relationships to popular media. The video's narrative logic, I realized in retrospect, effectively encapsulated GLAAD's institu-tional discourse about the inadequacies of the past relative to the con-temporary politics of inclusion. Seen in the context of Garry's speech to Bell Atlantic employees, which I discussed above, and earlier statements about GLAAD's evolution from "ragtag army" to "cultural movement," the choice of Stonewall veterans to open the video, while clearly meant as a tribute, also functioned as a way to mark the difference between the ostensibly limited strategies of the past and GLAAD's supposedly greater cultural power and effectiveness in the present.

This last point was reinforced later in the program when Seomin came onto the stage to introduce Garry and used the occasion to make claims about the value of his influence with media producers. "More and more," he said, "we find out about possible defamation before the cameras roll and, when we can, when the scripts are actually being written." The "really big question," he said, is "who? Who will these messages or images reach? What is their potential impact to do harm or to do good?" He went on to describe how he had intervened to prevent the recurrence of a character portrayed as a "clichéd sissy" on a wrestling program and cooperated with the producers of the Bill Maher program *Politically Incorrect* to stage a gay wedding. Seomin added: "We not only found them a handsome gay couple willing to wed on air, but we helped write their vows, we helped them with questions for the audience and even at the 11th hour we ran out and bought them wedding bands."

Seomin's contrast between a sissy and a handsome gay couple echoed some of the positive/negative binary oppositions of the video montage. It also continued the long tradition of assigning positive value to representations of LGBT people that combine as many of the following characteristics as possible: professional, attractive, gender-conforming, middle-class, typically white, preferably raising children, and in a committed monogamous relationship. It was no coincidence that the person Seomin was introducing, GLAAD's executive director, exhibited many of these characteristics herself. Indeed, Garry's self-presentation at the 2000 Media Awards in Los Angeles was especially illustrative of the tendency for LGBT movement organizations to choose leaders who present "the face of middle-class normality" (Gross 2001, xvi).

Unable to attend the ceremony that year because of "doctors' orders," Garry had videotaped a message in the sun-drenched kitchen of her suburban New Jersey home. In the video, she tells a story about her face-to-face meeting with Schlessinger, during which "Dr Laura" reiterated her public position that homosexuality is a "biological mistake" and leaned over to Garry to say: "But don't take that personally." At this point in the video, Garry paused for emphasis, and said: "Well, guess what? I'm here to tell you that it is profoundly personal. Because it's about our lives, it's about our careers, it's about our families. It's about gay teens fighting for their safety at school and in their neighbourhoods, it's about closeted men and women who can't talk about their partners for fear of losing their jobs. It's about my three kids and the world that they will live in. It doesn't get more personal than that." This segment, which was the climax of the video, emphasized the middle-class themes of individualism, career, family, and safety, all of which were also echoed in the evening's two best-received speeches.

The first such speech was by Gibbons, who in 2000 was hosting a talk show for Paramount Television, which had recently signed Schlessinger to a talk show deal of her own. In her acceptance speech for "Outstanding TV Talk Show," Gibbons skilfully deflected her corporate association with Schlessinger by using humour, directing her attacks at Schlessinger personally (as opposed to her employer), and emphasizing her credentials as a heterosexual ally to gays and lesbians. She began her acceptance speech by denying rumours that she had refused Schlessinger access to her dressing room on the Paramount lot and been asked for advice on hosting a talk show. "Dr Laura probably doesn't need me to teach her the difference between a grip and a gaffer," Gibbons joked.

Gibbons continued with a denunciation of the ways in which gays and lesbians are denied basic rights:

> I do think perhaps though that Dr Laura could use some coaching in learning the difference between the Bible and the Bill of Rights. The Bill of Rights ... the Bill of Rights and the Constitution ... those documents which are supposed to guarantee rights for all of us, but apparently not for gays and lesbians who everyday are losing their jobs, they're losing their homes, losing their health insurance, losing their children, all because of who they are. We can tax the pay checks – the government is very happy to take money from gays and lesbians – but apparently it is not quite capable of providing freedoms and basic privileges like the right to marry and the right to have a family.

By this point in the speech, Gibbons had the crowd on its feet. She went on to praise Jon and Michael Gallucio, former guests on her talk show who had recently celebrated their eighteenth anniversary together. She described them as "two people who were born to be parents" and whose home, she said, is built on "family values" of "tolerance, compassion, respect, encouragement, and love." In closing, she said: "There will always be places to tell stories that shine like beacons of light such as the Gallucios' ... Jon and Michael, they shine their light, as so many others did, on stage 26, *The Leeza Show*, at Paramount." It was a masterful performance: Gibbons had managed in one short speech to distance herself from Schlessinger's anti-gay views, win over her audience, promote herself and her show, and shield her employer from criticism.

The other celebrated appearance of the evening belonged to Taylor, who received the Vanguard Award, "presented ... to a member of the entertainment or media community who has made a significant difference in promoting equal rights for lesbian, gay, bisexual and transgender people." She appeared on stage wearing a black and white sequined gown, her jet-black hair raised in a mountain of curls, and began the speech by describing how she had "spent a lot of time with gay men" in her life, naming Montgomery Clift, Jimmy Dean, and Rock Hudson as "her colleagues, coworkers, confidants," and "closest friends." She added: "I never thought of who they slept with."[8]

Like Garry and Gibbons before here, Taylor's speech invoked "universal" themes like rights, freedom, marriage, love, God, and family: "I feel that any home where there is love constitutes a family and all families should have the same legal rights," she said to enthusiastic applause. Toward the end of her speech, she added: "What it comes down to, ultimately, is love. How can anything bad come out of love? The bad stuff comes out of mistrust, misunderstanding, and God knows, from hate and from ignorance. Thank God GLAAD works to fight this!" Taylor left the stage to a standing ovation, ending her short speech with the words: "That's why I'm here tonight: to celebrate you and your families. And to tell you to hang in there and to say once and for all of ... us [*sic*]: long live love!"

Not everything that was done and said at the Media Awards conformed to respectable themes like God, marriage, family, and country. For example, there was the (intentionally ironic?) performance of "Bad Reputation" by a bald-headed and tattooed Joan Jett ("I don't give a damn 'bout my reputation / You're living in the past it's a new generation"). There were a few moments of bawdy sexual humour, such as when butch stand-up comic Lea DeLaria pretended to make out on stage with Brooke Shields. And there were a few occasions for camp, such as a speech by a teenager who had been featured in the *Advocate* after

suing his high school for the right to form a gay-straight alliance. The
teenager's speaking style was all queen: exquisitely self-aware, affected,
funny, and serious all at once. He wore ostentatious designer eyewear,
lots of jewellery and shiny fabrics, makeup, and obviously tweezed eye-
brows. He was also the only person on stage that night to use the word
"queer," but the fact that he appeared after the ultra-masculine professional baseball player Billy Bean, who had recently come out on ABC's
20/20, only highlighted the gender normativity of nearly everyone else
featured on stage that night.

Another discordant moment was the speech given by Elton John at
the GLAAD Media Awards in New York in 2000. John was given the
Vito Russo Award, which "honors an openly gay or lesbian member of
the entertainment or media community for their outstanding contribution in combating homophobia." He began the speech by ranting about
the British tabloids and later declared that he wanted to "shove" his
award "up Dr Laura's asshole." Finally, after vouching he would do
everything in his power to get Al Gore elected, he said that he had once
met Barbara Bush and that she was a "pain in the ass," adding that, if
he could, he would have used the "C-word" to describe her. At that moment, I noticed GLAAD's director of special events visibly shifting in his
seat as an uncomfortable silence fell over the room. No doubt sensing
the discomfort, John explained that in his past political involvements he
had always tried to tailor his messages to mainstream audiences. "I don't
care what I say anymore," he declared. By the time John's appearance
at the Media Awards was broadcast on E!, all that was left of it was the
following sentence: "It's a very moving evening and one that reinforces
in us all that GLAAD do so much incredible work."

This editing out of discordant notes was also a feature of day-after
discussions about Media Awards events among staff and board members, who tended to focus on their perceived emotional impact. For
example, on the day after the 2000 Media Awards in New York, I
overheard a staff member say on the phone that the event had been
"moving" and had made people "feel good." At a board meeting the
day after an awards show in San Francisco, board members discussed
the "power" and "passion" of Garry's speech. Steward said that the San
Francisco ceremony had seemed "like the most heartfelt of the Media

Awards this year." That this emotional impact was also important to the organization's bottom line was made clear in the very next sentence, as Steward mentioned the fact that he had spent a great deal of time speaking with representatives from Absolut Vodka who "were gushing about how pleased they've been with the relationship." Another board member added that she had had a very similar conversation with people from Schwab, an investment services company, which had contributed at the $50,000 level for the first time in 2001.

These conversations about the Media Awards suggest that GLAAD's leaders were deeply aware of the importance for successful fundraising of eliciting certain kinds of affect from audiences. This played into a logic whereby the Media Awards were thought to be most successful when they counterpoised images of queer vulnerability – discrimination, violence, and exclusion – against positive and universalizing images of mainstream inclusion for which the organization could take credit. GLAAD, in other words, had a (financial) interest in maintaining and even heightening the polarity inherent in longstanding patterns of media representation that portray LGBT people either as victims to be pitied or as beacons of mainstream conformity and normalcy. Seen from this perspective, the cultural change for which GLAAD stood, paradoxically, depended on the reproduction of a status quo that tended to reinforce rather than challenge mainstream media's symbolic exclusion of many non-normative elements of the LGBT community.

In sum, in this section I have argued that, in both symbolic and economic terms, the Media Awards tended to (re)produce certain hierarchical divisions. The nominations and voting process, although presented as volunteer-driven, was weighted in favour of the (potentially self-interested) preferences of GLAAD board members and staff. The seating arrangements proceeded according to an economic and reputational logic that tended to reinforce attendees' class and status divisions. The imposition of a strict media pecking order reinforced the power of the larger mainstream outlets relative to local or community-based media. Finally, universalizing themes were privileged and contrasted with representations of queer vulnerability in ways that often reinforced mainstream media's tendency to ignore non-normative experiences of gender, sexuality, race, and class.

This is not to say that the Media Awards did not also contain moments of genuine "generosity, celebration, love, play, [and] community," as English (2009, 7) might point out. My account of the awards reflects the ambivalence of my own experiences of them as emotionally potent fundraising vehicles whose structuring assumptions about maximizing impact also unintentionally reproduced certain divisions and forms of symbolic erasure that prevail in mainstream media discourses and institutions. As GLAAD attempted to mediate between the diverse values and interests of LGBT people writ large and the more narrowly market-oriented values and interests of media professionals and their employers, it is hardly surprising that it found it easier (and more lucrative) to play by the rules of the more powerful partner in the game. But playing by those rules also had consequences that stood in tension with the ideals of inclusiveness espoused by GLAAD's third strategic imperative, "Harness the Power of Diversity."

### Harness the Power of Diversity: Branding Meets Activism

In 1997, early in her tenure as executive director, Garry initiated the complete overhaul of GLAAD's brand identity. She told me in an interview that the decision had less to with a visionary strategy than with sheer happenstance: "I think that there are people that look at what I have done in the last four years and some people would say: 'Boy, that was so smart that she did that when she did that because it set a tone, it created a feel and a kind of a personality for the organization at a very early point and that was really smart of her to have thought about doing that!' Well, the real truth is that it wasn't really strategic on my part." As she tells it, Garry had been in Los Angeles meeting with executives from the public relations firm Hill+Knowlton Strategies when "a hugely valuable pro-bono resource" fell on her lap. That resource was Enterprise IG, a company that specialized in branding.

With a client list that included Nike, Starbucks, and Monsanto, Enterprise IG (which has since rebranded itself as the Brand Union[9]) was among the largest of the corporate branding consultancies that emerged in the 1990s to help companies manage their public image and reputation. These consultancies were not traditional design shops, but developed total brand experiences that encompassed every aspect of the communicative interactions between a company and its consumers, employees, and investors through long-term strategies that encouraged people to develop an emotional connection to brands. The emergence of consultancies like Enterprise IG reflected and promoted a new emphasis on design in the corporate world and an understanding of brand image as central to business strategy.[10]

GLAAD's rebranding by Enterprise IG and the subsequent incorporation of its new image in an advertisement created for it by Absolut Vodka exemplify mutually reinforcing trends of the neoliberal era: the corporatization of activist organizations, on the one hand, and corporations' increasing emphasis on establishing long-term links with causes their customers care about, on the other. The trends come together in "cause-related marketing," a practice that "emerged in the mid-1980s as a strategic marketing tool for differentiating a brand and adding value to it," as Samantha King (2008, 9) explains in a book about corporate philanthropy and breast cancer organizations, adding that "companies and brands associate themselves with a cause as a means to build the reputation of a brand, increase profit, develop employee loyalty to the company, and add to their reputation as good corporate citizens."

Below, I argue that the visual identity Enterprise IG created for GLAAD expresses a brand essence that can be read as assimilationist, but which is better understood as expressive of a state-managerial discourse of diversity, particularly in the context of its incorporation in an Absolut Vodka ad. By the terms of this discourse, some differences can be symbolically harnessed for mutual benefit, but at the cost of excluding more expansive and challenging conceptions of diversity.

### Rebranding GLAAD

As Dauvergne and LeBaron argue in *Protest, Inc.*: "Over the last two decades activist organizations have increasingly come to look, think, and act like corporations," a point also made clear by Alexandra Chasin's (2001) earlier study of the marketization of the LGBT movement in the 1990s. For Dauvergne and LeBaron (2014, 127–8), moves by such nongovernmental organizations as CARE, UNICEF, the Red Cross, and the World Wildlife Fund to rebrand themselves are tied to processes of institutionalization by which organizations have enlisted the help of brand experts to help them compete for audiences, donors, and media attention. The process of developing a brand starts by attempting to determine the unique qualities that distinguish it from all other brands. Once established, "managing brand value and brand image" become "top priorities" for non-governmental organizations (127).

GLAAD's rebranding process began in 1997 with conversations with eight key individuals Garry selected from the ranks of GLAAD's staff, board, and large donors. They included Heffner, Klein (now a public relations consultant), two senior corporate executives (one from Showtime and one from Eddie Bauer), two executives from public relations and market research firms, and Howard Buford, who headed an advertising agency specializing in minority niche markets and was also a GLAAD board member. According to a memo, Garry's instructions to the participants were to assess "GLAAD as a product": how its members, donors, and partners perceive it, and its differences from other organizations. "How does GLAAD's unique selling position," Garry asked, "manifest itself in its print materials" and "in its logo?"

Through a series of brainstorming sessions, Garry's handpicked committee tried to distil GLAAD's essence. In an interview with me, Garry said: "I tried to get smart people in the room to try to think about this. It ended up being a very useful process and made me have to create a definition for the attributes that were meaningful to me about GLAAD ... I knew it had to be something that I cared about and that that was actually the most important thing ... and I was really clear I didn't want it to look like anything else." Based on this feedback, Enterprise IG developed five design proposals, one of which became the blueprint for GLAAD's new logo.[11] The design that was ultimately adopted consisted of a series of large circles on top of a row of smaller circles, which, read from left to right, appeared to come together through a process of mutual attraction to form a final larger circle (see figure 1).

There was one major difference between the chosen design at the proposal stage and the final version: in the proposal, the first larger circle was exactly the same size as the last one, or to put it differently, the smaller bottom circle appeared to have been absorbed by the larger top circle without modification. Garry said that she felt an immediate "emotional connection" to this original proposal but soon realized that it

# glaad

Figure 1 The GLAAD logo designed by Enterprise IG consisted of two rows of circles of different sizes coming together to form a final larger circle.

would not work because, she told the logo's designers, "the whole needs to be greater than the sum of its parts." In "logo land," she said to me, "that was like a big 'aha!' to them. They said: 'Oh my god, you're absolutely right!'"

Garry was careful to leave the interpretation of the final design, with its larger end circle, as ambiguous as possible. She told me: "When people say, 'what does the logo mean?' I always say the logo for me tells a story about change where the end is greater than the sum of its parts – and that's all I talk about." That deliberate ambiguity was partly a function of wanting the logo to be meaningful in different ways to different people, but it also spoke to Garry's desire to neutralize an assimilationist reading by which the larger circle appears to gradually absorb and eliminate the smaller one.[12] If a viewer were to substitute the idea of dominant heterosexual society for the larger circle and the idea of the minority LGBT community for the smaller one, the problematic implications of having a small circle join a larger one to form a final circle that is identical in size and shape to the larger were quite clear. Garry described this assimilationist interpretation as the "biggest challenge" she faced in selling the logo to her staff. In response to their concerns, she argued that altering the design to make the final circle larger than either of the first two circles changed the interpretation from "we want to be just like them" to "this process should result in something that is better for the connection."

The split in how GLAAD staff initially received the proposed new logo echoed historical debates in the LGBT movement between two polarized views of social change. In *Virtual Equality*, Urvashi Vaid (1995, 37) argues that the history of the gay and lesbian movement can be summed up as a conflict between those who aspire to the kind of social change that would radically redefine sexual norms and lead to the broadly inclusive integration of sexual minorities, on the one hand, and those who seek legitimation within existing social conventions and structures, on the other. These conflicting philosophical outlooks, Vaid suggests, continue to polarize gays and lesbians, even as their dialectical tug and pull propel and shape the movement's major debates and orientations, constituting an array of political cultures in the process.

The logo debate within GLAAD did not oppose two radically different theories of social change (the more radical view was largely absent) so much as reflect varying levels of (dis)comfort with the design's clearly assimilationist implications. Whereas in the earlier draft of the logo, the net effect of incorporating the minority was to make it disappear, which everyone agreed was a problem, the modified logo's larger final circle suggested the possibility that difference and sameness could eventually co-exist in the same expanded space. As such, it was a graphical expression of GLAAD's strategic plan's "we want in" priority.

As Garry put it to me, summing up her view of what GLAAD was working toward: "All of us together with our differences at the same table is a better table than each of these tables." In taking the analogy one step further, however, she unwittingly raised one of the problematic implications of a pluralistic conception of the process of social change, namely, that it ignores that sitting at the table is not a simple matter of wanting in, but of being asked to join and under certain conditions. She said: "We talk about the kids' table and the grown-ups' table and the much better table is everybody at the same table. When you get the ten-year-old at the table, the conversation is a lot more interesting with the forty-five-year-olds than it would be if you separate them." Perhaps, but the kids harbour no illusions about needing to behave or face being expelled by the adults in charge.

Having worked with Enterprise IG to create a logo that she and most of her staff liked or could live with, Garry met individually with about three quarters of GLAAD's board of directors to sell them on the design. Once the board voted to adopt it, the process of completely overhauling GLAAD's visual identity would eventually affect everything from its communications with media professionals and its members, to its letterhead, to the packaging of its Media Awards ceremonies, to its internal communications, to its website, and even to the design of the New York office, which moved to Thirty-Fifth Street in Midtown Manhattan in the fall of 2000. With the new visual identity worked out, the organization was ready, in the words of one communications staffer, to "get our brand out there."

At the time of my fieldwork, GLAAD was the LGBT movement organization that received the most corporate funding (about $1.5 million in 2000), which largely came from corporate marketing departments. For the twelfth annual Media Awards in 2001, Absolut Vodka paid $150,000 to be the principal sponsor and developed an ad vaunting its support of GLAAD (see figure 2). Absolut Vodka began to advertise to the gay and lesbian community in 1981, but it was the first time the brand had worked with a non-profit organization to create an ad, which appeared on the back cover of the *Advocate*, as well as in the trend-setting *New York* magazine.

The ad, which recalls a 1960s-era lava lamp, seamlessly integrated GLAAD's new logo with an iconic marketing campaign: the Absolut series of print ads, posters, and billboards employing the brand's distinctive bottle. The advertising agency that created the ad used a previous design for an Absolut Citron campaign from the mid-1990s, replacing the original citrus-coloured blobs in a lava lamp shaped like an Absolut bottle with blobs whose shape and colour corresponded to GLAAD's new logo (see figure 3).

As Naomi Klein (2001, 17) explains, Absolut is famous for developing "a marketing strategy in which its product disappeared and its brand was nothing but a blank bottle-shaped space that could be filled with whatever content a particular audience most wanted." Not unlike GLAAD, whose new globular branding lent itself perfectly to Absolut's

Figure 2 The Absolut ad developed for the 2001 GLAAD
Media Awards was the first time that Absolut created an
ad for a non-profit organization.

ABSOLUT CITRON.

Figure 3   The Absolut GLAAD ad was developed on the basis
of this existing ad for Absolut Citron from the mid-1990s.

lava-lamp treatment, "the brand reinvented itself as a cultural sponge, soaking up and morphing to its surroundings" (17). It was a match made in marketing heaven.

During a board meeting I attended, GLAAD staff and board members positively glowed about the ad and its placement, free of charge to GLAAD, in national publications. Later during the same meeting, Garry raved about GLAAD's success in raising funds from corporate sources: "Some of it feels like low-hanging fruit," she said (which seemed a propos, given that the GLAAD ad was based on an existing Absolut Citron campaign). Indeed, the Absolut ad was an expression of the kind of mutually beneficial relationships that the logo, with its gradual integration of separate spheres, illustrated; the perfect melding of cause and consumerism. Being an illustration of the ideals the GLAAD logo stood for, the ad was ripe for a 2001 GLAAD Media Award nomination in the advertising category. It won, further illustrating the circularity of the proposition that it served the interests of both GLAAD and Absolut.

Still, it is difficult to discern from this example of cause-related marketing exactly what cause was being served beyond a vodka brand's marketing objectives and GLAAD's interest in promoting its own visibility. The ad's semiotics were telling in this regard: GLAAD's logo, and what it stood for – the integration of differences in the service of a greater whole – appeared literally contained inside a corporate bottle doing double duty as a lava lamp whose connotations of 1960s counterculture suggested something about the corporate appropriation and commercial exploitation of the ideals of the new social movements of that era. This melding of brands told a story about social change in which the whole becomes greater than the sum of its parts via the market value accorded to gay and lesbian difference. As such, GLAAD's logo, and Absolut's ad, exemplified a "state-managerial" discourse of diversity, which values differences to the extent that they can be harnessed to a set of predetermined organizational objectives.

In her entry on "difference" in *New Keywords*, Ien Ang (2005) notes that, for the new social movements of the late 1960s onward, "difference is the basis and the condition of possibility of various oppositional forms of identity politics." Ang sees in the cultural politics of these new social movements a "romantic and/or militant" challenge to "the oppressive homogeneity imposed by the dominant sections of society" (84). These social movement demands for the political recognition of differences, she writes, have become "a ubiquitous and, increasingly, a normalized aspect of life in Western democracies" that has led to the development of an official discourse of multiculturalism, "which officially sanctions and enshrines ethnic, linguistic, and cultural differences within the encompassing framework of the state" (86). This "state-led recognition of difference," she concludes, "becomes the cornerstone of diversity," which she defines as a "bird's eye-view of the field of differences, which needs to be harmonized, controlled, or made to fit into a coherent (often national) whole" (86).

As a synthesis of the best practices literature on diversity management by the Rand Corporation[13] points out, three out of four Fortune 500 companies had launched diversity programs by the end of the 1990s (Marquis et al. 2008). However, the report conveys little sense that these diversity programs were created to redress grievances on the part of groups that have suffered discrimination. The literature, the authors assert, insists that diversity programs are most successful when they are presented and implemented with "appropriate motivations," which include improving a company's "bottom-line," enhancing the work environment, reducing turnover, reflecting customer demographics, improving employee satisfaction, and promoting flexibility in decision-making and problem solving (3).

The Rand authors further argue that "surface diversity," measured only in numbers, "will not be likely to contribute to workplace harmony," but must be "accepted and integrated into the firm's social and business fabric" and be made central to "business and operating goals." For this to happen, CEOs must be seen to be actively involved and committed to diversity goals; furthermore, internal marketing campaigns and diversity training "to win the support and enthusiasm of employees" should be carried out, and affinity groups should be formed to "encourage positive outlooks and allow employees to articulate their concerns in ways that are acceptable to the larger organization" (9). Such measures are the key to "transforming diverse individuals into integrated, highly productive work groups" (25). Left "unmanaged," the authors caution, diversity initiatives that simply involve increasing the representation of traditionally underrepresented groups are likely to result in "increased conflict and turnover among employees, with minority employees being the most likely to leave" (26).

What emerges, then, is a vision of difference stripped of politics and prescriptions for diversity whose explicit objective is to contain difference by means of practices designed to forge "unity" and "harmony," echoing GLAAD's insistence in its strategic plan on diversity as something to be "harnessed" or "knit together." As communications scholar Kevin Barnhurst (2007, 9) argues, corporate diversity initiatives "interpellate or call to *individuals* without acknowledging a history of devaluing collective identities: their class, race, ethnicity, gender or sexuality" (emphasis original) and require individual differences to be subsumed within a normative model of professional identity. Differences are not erased in this process so much as they are reproduced in ways that compel individuals to filter out aspects of their identities that organizational norms cannot or will not accommodate and emphasize (only) those differences that can contribute to an organization's bottom line.

In this chapter, I have examined three examples of how "unity is constantly and effectively created out of difference" (Grossberg 1997, 341). First, I examined how new arrivals to GLAAD de-emphasized confrontational tactics in favour of a public relations strategy designed to engage professionals like themselves, reshaping the organization in the process. Second, I described how the Media Awards employed a vast array of emotionally charged images, including of queer vulnerability, to ultimately construct a universalizing rhetoric that served fundraising and marketing objectives. Finally, my analysis of GLAAD's rebranding and its incorporation in an ad for Absolut showed the prevalence of a state-managerial discourse of diversity.

GLAAD's politics of access and inclusion, I have argued, required filtering out those differences that posed a challenge to the institutions to which inclusion was sought, even as more marketable differences were emphasized and incorporated into a greater whole. Although we might celebrate the fact that gays and lesbians have "come up from invisibility" since the 1990s and are increasingly integrated within society's dominant institutions, we also need to ask "how this inclusion is defined and on what terms it is granted" (Gross 2001; Clarke 1999, 84). As Eric O.

Clarke (1999, 2000) argues, inclusion within the public sphere is mediated by a set of norms and value relations that regulate and limit access. For some members of a minority to be included, others have to be excluded, meaning that, "rather than a transparent representation of minority concerns, inclusion entails fundamental transformations in a group's self-identified interests." The problem is that the fact of gaining access, the very process of winning (partial) inclusion, makes invisible the (typically heteronormative) "value determinations" that have gone into making some LGBT people visible and others not (Clarke 1999, 86).

In adopting "we want in" as their guiding principle, GLAAD's leaders had asserted their intention to get inside the corporate bottle and, with the help of Absolut Vodka's marketing department, promoted the idea that gays and lesbians were on the verge of enjoying the kind of warm, citrusy social acceptance that could only be granted by corporate America, arguably the dominant social institution as the sun was setting on the twentieth century. As I show in the next two chapters, however, clear bottles have limits, however invisible at times, and GLAAD's proverbial nose was about to hit the glass. In the next chapter, I explore what happened when GLAAD's corporate insider culture, and its attendant disdain for militant tactics, collided with a major grassroots mobilization against right-wing talk-show host Dr Laura Schlessinger.

---

## CHAPTER 3

# Insiders – Outsiders:
# The Dr Laura Campaign

As the only national gay and lesbian organization devoted to media advocacy, GLAAD projects itself as the mediating force between the profit-driven media industries, the ostensibly heterosexual mainstream, and a diverse constituency of gay and lesbian people. In so doing, it vies with other social agents who also have a stake in gay and lesbian cultural politics, which results in tensions that I will attempt to elucidate in this chapter through an account and analysis of the campaign to oppose the defamatory rhetoric of popular radio talk show host Dr Laura Schlessinger.[1] This campaign was, along with the Media Awards, a major focus of GLAAD's activities during my fieldwork in 2000–01.

At a time when GLAAD's leaders appeared confident that their new-found prominence in the movement signalled a new era of cooperation between gays and lesbians and the media industries, the Schlessinger campaign revealed that GLAAD could not sustain its fantasy of mainstreaming indefinitely. To function smoothly, the mainstreaming strategy – "we want in" – depended on two assumptions: that differences between LGBT people and media companies could almost always be worked out without confrontation, and that the differences among LGBT constituencies could almost always be harnessed to a common goal. In this chapter, I demonstrate the limits of the first assumption, which holds that insider tactics are the most effective means of dealing with media companies, while in chapter 4 I address some of the problems with the second.

The Schlessinger campaign is the story of how a small but well-connected group of activists challenged GLAAD's dominant position in the media activist field. In so doing, they forced GLAAD to adopt more militant, confrontational tactics than its 1999 strategic plan envisioned. The crux of the internecine conflict that I document in this chapter is summed up by journalist and activist Michelangelo Signorile, who claimed that GLAAD's Schlessinger campaign tactics were evidence that the organization had over-invested in professionalization. In a 9 May 2000 article in the *Advocate*, he alleged that GLAAD had gone too far in the direction of Hollywood insider, lost touch with its gay and lesbian constituencies, and compromised its ability to "apply pressure from the outside when needed." In contrast to his criticism of GLAAD, Signorile championed the ad hoc group of gay and lesbian activists called Stop-DrLaura.com (SDL), which he called "one of the most impressive weapons in the American lesbian and gay activism arsenal." More confrontational in its tactics, SDL made creative use of the Internet to recruit and mobilize activists, coordinate street protests and other forms of direct action, and pressure Schlessinger's corporate backers.[2]

My account of the Schlessinger campaign supports many aspects of Signorile's critique of GLAAD, but takes a wider view. The evidence argues against framing the campaign's success too simply and romantically as the triumph of outsiders and their confrontational tactics over insiders and their polite politics. GLAAD and SDL were constituent parts of a common field of relations, and I provide an account of the Schlessinger campaign that incorporates some of the subtlety missing from Signorile's highly partisan reporting and from the gay and lesbian press more generally. Viewing the Schlessinger campaign as a competition for cultural authority, instead of the triumph of outsiders over insiders, shows the extent to which SDL's challenge to GLAAD – although it shifted the dynamics of the campaign, altered the balance of power in the media activist field, and chipped away at the fantasy of mainstream inclusion for which GLAAD stood – represented only a partial challenge to the politics of mainstreaming.

## Insiders

GLAAD's involvement with Schlessinger began in 1997 when it began to receive complaints from some of its members that the syndicated *Dr Laura* radio program, with an audience base of twenty million listeners per week, had begun to feature anti-gay rhetoric. GLAAD set about to monitor the program and issued its first *Dr Laura*-related GLAAD Alert on 13 June 1997, in which it objected to Schlessinger referring to homosexuality as a "biological faux pas." GLAAD Alert, a weekly "activation tool," was the primary means by which the organization alerted its members to media content it wanted to praise or condemn. Schlessinger responded personally, and rather tartly, with a letter to GLAAD dated 7 July 1997, in which she wrote: "I do have a philosophical question for all of you in GLAAD. Is it possible to disagree with any, even a small agenda point of your organization, without being labeled 'anti-gay' or being accused of 'hate' or 'bigot' [*sic*] as I was portrayed in your offensive 'news' report about me ... ?" She ended her missive with the words: "You have become so invested in your cause that you shoot before you see the whites of anyones [*sic*] eyes. Shame on you."

Joan Garry began her tenure as GLAAD's executive director shortly after this letter was received and decided to attempt a conciliatory approach. She sent a letter to Schlessinger in which she repeated GLAAD's grievances, and added: "I would first say that I do regret that GLAAD did not take the opportunity to contact you directly regarding these matters. It has become apparent to us that in some circumstances, it makes more sense to sit down and have a conversation than to react without first speaking to them." Garry went on to say that GLAAD has "earned the respect of the news and entertainment industries" and that its agenda "isn't particularly militant – in fact it's sometimes downright moderate." She ended the letter by requesting a "free exchange of information between us, so that we all can do what we do to the best of our abilities."

In response to GLAAD's mollifying tone, Schlessinger agreed to a first meeting with Garry, which took place on 11 February 1998. The two decided to take part in a virtual town meeting hosted by AOL.com. Further attempts at dialogue broke down when Schlessinger decided to back out. Then, on 13 August 1998, Schlessinger announced on air that she was changing her position on homosexuality, but not in the direction that GLAAD hoped for: "I've always told people who opposed homosexuality that they were homophobic, bad, bigoted and idiotic. I was wrong. It is destructive." In response, GLAAD stepped up its "monitor and respond" efforts and encouraged its members to listen to *Dr Laura* and write to its producers. GLAAD also issued a written request for another meeting with Schlessinger, noting that, since their last meeting in February of the previous year, "your words about our community reaching twenty million people have become stronger and infinitely more damaging."

A second meeting between Garry and Schlessinger took place on 10 March 1999 in Schlessinger's Los Angeles office. The exchange was tape recorded by both parties. In August 1999, Schlessinger published an edited excerpt in the *Dr Laura Perspective*, her newsletter, which she introduced by praising Garry:

> I'd almost given up on the hope of ever having a reasonable dialogue with a gay activist – until I met Joan Garry ... Joan is a thoughtful, intelligent woman with a good sense of humor (I love those!), and she is the first gay activist I've ever come across who actually takes the time to try and understand my positions. Joan and I have substantial disagreements on many issues, but we respect each other personally and are willing to listen to each other ... As you might expect, we have a lot of differences. As you might not expect, we were also delighted to find some common ground.

Schlessinger went out of her way to characterize the meeting as a "reasonable dialogue" between individuals with "substantial disagreements" who "respect each other personally." By describing it this way, she made it seem as though her perspectives on homosexuality were matters about which reasonable people in a pluralist society might reasonably be expected to disagree.

A reading of the full unedited transcript, to which I was given access by a GLAAD staffer, suggests that Garry was willing, at the time of this meeting, to go along with Schlessinger's pluralist framing of the encounter. Midway through their discussion, Garry stated:

I think that we do need to engage people more in a conversation and I think that that's at the heart of this conversation and the others we have had ... I think that we have to go across, you know, that we are beyond the place in society where I stand on one side of the line and I shout and I scream and I wave my finger. I think I have to go across the line to the people who disagree and understand them. And I feel that that's part of my philosophy about the work. Is that it isn't all black and white ... What I hear is, and I will say, I feel that everyone is entitled to their own opinion about these things. And their own beliefs. I believe that. I would like to think that I'm respected for my own.

Combined with Garry's previous written assurance that GLAAD was not particularly militant, this statement about reaching out to one's opponents suggested her belief in a process whereby dialogue with an entrenched homophobe might lead to mutual understanding. Garry had begun the dialogue by trying to establish some common ground based on Schlessinger's well-known tagline, "I Am My Kid's Mom":

I think that you and I come to the work that we each do from somewhat the same place. Which is the basic premise of, you know, you are your kid's mom. And when I look at why I do the work that I do, I really do it for my family. That, you know, at the end of the day, I'd like to be able to say that I did something to help ensure that the world treats my kids well after I'm gone. ... And I guess that I just – I think that a lot of what you do is really about sharing your moral and ethical viewpoints to try to shape people and give them advice. And guide them.

Having attempted to establish some commonality on the basis of a shared devotion to family, Garry then called on Schlessinger to reiterate her position on homosexuality. Schlessinger's responses to this line of questioning can be condensed to two basic principles.

The first principle is based on an understanding of heterosexuality as biologically preordained, a belief that Schlessinger said is rooted in her doctoral studies in physiology. She told Garry: "We were meant to be heterosexual. That's obvious from our genitals. And how we reproduce as animals." And if homosexuality is not a choice (i.e., based on people choosing to act counter to their biological destinies), then it follows, according to her, that "it has to be a developmental error." In arguing the same point, Schlessinger also referred to homosexuality as a "biological error" or "mistake."

The second principle is Schlessinger's conviction, which she attributed to a conversion to Orthodox Judaism, that homosexual sex is forbidden by God. She based this belief on a reading of scriptures that condemns homosexual activity as an "abomination." Schlessinger saw (or represented) herself as defending the Judeo-Christian doctrine that underpins the laws and cultural norms of Western civilization. At one point in her discussion with Garry, she went so far as to quote Dostoyevsky: "Without God, all things are permissible." Nevertheless, she added, homosexuals should be treated with "decency," by which she meant that they should enjoy the same "civil rights" in such matters as employment, except in the case of schoolteachers and others in a position to "proselytize" to children. Homosexual relationships, however, because forbidden by God and based on a deviation from the intended biological script, should not, under any circumstances, be "legitimized" by society, such as through the extension of marriage or adoption rights or domestic partner benefits. A "society, a culture," she told Garry, "has a right and an obligation to set standards for the culture. I mean that is the way we have stability and civilization. And the most universal and eternal standard for that is God."

It followed from Schlessinger's line of thinking that the only options for those "challenged" by homosexuality were: (1) attempting to change through "therapy," or (2) leading celibate lives. Anything amounting to "acting out" on biologically disordered sexuality constituted a "forbidden relationship" that no laws should support, no matter how otherwise creative, intelligent, and loving the people involved might be. For these reasons, Schlessinger told Garry, homosexuals should be encouraged to seek "reparative therapy."

Confronted with Schlessinger's hard-line ideological and theological framework – one that, among other things, did not recognize her own hard-won second-parent adoption rights – Garry attempted to convey through the expression of her own hurt feelings the impact of Schlessinger's words. Schlessinger deflected Garry's attempts to personalize the discussion: "I'm back in the same position I was with you as last time. With you it's personal. With me it's philosophical. So, I feel bad, again." Garry responded: "I think that it's hard to … hear somebody say you're a biological error and not take that personally."

Garry decided to push the strategy of personalization a step further. She said: "I'm not here as an activist. I mean, I'm an activist because of my kids. Because I believe –" Schlessinger interrupted and scoffed at the notion that the executive director of a national LGBT organization was meeting her simply on behalf of her kids: "Okay, if you're not here today as an activist, then let's go shopping and be friends. Because I don't need this crap. You're here as an activist and we're discussing my position. If you are here as my friend, let's go eat. I don't want to do this. I don't want to be sitting and having you cry." Garry refused to relent, which led to this exchange:

> GARRY: I do this work because I feel like I'm an advocate for my kids. That I feel like I have …
> SCHLESSINGER: But that's not fair …
> GARRY: No, no, no. Please. You know what, I believe that I …
> SCHLESSINGER: You can't redesign the world because of your personal life. Where do you get off doing that? Where do you get off dictating to a culture because you want to legitimize your life. That's not right. That's not even intellectually fair. I'm not legitimizing my life. I'm standing up for what I think are cultural norms. You're defending Joan's life. We're not in the same discussion.

No matter how hard Garry tried to convince her counterpart that they shared many of the same values and that she too was a good parent, Schlessinger held firm to the two principles: homosexuality is biologically disordered and acting on it is immoral. Arguments that essentially proposed that gays and lesbians are "just like everyone else" had no persuasive influence.

Garry made little attempt to engage Schlessinger in debate on the substance (or lack thereof) of her arguments. On the question of nature versus nurture, Garry stated only that the matter is irrelevant to the question of civil rights, a point with which Schlessinger agreed to the extent that those rights are defined narrowly as pertaining to employment and the right to live in peace. When the "gay agenda" is defined to encompass things on the order of, "we should have the right to adopt babies as new-borns. We should have marriages. We should be rabbis," Schlessinger stated firmly, "that's wrong." On the matter of the biblical prohibition of homosexual acts, Garry pointed out the biblical support for polygamy, slavery, and stoning children who have disobeyed their parents. For each of these examples, Schlessinger had an elaborate rebuttal that (conveniently) contradicted literal interpretations or placed them in a wider historical context. Schlessinger, it became clear, was willing to allow for interpretative ambiguity only in relation to biblical matters with which she disagreed.

Meanwhile, with twenty million listeners and three million books in print, Schlessinger was riding a huge wave of popularity. To make matters worse for GLAAD, in early May 1999 Schlessinger was signed by Paramount Television, a subsidiary of CBS/Viacom, to develop a television talk show worth a reported $3 million to her personally; Paramount's overall investment was reported to be in the vicinity of $76 million, making this the most expensive launch in its history.

Despite GLAAD's best hopes for a non-conflictual resolution, the meetings between Garry and Schlessinger did not result in a scaling down of Schlessinger's rhetoric against homosexuality. GLAAD's continued daily monitoring of her radio program in the months following the announcement of the Paramount deal brought to light a marked escalation in the stridency of Schlessinger's on-air remarks. Here are three examples:

Rights. Rights! Rights? For sexual deviant [sic] sexual behaviour there are now rights? That's what I'm worried about with the pedophilia and the bestiality and the sadomasochism and the crossdressing. Is this all going to be "rights" too, to deviant sexual behaviour? It's deviant sexual behaviour. (9 June 1999)

If you folks don't start standing up for heterosexual marriage and heterosexuality pretty soon, that which you know as this country and family is going to be gone. (22 June 1999)

That men have to have sex with men is not something to celebrate. It's a sadness. It is a sadness, and there are therapies which
have been successful in helping a reasonable number of people
become heterosexual. (22 June 1999)

The boldness of that rhetoric, combined with the prospect of it reaching
a wider television audience, set off alarm bells. Schlessinger had become,
in GLAAD's estimation, the most dangerous homophobe in the nation.

## The Campaign: Phase I

Introduced as the new GLAAD director of communications at a board
meeting in September 1999, Steve Spurgeon presented a Schlessinger
campaign plan that aimed primarily "to stem the escalating influence of
Dr Laura's [sic] Schlessinger's homophobic advocacy." Spurgeon initially conceived of the campaign as having two phases designed to "educate Schlessinger about the consequences of her actions and words." In
the first phase, GLAAD would find and create opportunities to "challenge" her "anti-gay rhetoric," attempt to "persuade" her "syndicators
to regulate her," and "mobilize" the community "to educate Schlessinger
about her impact on real people." The second phase would "counter
the imbalance in Schlessinger's references and point of view" by encouraging allies in media, other advocacy groups, and members of the scien-
tific community to "counter Schlessinger's messages," "motivate" GLAAD's
"membership to monitor local coverage" and "respond with "letters to
the editor," and convene a "think-tank of high-level public relations
practitioners to suggest strategies."

GLAAD's campaign, as it was originally conceived, relied heavily on its
in-house professional skills and connections to monitor Schlessinger's
program; meet with her producers, syndication company, and Paramount;
forge relationships with experts from the medical/scientific community;
and supply media professionals with information on the controversy.
GLAAD's ability to become visible with its opposing messages, Spurgeon
hoped, would persuade Paramount to regulate Schlessinger. The more
high-profile media exposure GLAAD could get, the more influence it could
hope to have with Paramount in private meetings. The only role imagined
for the GLAAD membership was to monitor the local coverage of the campaign and respond with letters to the editor.

To build a credible case with media professionals and help maximize coverage of the issue, GLAAD developed a media kit that included full, unedited transcripts of some of Schlessinger's most vitriolic diatribes, along with corresponding audio originals on cassette tape. The cover letter stressed that GLAAD had begun by meeting with Schlessinger personally "to open an educational and relevant dialog with her and her listeners." It was also careful to portray GLAAD's response to Schlessinger's "incendiary commentary" as measured and reasonable: "We are registering our objections and point of view with those who air Dr Schlessinger's program. We have asked our members and friends to write directly to her and express their opinions and disdain – not angrily (which, frankly, she expects) but rationally and thoughtfully. We also are approaching other on-air personalities to consider our concerns in their upcoming programs and recurring topics. But it is you, of course, who can be a powerful voice." The letter closes by pointing out that GLAAD had provided complete, unedited transcripts so that it could not be accused of quoting Schlessinger out of context and to allow media professionals to draw their own conclusions.

GLAAD's first major effort to mobilize the gay and lesbian community was a GLAADAlert sent out on 3 August 1999 to 80,000 email addresses. Titled "Tell Dr Laura the Truth," it quoted a comment Schlessinger made during her March 1999 meeting with Garry: "If your organization doesn't agree with me then they will attempt to shut me down. Which, frankly, you've got to tell your people that when they do public attacks, it makes me more popular. It gets me more sponsors. It's counterproductive." In responding to this challenge, GLAAD instructed its members "to write to her and register your opinions as clearly and strongly as possible without rising to her 'bait,'" explaining, "she is expecting (perhaps even hoping for) angry letters with attacks as personal as those she directs." GLAAD received copies of nearly 1,000 letters within seventy-two hours of issuing its alert. Not one made it onto Schlessinger's radio program.

That same month, in August 1999, Spurgeon and GLAAD Entertainment Media director Scott Seomin attended a lunch meeting with two representatives from Paramount: John Wentworth, senior vice president of media relations, and Michelle Hunt, vice president of media relations. In an interview I conducted with the entire GLAAD communications team about the Schlessinger campaign, Seomin described the meeting in these terms: "It was very cordial. We brought them transcripts, a Dr Laura kit ... We said, look, you don't have to carry this torch, we can do it. This isn't going to go away. This isn't going to be a headline one day that says 'GLAAD is Mad!' and then it's going to blow over. It's going to be bigger than that." Spurgeon explained that he saw it as GLAAD's job to inform Paramount of the gravity of the situation. His discussions with insiders at the studio led him to believe that it had not taken Schlessinger's anti-gay rhetoric into account when it made the decision to give her a talk show. He told me: "I think they were absolutely enamoured with her numbers because she was the highest-rated woman nationally on radio. And frankly, I think Laura's reputation had not quite caught up with her in the mainstream yet. She had spent a lot of time giving really good advice and so forth, and she just became ... she switched over and I think they were still basing their opinion on Laura as being ... feisty, equally offensive to all kinds of persons, and she really had changed a lot." Could Paramount really have decided to invest $76 million in a talk show deal with Schlessinger and not taken her views about homosexuality into account, as Spurgeon believed? Or was the studio willing to wager that her views would not generate the kind of damaging controversy that would compromise ratings and advertiser support? Spurgeon gave Paramount the benefit of the doubt and held firm to the idea that studio executives could be swayed through tough but polite discussions.

Spurgeon and Seomin saw their meeting with Wentworth and Hunt as an opportunity to tell Paramount that it had bought itself trouble. Paramount, however, did not react as GLAAD had hoped. As Seomin explained: "We don't believe that John took that [message] to [chairman] Kerry McCluggage and [president] Frank Kelly ... I believe he just felt that he did his job so he could say: 'Well, I had lunch with the guys at GLAAD so I could hear them out.'" Meanwhile, a request to meet with the upper echelons of Paramount, which the studio had agreed to in principle but had not yet scheduled, was beginning to stagnate. It was time for GLAAD to crank up the pressure.

By this point, GLAAD had hoped to generate significant LGBT press coverage of its Schlessinger campaign. Spurgeon recalled that GLAAD was not successful in piquing the interest of LGBT media outlets, something that became a bit of a sore point: "We had tried like hell to get a

couple major [gay] publications to work this story and to get some interest and momentum going on it. [They] couldn't have been more
bored, couldn't have given us a bigger yawn. It was sort of like, yeah,
yeah, call us when it's something a lot bigger. So, where we would have
broken the story in the gay press, we couldn't get any interest." This
lack of interest was perhaps not surprising given that, as Larry Gross
(2001, 247) writes, "the lesbian and gay press is torn between acknowledging its historic role as a committed advocate for the interests
of a marginalized community and a desire to be seen as fulfilling the
professional role of objective journalism." It may be that GLAAD's
Schlessinger campaign was not yet a story for national gay journalists
because it was not yet a story for mainstream journalists. To act otherwise would have been to break the story because GLAAD asked them to,
something that went against gay journalists' professional desire to be
seen as just as objective as their mainstream counterparts.

Spurgeon and Seomin turned to the *Los Angeles Times*, which, Spurgeon said (snapping his fingers), "snapped like that with it." "As it
turned out," he adds, "that was exactly the lever to push." Seomin contacted Brian Lowry, the *Times'* television columnist, who on 11 January
2000 described GLAAD's concerns about Schlessinger's upcoming television program and the reactions of some gay employees at Paramount.[3]
The column generated considerable national media interest and, for the
first time since GLAAD's campaign began, led to the widespread dissemination of some of Schlessinger's most inflammatory rhetoric. GLAAD
communications manager Sean Lund told me that breaking this story
was not a simple matter of calling up a friendly reporter: "This would
not have broken in the *Los Angeles Times* if we had not done the meetings with Laura ... and mobilized the gay community to try and educate
Laura. Our entire strategy ... was about building credibility with not
only the gay press but with the mainstream press and with the American public." Interest in the campaign on the part of both mainstream
and LGBT media exploded. Lund said, "we probably sent out ... better
than 150 press kits with audiotape within two months of that story."
Ironically, many of the reporters now requesting information were the
same LGBT reporters who had previously turned down the story.

The media attention had another desired effect: Paramount finally
scheduled its top-level meeting with GLAAD. The discussions, lasting

three hours, took place on 14 February 2000 and involved senior executives of Paramount Television, the co-presidents of Paramount Domestic Television, the head of Paramount Syndication, the executive
producers of Schlessinger's radio and television shows, and Garry and
Spurgeon. GLAAD's objectives for this meeting, consistent with the campaign strategy Spurgeon outlined, were to demonstrate to Paramount
how extreme Schlessinger's rhetoric had become and persuade the studio to institute a zero-tolerance policy on defamatory speech (including
words like "deviant" and phrases like "biological error"). As Garry told
Lowry after the meeting: "All we're asking is to be heard up front, while
they're still developing this ... It's really to educate them, to give them
the full picture of who she is and the kind of things she's saying."[4]

The meeting produced only assurances from Paramount that Schlessinger's views on homosexuality would not go unopposed and that discussions of homosexuality on her show would cite credible research.
Paramount did not agree to GLAAD's third and most important request,
a guarantee that defamation of the sort Schlessinger was now known
for would not be tolerated. A joint public statement issued after the
meeting characterized it as "a positive exchange of differing perspectives." Although it also stated "the dialogue with Paramount executives
is expected to continue," the statement did not indicate when further
discussions might take place. Schlessinger's program, it said in the
vaguest of terms, would "vary from Dr Laura's successful radio show"
and offer "many points of view, derived from a variety of sources, guests,
and a studio audience." Beyond this statement, the parties agreed not to
discuss the meeting's specifics with media.

The statement, lukewarm as it was, created a stir in conservative circles. Responding to criticism that Schlessinger and Paramount had
"caved in" to pressure from GLAAD, a spokeswoman for Schlessinger
told the conservative *Washington Times*: "It's not true that Dr Laura ca-
pitulated to anyone or anything ... that's totally wrong." An "unidentified spokesman" is also quoted saying that Schlessinger retained "total
control" over content.[5] These statements to the *Washington Times* con-
travened the agreement to avoid discussing the meetings with media and,
in Spurgeon's view, deliberately misrepresented them: "I believe ... when
Schlessinger's representatives went back to [her], they quickly deduced
what the agenda was going to be for the next meeting [i.e., to convince

Paramount to institute a policy of zero-tolerance for defamation]. And the screws were going to come down on Paramount. I think they didn't want that meeting to happen. So they misrepresented." Schlessinger's public relations team's statements left GLAAD in the embarrassing position of appearing as though its insider efforts were not bearing fruit. Its strategy thus compromised, the organization soon found itself vulnerable to attack from within the gay and lesbian community.

## Outsiders

On 19 February 2000, Signorile interviewed Garry on the Internet-based GAYBC Radio Network. Conceding the point that Schlessinger's rhetoric had not improved since she met with her, Garry spent much of the interview defending GLAAD's strategy, which at that point was still "to work with Paramount to make sure that they create a balanced show." Signorile criticized this strategy as "corporate" because it consisted of meeting behind closed doors and asking for "balance" instead of calling for the show to be cancelled as a matter of principle: "Would it be okay to put a racist talk show host up there," he asked, "as long as there was a differing viewpoint [offered], as long as they had someone come on and say, 'No, blacks are okay?'" He questioned GLAAD's unwillingness to call on the community to pressure Paramount, implying that the strategy appeared designed to keep the organization in Paramount's good graces. Garry did little to dispel this impression by repeatedly invoking the importance of holding on to GLAAD's "place at the table," and the unprecedented "opportunity to make sure the show is fair, accurate, and inclusive." GLAAD had never before enjoyed this level of access, Garry argued, and there was still an opportunity to use that access to convince Paramount to control Schlessinger's speech. To mobilize the community against the studio, she suggested, would be premature, since it would compromise GLAAD's ability to engage in this kind of dialogue. Signorile responded with a scathing critique:

> Joan, with all due respect, do you know what I think? This corporate strategy, which is what you're using, doesn't seem to be working. It's proved wrong. This woman is not going to let them mould her and reshape her show ... You've not summoned up

the troops. You've not blasted Paramount and scared them in the way other minority groups have scared them from putting on defamatory shows. You've not demanded this show not be aired. It all seems to deny GLAAD its activist past ... In the end you only get the access by having power, and you only get power by flexing muscle, and that means putting pressure – instead you use this corporate strategy that only gives an illusion of access and allows them to buy time, and to screw you over – and to buy you too. I don't know, maybe Paramount has some investment in giving you money for tables at your events, or something, I don't know. This strategy has GLAAD dropping the ball, losing critical battles.

Keeping her cool, Garry answered: "I respectfully disagree with you Michelangelo. The one thing you didn't talk about is respect. GLAAD has a tremendous amount of respect within the industry. GLAAD's voice is respected, whether we're celebrating the things they do right or calling them to task."

Within a few days of this confrontational interview, an email from an unidentified source began to circulate on the Internet. It began with three simple words and as many exclamation marks: "STOP DR. LAURA!!!" This was followed by a list of media personalities who had been fired or otherwise disciplined by corporate entities because of insensitive or offensive language directed at minorities: "When Atlanta Braves pitcher John Rocker belittled 'queers' ... he got suspended. When *60 Minutes*' Andy Rooney belittled Native Americans ... he got suspended. When golf announcer Ben Wright mocked lesbians ... he got fired." Using the same phrasing, the text went on to list the consequences of one writer's "denigration" of Asians, a sports team owner's "disparagement" of African Americans, and a football player's "attack" on gays. The list ended with a statement meant to illustrate a double standard: "But Dr Laura calls gays 'biological mistakes' ... and she's getting a TV show from Paramount." While GLAAD had thus far instructed its members to write polite letters to Schlessinger and avoided calling on the community to act against Paramount, this email, which spread like wildfire in a matter of days, was designed to get gays and lesbians everywhere riled up. Its call to action was straightforward and expressed in capital letters, the online equivalent of shouting from the rooftops: "EMAIL PARAMOUNT NOW AND DEMAND DR. LAURA BE DROPPED."

On 28 February 2000, GLAAD responded with "A Letter from GLAAD Executive Director Joan M. Garry." It began by acknowledging criticism of GLAAD's approach to the campaign: "During the last two weeks, some of you have expressed concern about GLAAD's recent work concerning Dr Laura Schlessinger and her move to television. Although some of this criticism has been hard to hear, we know how important it is to listen. And we've been listening." Garry went on to describe GLAAD's work on the campaign to that point, and rationalized waiting to call on Paramount to drop the show:

> Our plan has been intentional from day one. We have always believed that there were series of cards to play and that it has been our responsibility to play each of them. We are all working toward the same end – to ensure that Dr Laura does not spew her homophobic rhetoric to television audiences and that media professionals are held accountable for portraying the reality of our lives. And we started this work far enough in advance to have meaningful conversations with Paramount before her show even went into production.

Garry then gave an account of GLAAD's meeting with Paramount representatives and argued that the organization had "made solid progress." On the most important point, GLAAD's request that Paramount guarantee it would not tolerate defamatory language, Garry admitted that work remained. She also admitted that the organization had "not given the LGBT community enough information about what we've planned and about what we as a community can do together." At the end of the letter, Garry informed readers that GLAAD had sent a letter to Paramount requesting a second meeting within seven days and a written assurance "that Paramount has a zero tolerance for defamation directed at the gay and lesbian community." Failing that, Garry wrote, GLAAD would "call on Paramount to pull the plug on 'Dr Laura.'" For the first time since the campaign began, Garry called on the GLAAD membership to "put pressure on Paramount" by writing letters to its chairman.

The next day, 29 February 2000, GLAAD published a full-page ad in two entertainment industry trade publications, the *Hollywood Reporter* and *Daily Variety*.[6] Addressed to media professionals, the ads aimed to create pressure from the inside – from within Paramount and elsewhere in the media industry – and to embarrass the studio's executives. In an interview, Spurgeon explained: "We were smarting from the Laura camp having screwed us out of our next meeting, you know, and the fact that Paramount didn't have any more control over the Laura people ... The ad was really to make Paramount sit up and go 'who the hell is driving this bus? Is it going to be Laura or is it going to be us?' We had to strike some discord. We had to try to start to divide and conquer and bring a wedge between Paramount and Premiere Radio Network. And the ad was to make Paramount look as foolish as possible." At a cost of a few thousand dollars, the ad continued to let Schlessinger speak for herself. Its heading stated: "Dr Laura says: 'I have never made an anti-gay commentary,'" followed by, "Oh, really?" and four word-for-word excerpts from her radio program. In these statements, Schlessinger called homosexuality "destructive," a "dysfunction," and "deviant," linked it to pedophilia, bestiality, sadomasochism, and cross-dressing, and suggested that "gay" is to "homosexuality" as "ethnic cleansing" is to "murder." The last quoted segment made a case for why society "should discriminate against certain behaviors": "man-on-man and woman-on-woman sexual activity is a deviant sexual orientation, and does not promote any of the values set forth biblically." The ad ended with a simple statement of fact – "Paramount Domestic Television will bring Dr Laura to TV this fall" – and a simple directive: "Tell Paramount what you have to say." Seomin said about that final directive: "We didn't give any phone numbers because everybody in this industry knows people at Paramount." Spurgeon added: "It was so that when ... whoever went to lunch that day was going to be embarrassed by a question, and it was going to point a lot of fingers at Kerry McCluggage: 'What the hell did you put us into and how do we get out of this?' Because no studio likes to be embarrassed and we wanted to embarrass them."

Other ads designed to raise mainstream awareness about Schlessinger's anti-gay rhetoric, by the San Francisco-based Horizons Foundation and the online "journal of opinion" TomPaine.com, appeared in newspapers around the same time. The most important was the full-page Horizons ad, which ran in the *New York Times*, the *Los Angeles Times*, and the *San Francisco Chronicle*. The ad and placements, which Horizons paid for in part through a special appeal to its major donors, probably cost a few hundred thousand dollars, according to Spurgeon. It centred on the idea that "Dr Laura Schlessinger's anti-gay commentaries are harmful to our children" and appeared in conjunction with an "open letter" to Schlessinger, available online, signed by more than 150 prominent organizations and individuals in the fields of health, religion, child welfare, and civil rights "inviting her to use her wit and intelligence to help kids by speaking out against anti-gay prejudice and violence."

The Child Welfare League of America, the National Mental Health Association, the American Civil Liberties Union, and the National Organization for Women all signed the letter, as did most major gay and lesbian movement organizations. GLAAD was invited to add its imprimatur as well but declined because, Spurgeon told me, it decided the ad's focus and timing were ill-considered. Going after Schlessinger on the topic of harm to children, GLAAD's leadership thought, was not a sound strategy because of Schlessinger's credibility as a strong advocate for children. Spurgeon also told me that GLAAD's leaders did not believe it was cost-effective to try to reinforce a message about Schlessinger's rhetoric that had not yet taken hold in the mainstream. Nevertheless, the high-profile ads generated an unprecedented amount of regional, national, and international press about the escalating campaign against Schlessinger. There was now no question that the gay and lesbian community's grievances against her had become a matter of public debate.

On 1 March 2000, the ad hoc coalition that disseminated the STOP DR. LAURA email launched StopDrLaura.com (SDL), a website that also gave the coalition its name. SDL founders John Aravosis (an Internet consultant), Alan Klein (a former GLAAD communications director), William Waybourn (the former GLAAD executive director), Robin Tyler (an activist and comedian), Joel Lawson (a public relations consultant), and Scott Robbe (a TV/film producer and director) took the position that calling for anything less than the cancellation of *Dr Laura* amounted to capitulating to an unacceptable double standard: no television studio would give a platform to an avowedly racist or anti-Semitic host, they argued, so why was a studio giving an unrepentant homophobe a national talk show? The response to this framing was immediate and overwhelming: within three days of going online, the site, designed to become the hub of a grassroots mobilization campaign, logged more than a million page views.[7]

Visitors to SDL were greeted by a then-state-of-the-art Flash animation designed by Aravosis. It began with the phrase "Are you?" in white lettering against a black background, followed by a succession of words describing identities or characteristics such as straight, addicted, Black, Jewish, blind, afraid, smart, fat, blonde, cute, etc. The words faded in and out very rapidly, ending with "gay," which remained on the screen for a few seconds before it was replaced by: "Are you a biological error? Some people think so."

Under the heading, "StopDrLaura: a coalition against hate," the website featured a close-up photograph of Schlessinger edited to appear as if lit from below, making her look like the caricature of an evil harridan. To the right of her face was a scrolling list of some of her most infamous quotations about homosexuality. Having interpellated its visitors and riled them up, the site then directed them to take action in a variety of ways that initially focused on participating in protests and flooding executives at Paramount and its parent company, Viacom, with phone calls, faxes, and emails. Adopting aggressive tactics from the beginning, SDL published the direct telephone lines and email addresses of key executives with the goal of overwhelming their communication systems. SDL reported that the phone number of a senior Paramount executive had changed within a day of being posted and that the studio had been forced to temporarily shut off all but the internal portion of its email system.

With SDL pulling the grassroots out from under her feet, Garry called an all-staff teleconference on 3 March 2000. There was a palpable sense in the New York office that this call was coming at a time of crisis for the organization. All-staff calls, which took place every month or so, were normally routine affairs. They usually lasted no more than an hour and were a way for Garry to inform staff of management decisions, boost morale, boast about accomplishments, mark anniversaries, and help the various parts of a decentralized organization feel more connected to one another. This conference call stood out as anything but routine. Coming as it did in the midst of SDL's community mobilization, it was Garry's first opportunity to let her staff know that GLAAD's campaign was entering a new stage. I recorded in my field notes that she declared: "One of the things I've come to grips with in the last two weeks is that we have to be mindful of our goals with Paramount, but also mindful of our obligations to the community." Within the next two weeks, she predicted, GLAAD would either claim victory on the basis of an announcement that Paramount had agreed not to tolerate defamatory rhetoric, or add what she called "significant influence" to the voices calling for the program's cancellation.

The anticipated Paramount response to SDL's mobilization came on 10 March 2000 in the form of two media statements. The first, by Schlessinger, said: "I never intend to hurt anyone or contribute in any way to an atmosphere of hate or intolerance. Regrettably, some of the words I've used have hurt some people, and I am sorry for that." The second, by Paramount, affirmed "a commitment to present society's issues without creating or contributing to an environment of hurt, hate, or intolerance." Was Schlessinger's statement an apology? Was Paramount taking a zero-tolerance stance against defamation, as GLAAD hoped?

SDL's leaders dismissed the statements as half-hearted and announced a 21 March protest in front of the Paramount gates. GLAAD's leaders reacted with carefully worded optimism. They wrote: "We are encouraged that Schlessinger has listened to the concerns of GLAAD, others in the lesbian and gay community, and other fair-minded people about the hurt caused by her words. GLAAD welcomes Schlessinger's new public commitment to conduct her self-proclaimed moral and ethical advocacy in an environment free from hate and intolerance. We will be listening to and watching her current and upcoming radio and television broadcasts to be sure she is true to her word." It did not take long for Schlessinger's apology, such as it was, to fall apart. On 15 March 2000, a column by conservative columnist Don Feder in the *Boston Herald* quoted her saying that her statement was a clarification and not an apology. Feder wrote: "She will continue to recommend reparative therapy (for homosexuals who want to change), to oppose same-sex marriage and adoption, and [to] champion Judeo-Christian sexual ethics."[8]

Feder's column appeared sixteen days after GLAAD issued its seven-day ultimatum to Paramount. There had been no second meeting with Paramount executives, and worse, the statements by Schlessinger and Paramount appeared like little more than evasive rhetorical manoeuvres now that Schlessinger had recanted her apology. With little hope left for a continuing dialogue with the studio, GLAAD issued a statement on the same day as Feder's column was published: "GLAAD now has no assurance that Schlessinger will not publicly defame lesbians and gay men in

her radio or upcoming television broadcasts ... GLAAD now calls upon
Paramount to ... [abandon] its plans to produce and distribute any program featuring Laura Schlessinger."

With the announcement that GLAAD would join SDL in front of the
Paramount gates, the Schlessinger campaign entered a new stage that
had GLAAD engaging in public protest for the first time since 1995. The
campaign would continue, but its tactics would shift to a wider set of
targets: television critics, local UPN and CBS affiliates, and advertisers.

### The Paramount Decision

Back on 20 February 2000, the day after Signorile had accused her of
having been bought by Paramount, Garry sent out an email to GLAAD
development staff raising the issue of Paramount's contributions to the
Media Awards. Paramount Television Group, which produced Schlessinger's television program, had purchased a $7,500 table at the Media
Awards in Los Angeles, while Paramount Pictures, which was nominated for the film *Election*, had sponsored the awards at the $50,000
level. A conference call involving Garry, Julie Anderson, Spurgeon, Jason
Burlingame, and Cathy Renna was held on 21 February. The consensus
coming out of that meeting, reportedly based on staff members' assurances to themselves that corporate gifts never influence GLAAD's decision-making, was that the organization should hold on to the money.

This decision was questioned the following month during a conversation between Garry and the then-co-chairs of the board, David Steward and Gene Falk. While Steward agreed that the money should not be
returned, Falk argued that it would be a serious mistake and a potential
public relations disaster to hold on to it. Given the disagreement, Garry
arranged for a conference call of the executive committee on 29 March,
which resulted in a motion to return the Paramount money. The motion
failed by a vote of three to four, a close split that left the executive committee nervous about an issue it considered delicate and important. It decided to meet again two days later, after Garry had spoken to two key
allies working at Paramount: David Lee, executive producer of *Frasier*
and a generous contributor to GLAAD, and Joe Lupariello, a GLAAD
board member and the president of Leeza Gibbons Enterprises, which
was affiliated with Paramount. Garry also called another management
team meeting, which focused on the potential negative press that ac-

cepting the Paramount money might engender. Following that discussion, the management team reached a new consensus. The issue was put to a second vote at the executive committee level, which passed a motion on 31 March 2000 to return the money. It also decided to extend complimentary Media Awards invitations to the producers of nominated Paramount-produced content.

The decision to return the money generated controversy among GLAAD board members, some of whom objected to the decision and/ or the lack of full board involvement in making it. The controversy resulted in a flurried exchange of emails, one of which, from Howard Buford, head of an advertising agency named Prime Access, offers a glimpse into the content of the discussions at the executive committee level. Buford, who provided me with a copy of his email, wrote with the passion of one who has "participated in rallies and marched [in] demonstrations since I was 5 years old because of my parents' involvement in the civil rights movement." He described the campaign against Schlessinger as a "defining moment for GLAAD" and as an issue that is "ours and ours alone" whose "savvy handling ... can make GLAAD the premier gay and lesbian community advocate." Buford then lent his marketing expertise to an analysis of why returning the Paramount money was the right decision. He wrote: "This battle is reaching lesbians and gay men out to the suburbs of Topeka. And it is reaching the kitchen and dining room tables of 'everyday folk.' Neither of these groups knows us as people. They only know us by our actions and the appearance of our actions. And as such, we have to understand the importance and power of our actions as symbolic gestures." The letter went on to summarize two sets of arguments some staff and board members had made in favour of keeping the money: First, that Paramount is a wholly owned subsidiary of the Viacom media empire, which also includes CBS, Showtime, MTV, and other media entities who donate money to GLAAD. To be consistent, would we not also have to return all of that money? Where do we draw the line? Are we at war with all of Viacom? Second, that returning the money might compromise "the possibility of continued conversations with Paramount" and "make [talk show host] Leeza [Gibbons] uncomfortable."

Refuting both arguments, Buford offered that the "only value of this gesture [returning the money] is as a piece of communication," and that "we have to be seen as doing the right thing." He wrote: "We must focus on the Paramount brand name. And our actions must be informed by this focus. Anything else is confusing to the outside world and, ultimately, untenable. To win, we must frame this argument appropriately and winnably."

In an interview, I asked Buford to elaborate on his reaction to the argument that GLAAD would be accused of hypocrisy if it continued to accept money from Paramount's parent and sister companies:

> I remember having a very contentious ... exec committee conversation about, "yeah, but they're part of Viacom and do we boycott Viacom," and I said, look ... this thing will be decided in the court of public opinion. You know, all this stuff about, yes it's CBS and you're not boycotting CBS and you're being hypocritical ... that's a whole intellectual, unimportant, jack-off, bullshit argument that people in the streets are not going to understand. And the burden is going to be on somebody else to try and explain how CBS is connected to Viacom who owns Paramount ... That's not something that people get. You gotta be very clear and be very focused on it. So we were able to focus on not accepting money from Paramount.

As a matter of tactical positioning in the campaign, Buford argued that the money had to be returned not so much as a matter of principle, but because, he wrote, "on the surface, accepting money from Paramount does not look good to the outside world. In fact, it looks bad. Just as bad as a political candidate taking corporate money when about to vote on policy affecting that corporation's interests." If GLAAD's critics still chose to take on GLAAD for taking money from Viacom, Buford stated, "the burden of explanation will fall on them, not on us," which he argued would allow GLAAD to prevail in the public relations battle.

Buford's framing of the debate as a public relations battle carried the day, but broader questions of principle concerning corporate donations arose in the subsequent GLAAD board discussions. Some questioned what it meant for GLAAD to accept money from companies like Coors, which is linked to religious conservative interests, or Brown & Williamson, which manufactures cigarettes. One board member asked: if returning

Paramount's money "means that we disagree with them," does accepting money from other corporations mean that GLAAD agrees with everything they do? Another volunteered that a different way to pose the question was: "Should we accept money from everybody?" As board members raised these questions, however, they were careful to assert as self-evident that GLAAD is never "influenced" or "handcuffed" by corporate money, even as they acknowledged that such financial relationships could get "dicey" and cause "problems," particularly around the perception that money could buy GLAAD's "silence." In the end, the board concluded that returning the Paramount money was not a problem, as long as it did not amount to an admission that corporate donations are in any way linked to GLAAD's decision-making. The rationale was that they simply could not afford to waste valuable time and organizational energy defending a decision to take money from a "brand" they had "soiled." Said one board member: "To be consistent, we had no choice but to do this."

If GLAAD had soiled Paramount, it was because its leaders had recently called for Schlessinger's show to be cancelled and had begun to openly criticize the studio for its refusal to regulate her. In a speech to the SDL-organized rally on 21 March 2000, which over 500 people attended, Garry stated that Schlessinger's recanted apology had made clear that she "cannot be held accountable for what she says publicly." "If she can't be controlled," Garry said, "she must be stopped." If Paramount would not "accept [its] corporate responsibility and drop this show," then it had "bought itself a seven-month battle." This was a very different tone for GLAAD, and it signalled a new willingness to take stronger action and become more responsive to grassroots concerns.

Buford told me that this shift in tone and strategy came about as the result of the board's growing recognition that "we had a real grassroots faction that we had to deliver some results on or show some action on … I was saying … has anyone been to the Internet and seen what's being said about GLAAD out there? I said, you don't think that's alarming? You don't think that's upsetting that they're saying that we're not doing anything, that we're all basically looking for jobs in media and so we're not going to ruffle feathers. You don't think that that's going to have repercussions?"

## "We're GLAAD and We're Smart and We Know What We're Doing."

The criticism directed at GLAAD from within the movement was given a much broader platform in a 9 May 2000 article in the *Advocate* by Signorile. In "Takin' It to the Streets," Signorile condemned GLAAD's insider tactics and credited SDL with having mobilized large numbers of gays and lesbians in opposition to Schlessinger. Signorile, who did not disclose his own involvement in SDL, began by contrasting the group's direct action pressure tactics with GLAAD's monitoring, letter-writing campaigns, and meetings with corporate executives. He suggested that a desire to preserve a good relationship with Paramount, including its financial relationship, had caused GLAAD to "become frozen in its tracks." He also characterized as "strange" the fact that the "well-established, well-funded" organization had been so slow to ask its membership to apply pressure on Paramount. Listing the various corporate credentials and media ties of GLAAD staff and board members, Signorile argued that GLAAD's leadership had lost its connection with activism: "An activist group run exclusively by people from inside the industry," he writes, "has a will to do just one thing: be inside the industry." While he was encouraged by the fact that GLAAD had decided to return Paramount's money, join the direct protest, and appoint Renna to work with local groups to help organize further protests, he dismissed these moves as "showy gestures" and suggested they were little more than "damage control" for fear that GLAAD's "reputation is being tarnished and its turf being moved in on."

I was in New York the week this article was published, as was Spurgeon, who was meeting with the editorial board of the *New York Times* to discuss ways to incorporate gay and lesbian issues and perspectives in coverage of the upcoming November elections. After that meeting, he and junior communications staffer Wonbo Woo invited me to join them on a coffee break. Though I had not known Spurgeon for very long at this point, I had been immediately struck by his avuncular manner, which he expressed on this occasion through stories about his days in a small Midwestern liberal arts college where, he delighted in telling us, he had belonged to a fraternity. He joked that he initially thought he had been chosen because he was cool but soon figured out that the fraternity needed him because his grades brought up its average. It was clear from his story that this had been a challenging period for him, so I asked why he had wanted to join the fraternity in the first place and why, if being in that environment had been so painful, he had decided to stay there. He answered that he had thought that joining would prepare him for the heterosexual, male-dominated business world. "And did it?" I asked. Yes, he answered, except that the business world turned out to be much worse.

As we returned to the GLAAD office, I was invited to join the two staff members as they brainstormed about how best to respond to the Signorile article. Spurgeon was visibly upset and looking to let off steam. He also knew that Woo, who approached his work from the kind of perspective that Signorile and SDL advocated, would give him some insight into how the article might be received in LGBT activist circles. What transpired was a substantive, sometimes passionate debate about GLAAD's political philosophy, strategies, and tactics.

It was immediately clear from the discussion that Spurgeon felt personally attacked by Signorile's article. He stated that Signorile, who has been involved in and writing about the gay and lesbian movement for many years, had an axe to grind with people like himself who had joined more recently. He accused Signorile of holding a nostalgic view of street protests as signifying some sort of authentic activism that GLAAD's insider tactics fell short of, and took issue with the journalist's contention that SDL had achieved success in the campaign that had thus far eluded GLAAD: "None of us has had success," he told Woo and me, because no one had stopped *Dr Laura*. Direct protest, he said, is only one tactic and among the least effective. Those who value protest above everything else are making a mistake by forgetting that there is space in the movement for other strategies and that tactics need not involve either/or choices. "There's a reason it's called a movement," Spurgeon said, "it rolls on."

Woo responded that he read Signorile's article not as an example of an old-fashioned activist refusing to change with the times, but as a criticism of some of the dangers of the changes GLAAD's insider activism initiated. Signorile, he said, "is questioning the nature of the changes we're supporting." He thought the article had some valid criticisms in pointing out, for example, that GLAAD had not had "enough contact with the community" and "lost touch with the people we represent." Spurgeon balked at this notion and said that people who make this argument tend to define community as narrowly made up of "granola activists," "full-time queers," and "ghetto homosexuals" who live, work, and socialize exclusively in gay enclaves like West Hollywood. By adopting this definition of the community, he argued, "we shut out the Steves," by which he presumably meant people like himself who see themselves as more integrated within mainstream society.

Woo pointed out that "by not communicating with anyone" about what it wanted from Paramount, GLAAD was not including the Steves any more than the granola activists. For Spurgeon, however, GLAAD had no particular responsibility to inform the community of its plans or to consult it about what it wanted: "GLAAD," he said, "was formed to get on the inside" of the media industry. "We had a longer line to play," he said, "but the community didn't trust us." Woo interjected that it was difficult to ask the community for its trust when GLAAD was not informing it of actions taken on its behalf. "They didn't need to know," Spurgeon answered, because making that kind of information public would have made it impossible to negotiate anything.

Spurgeon added that, going into the meeting, GLAAD knew that "they [Paramount] weren't going to just roll over." GLAAD's initial position, he explained, let it get in the door and begin a process. There were eight months left before the show would air and GLAAD understood that it would take time to get results. Spurgeon said he was convinced that if GLAAD had been able to continue its discussions with Paramount, "we would have been further ahead than we are now." Instead, he lamented, by being forced to participate in direct protest, "we closed the door we worked so hard to open" because the "community wouldn't allow us to continue." Yet, "Paramount was listening to us" and had already agreed to two of the three requests that had made up GLAAD's initial negotiating position: the studio affirmed that Schlessinger's views on homosexuality would not go unopposed and that discussions of homosexuality would cite credible research. Further negotiations, Spurgeon believed, could have led Paramount to take a hard line against defamatory rhetoric, despite Schlessinger's assertions that she would remain in control of her show. "It doesn't always have to be taken to the streets," Spurgeon said.

Woo asked if the message that Spurgeon wanted to convey in his response to the Signorile article was that the world has changed and that GLAAD is playing by new rules. Spurgeon offered that yes, the movement is now in a position to deploy a wider array of tactics and direct protest has its place in that arsenal. The problem, he said, is when people "hold that [protest] up as a mantra." This led Woo back to his central point, which was that Signorile's article addresses a "fundamental conflict" for which other LGBT organizations, like the Human Rights Campaign, have also been criticized. Woo described it in this manner: "How can they claim to represent anyone in the community if people don't know [what happens behind the scenes]?" He added: "There are aspects of our work that are suspect in the same way."

To Spurgeon, by contrast, what mattered most about the organization's access to corporate decision-makers was that "GLAAD isn't in the dark anymore" after "trying so hard" for years to manoeuvre itself into a position where it could legitimately claim to have some influence. It did not achieve this, Spurgeon said, by asking the community about how it wanted to proceed, but by bringing on board people who know how to work within the system. He named Seomin as an example of someone community members are suspicious of but who is extremely effective in his insider role: are we better off, Spurgeon asked, doing our letter-writing campaigns or "having ... Scott sit in a meeting with the producers of a show to make sure that something doesn't get on?" The problem is, "you can never tell people enough about those meetings" because they always say that "Scott didn't ask for enough" or that he's not really "playing for the LGBT community." And it is true, Spurgeon said, that Seomin is not really playing for the community: "He's playing for how we are perceived outside the community."

This last statement had Woo shifting uncomfortably in his seat. He asked Spurgeon to elaborate. Spurgeon responded with an analogy: it's the difference between "singing to the choir" and "singing so that you can be heard outside the church." Fair enough, said Woo, but "don't we exist to serve the community?" Spurgeon started to say no and then swallowed his words. After a short pause, he stated: "We exist to serve the community by working outside the community."

An example of serving the community by working outside the community came later in the conversation when Spurgeon explained why he thought it was not feasible to call for *Dr Laura*'s cancellation. We recognized, Spurgeon said, that the show is a $100 million investment by Paramount and "you don't pull a show" with that much invested. Secondly, McCluggage, the executive who wanted and approved the show, and whose wife reportedly loved *Dr Laura*, was not about to lose face by allowing it to be cancelled because of protests. There is "less shame," Spurgeon said, in letting the show go on and "letting it die" of its own accord. Thirdly, McCluggage was involved in a power play as a result of the 1999 CBS-Viacom merger and stood in the weakest position among three people with similar jobs. He could not afford to bow to special interest groups. Given this analysis of internal goings-on at Paramount, GLAAD's strategy was to force the studio to create a "sanitized, face-lifted, derma-brasioned, version of the show." In other words, Spurgeon had hoped to wield GLAAD's influence in such a way that Paramount would create a show so bland and so devoid of the persona that has made Schlessinger a success on radio that it would be seen to have failed on its own, which would allow Paramount (and McCluggage) to save face and GLAAD to preserve its relationship with the studio. Said Spurgeon: "They [Paramount] could have used us to make the show bad." He added: "Could I have explained that to the community? It would have given away our whole strategy."

In Spurgeon's estimation, then, the community's lack of trust in GLAAD's strategy resulted in an unnecessary and premature resort to direct protest: "We played our cards too fast" and "lost our sense of momentum." The "only things left" are "to go after advertisers ... and individual stations." But "we're still in May," he said, and it would have made more sense to "build pressure." Instead, without consultation with GLAAD, SDL pulled out all the stops. But "where do they have to go?" "There is no strategy coming out of StopDrLaura.com," he stated, "only instant gratification." From Spurgeon's perspective, SDL's haste in employing aggressive tactics belied the absence of a long-term plan to deal with Schlessinger's homophobic rhetoric. Confronting Paramount, he believed, would only succeed in making activists feel good about themselves and would damage the movement's longer-term prospects with the studio.

Wrapping up their discussion, Spurgeon and Woo resolved to write a letter to the *Advocate*, which Woo would draft (because, Spurgeon said, Woo had a "certain sensibility" that made him the better choice to respond), and to "come up with our own last word" to be published elsewhere. What Spurgeon had in mind was not a direct response to Signorile's article, but reflection that would lay out the philosophical underpinnings of GLAAD's tactics. "We have to lead thought, we can't pander to the lowest common denominator," Spurgeon said. "I'm so proud of the work we do," he added, describing GLAAD's work as "smart" and "well-intended." It was important to him, therefore, that its response not come across as a mea culpa or an attempt to mollify: "Why do we need to placate anyone? We're GLAAD and we're smart and we know what we're doing."

Spurgeon struggled at various times over the course of many months to write a think piece that would not seem overly defensive or concede too much to GLAAD's critics, betray the hurt feelings of many staff members, or constitute an ill-mannered counter-attack on SDL. It was a difficult balance to strike, and Spurgeon was never fully satisfied that he had found the right tone. Although GLAAD had negotiated for some space on Gay.com, where Signorile had continued his attacks, the article Spurgeon had in mind was never published.

## The Campaign: Phase II

It was clear by the June 2000 board meeting that SDL had forced GLAAD to change its approach to the campaign. Despite Spurgeon's convictions about GLAAD's responsibility to lead thought, the revised campaign plan he presented to board members bore striking similarities to SDL's strategic and tactical orientations. GLAAD's new objective for the campaign, which had previously been "to stem the escalating influence of ... Schlessinger's homophobic advocacy," was now "to persuade Paramount Domestic Television to drop this show." The main tactics, which had previously focused on negotiating with Paramount while generating favourable mainstream media coverage, were now: (1) to exert pressure on CBS/UPN affiliates, and (2) to compel advertisers to withdraw from the program. The strategy document Spurgeon presented revealed both the extent to which GLAAD had been compelled to redefine its objectives and his personal ambivalence about them: "We must drive toward [persuading Paramount to drop the show] regardless of whether we see this as attainable. I say this for two reasons: I see it as our responsibility to do what we [can] to ensure that defamation ceases. The work we do toward that end has meaning and value regardless of the ultimate outcome – in community organizing, raising awareness of pervasive discrimination, just to name a few." By questioning "whether we see this as attainable," Spurgeon cast doubt on the feasibility of an objective he had not initially favoured. Having adopted a position that conflicted with GLAAD's usual insider stance and tactics, he had little choice but to justify it in terms of its intrinsic value for community organizing, regardless of whether or not he believed it was the right course of action.

In an interview with me, Spurgeon emphasized that if the initial campaign was focused on negotiation with Paramount and generating mainstream media coverage, it was because GLAAD had its eye on what he called the "ultimate" audience: women in the eighteen-to-forty-nine demographic that Paramount identified as its target market for *Dr Laura*. Spurgeon told me that he conceived of Schlessinger's audience as women from lower-middle-class backgrounds who were stay-at-home mothers, or swing-shift or part-time workers with incomes up to about $30,000 a year. This demographic, he told me, is made up of "folks who will respond to straightforward education." "All kinds of demographic studies," he said, suggest that women in this audience "like to make their own decisions, they like to think they make smart decisions ... So by giving straightforward information about Laura and her positions, it allowed people to feel that they were coming to their own conclusion about Laura."

SDL's arrival in the campaign, Spurgeon argued, came just as GLAAD had begun to make inroads with its target audience of potential Schlessinger viewers. "The ultimate thing," he said, "was to cripple the show with viewers and with advertisers and at that point, it was like, there needs to be more pulling people in to our position before we raise our fists up in the air." If GLAAD decided to join SDL in protesting Paramount, Spurgeon acknowledged, it was because SDL's success in rallying gay and lesbian community members was beginning to threaten GLAAD's position with its "home-base audience." "We couldn't lose the base within the gay and lesbian community," he said. "We had to give them something," and at the same time "preserve our potential to do right by another audience," which he described as a "dilemma."

As part of the second phase of the Schlessinger campaign, GLAAD arranged to meet with local station managers in the top ten television markets in the United States. Renna spearheaded this initiative and organized or participated in several local "visible press opportunit[ies]," small-scale protests designed to give media images to accompany local campaign coverage. In New York, the only top-ten market where it was unsuccessful in meeting with station managers, GLAAD, along with SDL and about a dozen community groups, participated in a rally that attracted over 400 people.

GLAAD approached affiliate meetings with the objective of getting "at least one station to drop her show." It also saw the meetings as an opportunity to educate station managers about the controversy (most, in Spurgeon's estimation, were "painfully unaware" of Schlessinger's rhetoric) and to encourage them to "raise concerns" with the local press and Paramount, which might feel further compelled to regulate Schlessinger's speech. GLAAD began each meeting by playing an audiotaped excerpt of one of Schlessinger's most incendiary monologues and, in Renna's words, watched as the station managers' "jaws dropped." As Spurgeon wrote in an update to the campaign's strategic plan: "Station managers we have met with have been very receptive to our message. Many of them have described feeling blindsided by Paramount Domestic Television and felt that they were not given sufficient information about what they were buying ... We have also been very successful in getting station managers to talk to the press about their newfound concerns. Several key station managers have been openly critical of Paramount and have indicated that they are in the process of reconsidering their decision to air the show." In an interview, Renna talked about the benefits of meeting with affiliates in terms of local activism:

> I think the strategy was very similar to why we met with Paramount first, with the added benefit of really giving local activists a chance to put themselves on the map with this ... We were instrumental in getting the access because of our visibility around this issue and having the resources to walk in there with local activists and really get the stations to sit up and pay attention ... I can't tell you how many folks weren't aware ... of how to go

about really preparing for a meeting of that significance ... and dealing with media at that level and then maybe dealing with media coverage of a protest. It was a real opportunity to use Schlessinger as a vehicle to grow grassroots media activism work ... and it did make a huge impact because there was a follow-through at the stations, people have continued relationships with them, coverage on other things is much better because now they've actually met physical people in their town who are gay and lesbian who they can talk to about other stuff.

For some activists, however, GLAAD's approach to the station meetings smacked of the kind of paternalism whereby, when it suits its purposes, a national organization with little regional presence parachutes into a locality and imposes its will.

For example, SDL organizers in Chicago issued a press release two days before their planned protest of the local CBS affiliate. The release stated that the coalition of activists organizing the protest would, as a matter of principle, "settle for nothing short of Schlessinger's cancellation," accused GLAAD representatives of "trying to substitute themselves as brokers for the local movement," and objected to the "needless concession" of a "negotiating posture which included having the program air as a 'fall-back position.'" These activists, in other words, accused GLAAD of not only trying to take over, but also being too willing to treat *Dr Laura*'s broadcast as inevitable. Having defined the cancellation of the local affiliate's contract with Paramount as the only morally acceptable outcome, these activists held that the cost of maintaining access was too great. Activists claiming to act on behalf of the gay and lesbian community, they held, should not compromise on the principle that the show should be cancelled. For GLAAD, taking a view it saw as pragmatic, the opportunity to create relationships between local activists and station managers was too good to pass up, especially given the virtual certainty that the show would air and the possibility that the meeting might further encourage Paramount to regulate Schlessinger's speech.

Recognizing that it would not be able to organize meetings with every affiliate, GLAAD also created a "Local Laura Activism" resource section on its website to support activists interested in mounting a GLAAD-style campaign in their own communities. The section contained contact information for every affiliate that had signed up to carry *Dr Laura*, as well as primers on how to communicate effectively with media and "plan for, ask for and conduct a productive meeting" with station managers. GLAAD also made available transcripts of Schlessinger's monologues and examples of its ads, statements, speeches, Q&As, letters, and fliers to use as templates. As *Dr Laura* went to air, the section was revamped as a "monitor and response" initiative. Visitors were encouraged to watch the show, make a note of advertisers, sign up for GLAAD's email updates, ask advertisers to drop their sponsorship, and continue to work with local media to generate stories about the controversy.

On the advertising front, GLAAD's primary strategy was to reach media buyers who, in late May of each year, begin to make purchasing decisions about the fall television season. Based on that knowledge, it developed an ad to target advertising professionals with the message that there were other ways to reach *Dr Laura*'s demographic. The goal was to build on the now highly visible controversy and convince advertisers to "buy around" the program by giving them specific reasons to find it objectionable.

It helped GLAAD's work with advertisers that just one week before the ad first ran in trade publications, household products giant Procter & Gamble, which had signed on as a major sponsor of *Dr Laura*, announced it had reversed its decision. On 16 May, the Cincinnati-based company released a statement that said: "There has been controversy surrounding Dr Laura on a number of topics. We've chosen not to be involved with a show that will require time and resources to deal with this kind of controversy. The focus of the show is intended to be responsible parenting. As we've studied it more closely, we've decided it isn't possible to separate the broad range of Dr Laura's opinions from the specific focus of this program. Stepping back, today there are lots of programming options, and we've decided there are better ones for us." In interviews commenting on the decision, a P&G spokesperson added that the company would also no longer sponsor the radio program.

This decision by the world's largest advertiser was a major victory in the battle to convince companies not to sponsor *Dr Laura*. P&G had come under intense pressure from both GLAAD and SDL when it initially announced its sponsorship on 8 May. GLAAD asked its membership to write, phone, or email the head of P&G and spoke with the corporation's gay employee group, local community organizations in Cincinnati, and major P&G stockholders to encourage them to voice concerns about the decision to advertise. SDL, for its part, had thousands of visitors to its website bombard P&G with emails and phone calls.

On the heels of P&G's momentous decision, GLAAD rolled out a second ad directed at industry insiders. The prominent full-page ad ran in two phases, once on the Wednesday before Memorial Day weekend in the *New York Times* and the *Los Angeles Times*, and once the following Tuesday in the major media industry trade publications (*Variety*, *Advertising Age*, *Adweek*, *Media Week*, and *Broadcasting and Cable*), so that industry decision-makers would again be confronted with it upon returning from the long weekend.[9] Although the ad was the single most expensive element of GLAAD's Schlessinger campaign, the organization used Buford's connections to the advertising industry to reduce the total purchase price to about $200,000, or about one-third of the normal cost of advertising in these publications. This was a significant unbudgeted expense for GLAAD, but its perceived importance was such that within a few weeks the organization was able to secure additional pledges of as much as $50,000 from key major donors, which paid for close to the entire cost of the advertising.

GLAAD's leadership worked with Buford's advertising firm to develop the ad, which, once again, employed the strategy of using Schlessinger's words against her. The top read: "Ad time with 'Dr Laura' is for sale. Here's what you're buying." As in the first ad, the middle of the page featured direct quotes from various print and electronic media. This time, however, GLAAD decided to broaden the ad's focus to include some of Schlessinger's views on women. As the June strategy document had explained, the goal was to present the controversy as a "universal issue, not just a particular agenda of the gay community." Hence, the lead quotation, titled "Dr Laura on women," read: "There is little reason left for society to respect women as it once did. Women get knocked up. They don't marry. They have abortions. They go to bars. They get knocked up again." The rest of the quotations followed the "Dr Laura on..." format, quoting Schlessinger's commentary about women in the workplace, single mothers, and the alleged threats posed to society by the "decline of the traditional family." There was only one section about gays and lesbians, which consisted of Schlessinger's characterization of homosexuality as "destructive" and an excerpt of her radio monologue comparing "sexual deviant sexual behavior [*sic*]" with pedophilia, bestiality, sadomasochism, and cross-dressing. The quotations were followed by a short paragraph summing up why advertisers should stay away from *Dr Laura*: "Laura Schlessinger has angry and hurtful things to say about all kinds of Americans. Many advertisers don't realize how alienating her program has become. Consumers judge brands by the company they keep. Aren't there better ways to reach women 18–49, or anyone else?" The last sentence of the ad, in bold, read: "'Dr Laura.' We don't buy it." The logos of five organizations appeared at the bottom of the page in the following order: the National Organization for Women, the National Center for Community and Justice, the National Mental Health Association, GLAAD, and People for the American Way. The National Association for the Advancement of Colored People and the Anti-Defamation League were asked to add their imprimatur, but declined.[10]

Buford told me in an interview that a great deal of thought went into the ad: "Everything in there just sang in just those three or four sentences," he said. Referring to the sentence that read, "Schlessinger has angry and hurtful things to say about all kinds of Americans," Buford added:

> That is so thought out, that one sentence. She's being hurtful. People don't like people who hurt other people ... And she's angry. She's angry and she's lashing out. And everybody better stand back because you're not safe either. The copy that came out of GLAAD was: "Laura Schlessinger has angry and hurtful things to say about all kinds of people." I said no. Because people don't care so much about what people do to other people ... But they care a lot about what people do to Americans. So we changed it to Americans.

Although there is no way to measure how many companies decided not to purchase advertising on *Dr Laura* as a result of the ad, Buford points to some anecdotal evidence recounted to him by a colleague in another firm: "Someone told me that ... a straight white woman where he worked had ... ripped that ad out of *Ad Age* and put it on the bulletin board in her office in the advertising department somewhere on Wall Street."

In an interview, Seomin told me another story to illustrate the ad's impact:

> I got a clandestine phone call from somebody in the ad com-
> munity who wanted to call my cell phone, or a home phone,
> didn't even want it on the record that they were calling here at
> GLAAD ... And I thought, this is fun, and I had to go down to
> my car and get my cell phone and they called me back. They
> wanted to meet and I said okay. They said that they were from
> an ad agency and they represented a lot of consumer goods,
> health and beauty and women's products. We actually met in a
> Marie Callender's [a restaurant chain], I mean it was very clan-
> destine ... I couldn't go to their office. In fact, I was waiting for
> them to give me a keyword to say ... I brought them [GLAAD's
> Dr Laura] kits ... We came for the food, we stayed for the pie
> ... I was there for three hours, I mean the waitress was pissed:
> she wanted that table turned! I answered so many questions ...
> And, you know, it didn't take a genius ... to find out who they
> represented ... but these were people who literally ... said: we're
> not going to buy on Laura.

Adding to the impact of the ad buy was the fact that GLAAD was able to convince the two main advertising trade publications to publish editorials about the controversy. The editors of *Advertising Age* wrote:

> As long as radio and TV programmers bid for audiences with pro-
> gram hosts that champion one side in political or social issues that
> divide the country ... advertisers will have choices to make, and
> the decisions will be hard to avoid ... P&G could have advertised
> on the show, weathered protests from gay groups and sold some
> Tide – at the cost of being associated with Dr Laura's message of
> derision and division. That's a steep price and, as it turns out, more
> than P&G cared to pay. Other advertisers should pay attention to
> P&G's words: there are indeed "better" program options.[11]

*Adweek*'s Debra Goldman, for her part, took a more ambivalent view, and noted, "encouraging advertisers to legislate the limits of public speech," even in the service of a "good cause," tends to contribute to a bland media landscape that "offends no one." Still, she wrote, "the world could do without a Dr Laura TV show" because Schlessinger "is stupid, simple-minded and grotesque – qualities with which television is already well-supplied."[12]

The visibility of the ad campaign also helped the GLAAD communications team generate high profile mainstream media exposure in the months that followed. The esteemed *PBS News Hour* featured a fifteen-minute debate on 15 June 2000. Spurgeon and Garry secured a full-page opinion piece published in *Time* on 17 July as a rebuttal to an interview that they considered overly deferential toward Schlessinger. Spurgeon also worked with the producers of NBC's *The Today Show* on what became a seven-minute segment on 8 September devoting exceptionally long coverage to the Schlessinger controversy. All the media attention to the controversy, from GLAAD's perspective, amplified the message in the ad that buying on *Dr Laura* was a bad business decision.

## Clash of the Activists

Like GLAAD, SDL targeted advertisers and local affiliates. The group also coordinated protests in thirty-four cities, some of which GLAAD also took part in, and instructed website visitors – who numbered in the hundreds of thousands for a total of over fifty million page views in 2000 – to call and email Paramount. The group's total budget of only $18,000 (the work was performed by unpaid volunteers) was largely financed by T-shirt sales and individual donations, although, according to GLAAD staffers, the Human Rights Campaign gave the group a $5,000 grant approved by its communications director (and former but short-lived GLAAD/LA executive director) David Smith.

Some of the SDL protests coincided with *Dr Laura*'s premiere on 11 September 2000. GLAAD's leaders chose not to support these protests because, they argued, they would only call attention to the program and boost its initial ratings. In response to GLAAD's non-participation, SDL's Aravosis fired off a six-page position statement emailed to the activists and media professionals subscribed to a list maintained by gay journalist Rex Wockner. The statement accused GLAAD of secretly reverting to its initial position that *Dr Laura* could be deemed acceptable so long as it did not defame gays and lesbians. SDL's position, by contrast, remained that the only principled response to Schlessinger's track record and ongoing public comments condemning homosexuality was to call for her show's cancellation; it simply was not enough to have Paramount regulate Schlessinger's speech.

If GLAAD had truly joined the forces calling for the cancellation of Schlessinger's program, Aravosis asked, why had Seomin been quoted in the *New York Daily News* on 7 September 2000 as saying GLAAD was satisfied that *Dr Laura* would not be defamatory? Seomin told the *Daily News*: "From the beginning, GLAAD has asked for Schlessinger to stop using rhetoric that's damaging to the gay and lesbian community. And from the shows we've seen in person, that's exactly what she has done." Was GLAAD declaring a kind of victory, Aravosis asked? And if it was so concerned about not generating publicity for Schlessinger's show, why had Garry given an interview to NBC *News* just three days before the premiere?

In a rebuttal that was also distributed to Wockner's subscribers, Garry expressed dismay at the harsh tone of Aravosis's statements and regret that he had not raised his concerns with her directly before making his accusations public. "Criticism,' she wrote, "will and should always have a place in our community ... But when criticism 'for the good of the cause' isn't, the criticism can just become rancorous and self-serving." As her tone made clear, the internecine battle with SDL was beginning to take its toll on many GLAAD staff and board members.

The sense that the communications staff felt under attack, beleaguered, and exhausted by the campaign and the competition between GLAAD and SDL was palpable as I carried out my fieldwork in the Los Angeles office in the fall of 2000. It was evident in Spurgeon's occasional frustrated outbursts, Seomin's retreat behind the closed door of his office, communications managers Nick Adams's and Lund's obvious stress as they put in long hours day after day, week after week. It was evident, also, in the way Spurgeon began a staff meeting in late October 2000 by sounding a note of exasperation about the fact that Schlessinger was, as always, it seemed, the first item on the agenda. On that day, Spurgeon acknowledged the cumulative toll of the campaign and of the tensions with SDL when he said it felt like the communications staff were running out of steam. His frustration had also been obvious at the previous month's board meeting when he repeated the inside joke that StopDr-Laura.com was really "StopGLAAD.com."

The sources of SDL's barely concealed animosity toward GLAAD could be traced in part to the fact that at least three of SDL's leaders had strained relationships with the organization. Waybourn had been its first national executive director, and had handed Garry an organization on the verge of financial collapse. Klein had served as GLAAD's communications director under both Waybourn and Garry, and was said to have left the organization on bad terms. Aravosis had reportedly tried – unsuccessfully – to develop a business partnership with GLAAD and a major Internet company. Spurgeon told me that when he confronted Aravosis about why he had blindsided GLAAD with SDL, Aravosis answered: "I wanted to fuck you for leaving me out in the cold."

GLAAD communications staffers often discussed how they had not expected the backlash from within the community. As Lund told me in an interview: "Some people in this thought that there was a finite amount of power, visibility, and promotion available through this, and that's how they played the game." In contrast to what it saw as SDL's competitive framing of the campaign, GLAAD sought to affirm a pluralistic view of movement politics. Garry's rebuttal to Aravosis's attack, for example, stated: "For our movement to have different dimensions, I don't believe we all should see and do things the same way. Working to combat Schlessinger has taught me that there is room here and a need for a variety of tactics and objectives." Spurgeon also made this point in an interview with me in which he disavowed GLAAD's dominant position in the gay and lesbian media activist field: "The point is that everybody can have a point of view ... What really baffled me was, you know how on those games you get for kids that say, 'any number can play' or 'appropriate for any age'? That's kind of how I looked at this. GLAAD had a strategy that was consistent with its mission. If somebody else wants to do something ... that's what somebody else wants to do ... What I didn't understand was why the anger was directed at GLAAD instead of just going out there and doing whatever it was that they thought needed to be done." Whereas at an earlier stage in the campaign, he had spoken of GLAAD's obligation to lead thought, faced with SDL's success, Spurgeon was now espousing an equality-of-perspectives point of view. Garry summed up the frustration underlying Spurgeon's comments at the September 2000 board meeting: "Here we all are fighting for a place at the table and our own table isn't a very welcoming place."

Might the source of the tension between GLAAD and SDL have been that everyone was fighting for the same place at the same table? Renna suggested as much when she told me in an interview: "There's a sort of resentment of folks who are coming into the community with different sets of skills and experiences. And I think that there's ... folks who are ... you know, feel like they're losing some grip on some of the power ... and that there's some resentment of that and there's some anger at that, and I think that drives sometimes some of the disagreements in the community in a way that's not healthy." Renna, whose role in the Schlessinger campaign was focused on relations with the LGBT community at large, was quick to add that SDL's animosity toward GLAAD did not necessarily trickle down the ranks. She perceived a "desire on the part of the ... coterie of national [SDL] organizers to find places where we didn't agree," but counters that on the ground, local activists she met with across cities were more willing to work in tandem with GLAAD.

Some staff and board members privately acknowledged that GLAAD was "in competition with StopDrLaura.com" and were concerned with how to "scoop" SDL and "get quoted first" in articles about the Schlessinger controversy. Though GLAAD's leaders publicly espoused a pluralistic, "anyone can play" understanding of movement politics with regards to this issue, they recognized an institutional need to consolidate and strengthen their dominant position in the field of gay and lesbian media activism. For example, in a meeting, one long-time board member wondered aloud what GLAAD might do to better "manage ... differences of opinion" in the movement, which he said "have always existed." He asked whether there was a need to think about ways to "strategically and maturely ... deal with the fringe" since it will "always be there." He added, with a wry smile, that GLAAD had "success in managing ... different chapters with different ideas" during its transitional period, which another long-time board member, affecting the speech tones of a science-fiction alien, immediately rephrased as "you have been assimilated." A third board member added that the value of more radical groups like SDL was to make "GLAAD look more reasonable," something that improved its chances of meeting directly with people in positions of power who preferred to deal with it rather than with more adversarial groups. In any case, this board member added, "we'll be around next year, they're not."

That long-term institutional outlook made it in GLAAD's interests to take the high road with regards to the tensions with SDL. During one board meeting, for example, Spurgeon discussed an article in *Variety* that quoted SDL extensively but ignored GLAAD altogether. Spurgeon said he had made some inquiries and was informed by a reporter that Aravosis had been telling journalists that "GLAAD is not doing anything" in the Schlessinger campaign. He expressed frustration at this turn of events and said that he was tired of "turning the other cheek." Still, he concluded, there was "no upside" to talking publicly about SDL's attacks on GLAAD: doing so would only exacerbate the tensions and distract from the long-term goal of stemming the tide of Schlessinger's defamatory rhetoric.

## Campaign Outcomes

Schlessinger's television program premiered on 11 September 2000 to universally terrible reviews, almost all of which, GLAAD staffers noted with satisfaction, referred to the controversy over her views about homosexuality. Seomin had planted the seeds for this critical drubbing when he attended the Television Critics Association conference a few months earlier and distributed GLAAD's *Dr Laura* media kit to over fifty critics. In one widely syndicated review, "A Case of the Creeps: 'Dr Laura' on UPN Looks Better on Radio," Tom Shales derided Schlessinger as "somewhat defanged and declawed yet still obnoxious, bossy and self-righteously abrasive" and called the show "not distinctive and certainly not a dynamic addition to the daytime talk show population." The review also made clear that Schlessinger's public image had taken a dramatic turn for the worse. Shales wrote that the show consisted mainly of "Dr Laura preaching, hammering home her dogmatic beliefs, trotting out people who support her and dismissing or bullying those who don't ... Whatever surgical or cosmetic wonders were employed to give her a somewhat youthful face failed at about the chin line. Sometimes she tries to hide her saggy, baggy wattles with turtlenecks so high they almost reach her lips, but she still looks, well, creepy. Her speaking style is strident, she rarely shows compassion, and she is anything but a comforting presence. She's the anti-Oprah."[13] Despite the ratings boost the controversy over the show might have brought, GLAAD reported through "Laura Watch" that it premiered with a low 2.0 Nielsen household rating, which meant that just 2 per cent of US homes had tuned in to *Dr Laura*. By contrast, Oprah Winfrey's program rated a 5.6, down considerably from the previous year but still dominant in the afternoon market.

The program also suffered from a distinct lack of national advertisers. The few that did advertise came under intense pressure to drop their ads almost as soon as they aired. Both GLAAD and SDL's websites were quick to list contact information for these companies, many of which pulled their ads within days and often claimed that they had never intended them to run on the program in the first place. After just two weeks, amid declining ratings and an unmistakable advertiser exodus, Paramount announced that it was stopping production of the show for "retooling." The program reappeared a week later with two new national sponsors, including Pillsbury Company, which announced it was pulling out just one day after its first ad appeared. On 4 October, four Canadian television stations owned by CanWest announced they were dropping the show.

Undoubtedly feeling the pain of recent events, on 11 October, Schlessinger published a full-page ad on the back cover of a special issue of *Variety* devoted to the topic of gays and lesbians in Hollywood. Titled "A heartfelt message from Dr Laura Schlessinger," the ad, which ran two days after Yom Kippur, the Jewish Day of Atonement, again fell short of an explicit apology, but made overtures in that direction. Schlessinger defended her pseudo-clinical language as an expression of her religious views but also acknowledged some fault: "While I express my opinions from the perspective of an Orthodox Jew and a staunch defender of the traditional family, in talking about gays and lesbians, some of my words were poorly chosen." She then subtly tried to shift the blame and cast herself as the victim of a deliberately provoked misunderstanding: "Many people perceive [my words] as hate speech. This fact has been personally and professionally devastating to me as well as to many others. Ugly words have been relentlessly repeated and distorted for far too long ... I deeply regret the hurt this situation has caused the gay and lesbian community."

Through an inside contact at *Variety*, GLAAD obtained a faxed copy of Schlessinger's ad a day in advance of its publication and therefore had plenty of time to formulate a response, call up reporters, and help shape the coverage. In "Laura Watch," GLAAD's leaders explained:

We realized that if the ad were to hit the stands without comment, the media would likely characterize it as another "apology," even though Schlessinger did not actually apologize for her defamatory comments in the text of the ad. In an effort to place the ad in context, GLAAD proactively contacted the national media in a day-long outreach effort, reminding them of Schlessinger's earlier, recanted apology and encouraging them to take a closer look at what she actually had written. We were careful to discuss the ad as an "admission" (and a qualified one at that), not as an apology – especially since Schlessinger's camp was not calling it an apology either when speaking with the media.

By GLAAD's own account, that strategy produced high-profile, national media coverage of Schlessinger's ad that incorporated GLAAD's perspective and was successful in casting suspicion on her motives. In its coverage of the ad, PR *Week* noted GLAAD had been "typically speedy" in "issuing a same-day press release rejecting Schlessinger's apology and refuting her arguments."[14]

*Dr Laura*'s death knell began to sound during the November sweeps period, when major affiliates in New York City, Los Angeles, Chicago, Philadelphia, San Francisco, and Dallas, among others, began shifting *Dr Laura* to late-night time slots. Other affiliates soon followed suit, prompting Spurgeon to joke around the office that Schlessinger had expanded her audience to "breast-feeding mothers and insomniacs." Lowry reported in the *Los Angeles Times* that since her move to late night, Schlessinger had averaged a 0.6 share, or a measly 30,000 viewers.[15] By this point, the only advertising left on the program was an odd assortment of psychic hotlines and "exclusive TV offers" for such items as talking beer openers, Anne Murray CDs (ironic, given Murray's lesbian following), and Madame FiFi's Love Plant, which, for only $19.95 plus shipping and handling, promised its buyers some "magical love seeds, love pellets, [a] love scroll and a pot." The only advertising left, in other words, was for remainder ads that run only when no other advertisers can be found to purchase time at regular rates. A GLAAD staffer even discovered that two of the companies advertising on *Dr Laura* had federal lawsuits pending against them for dishonest business practices. In total, GLAAD and SDL documented that over 170 companies pulled out of advertising on *Dr Laura* over the course of the campaign, not to mention the unknown numbers that decided not to advertise in the first place. A further thirty companies reportedly dropped their ads from Schlessinger's radio show, even though there were no targeted activist efforts in that direction, resulting in a reported revenue loss of some $30 million for Premiere Radio Networks.[16]

That even her radio show was financially hurt due to the campaign was made abundantly clear on 17 November, when Schlessinger resorted to begging for advertisers during the broadcast. That day, Adams and Lund beckoned Garry, Spurgeon, and me to Spurgeon's office where Lund pressed play on a portable tape player, a look of barely concealed glee lighting up his face. We heard Schlessinger trying to sound upbeat while making a remarkable and desperate-sounding plea for advertisers: "If you own any kind of a business, you have things or services or what-have-you, and you would like to be a sponsor and/or of my radio show and/or television show [*sic*] – locally or nationally, depending upon how successful you've been and wanna get! – all you have to do is fax me here. I can pass it to the right people." Garry's jaw dropped in an expression of utter astonishment as she looked around the room as if to confirm that we had all heard the same thing. Schlessinger went on to say: "There's just one thing I have to remind you of: there's something very usual ... unusual ... about my radio show and TV show, and that is that they basically both support and promote traditional values. This makes it very dangerous, because there are other forces that bear against traditional values." And then came the punch line: "But beware, the bad guys are going to beat on you. You have to have a spine to stand with me." Everyone in the room, including me, burst out laughing. If the move to late-night time slots had sounded like the beginning of *Dr Laura*'s death knell, this had sounded like the final nail in the coffin.

As though to confirm that impression, Melissa Grego wrote in the 11–17 December issue of *Variety* that *Dr Laura* had become a case study in "how to fail in syndicated television." She attributed the show's dismal showing to a "toxic mix of protesters' rancor, advertisers' anxiety and Paramount's misguided spending." The most expensive new show in Paramount's history had become its most disastrous failure, incurring "a loss said to be in the seven-figure range." Grego suggested that the "debacle" surrounding *Dr Laura* might have industry-wide repercussions by casting "fresh doubt ... on the practice of picking shows without a pilot or a tape. Although tape has always been something stations have liked to see, it has become a higher priority for stations burned by 'Dr Laura.'" As for Schlessinger herself, Grego noted, "her reputation as a respected, tough child-and-family advocate has been transformed into one whose 'advice' could be considered hate speech."[17] Sketch comedy shows and late-night talk show hosts poked fun at Schlessinger, who became a punch line at the 2001 Oscars ceremony, courtesy of host Steve Martin: "The Straight Story ... is the story of Dr Laura Schlessinger," Martin joked. "She couldn't be here tonight because she couldn't get anyone in town to do her hair and makeup." Most memorably, perhaps, Schlessinger was satirized on the *The West Wing* as a conservative Christian radio host upbraided by Martin Sheen's fictional President Bartlet. The season two segment, which was based on an "Open Letter to Dr Laura" then making the rounds online, took "Dr Jenna Jacobs" to task for calling homosexuality an abomination on the basis of her highly selective reading of the Old Testament.

On 29 March 2001, Schlessinger taped *the* final episode of her television program's first season. The next day, Paramount, having fulfilled its contractual obligation to produce one full season of *Dr Laura*, quietly announced it was cancelling the show. Post-cancellation analyses by television critics tended to attribute the program's failure to the fact that Paramount and Schlessinger had simply produced a bad show, but acknowledged that protest had also played an important role. Schlessinger, in a written statement, said: "I believe it could have earned a substantial audience in time, but the television advertiser boycott precluded that." Another measure of the success of the GLAAD and SDL campaigns was that, throughout the run of the program, Schlessinger avoided any mention of gay and lesbian topics, with the single exception of an oblique reference to a television commercial with lesbian content.

Buford, who earlier in the campaign had been angered by some board members' reluctance to take strong action against Schlessinger, ended up pleased with GLAAD's efforts. Referring to his fellow board members, he said: "They really came around. They came around big time." He described the work with advertisers as particularly significant for the long term:

I think something that has actually been achieved in this effort is you can't assume that you can make a name for yourself out of defaming homosexuals. You better think twice about it. And they're more in the column of, now in the US, this group, our community, is more in the column of Israel and other people who you don't, quite frankly, who you don't fuck with, because the word is out there and the feeling is that you don't fuck with them because they will get you and you will not be able to get away with it. Whereas we used to be in the other column of easy hit, easy mark, you know, trash them, build yourself and move on. I think that has fundamentally changed in this country as a result of that. And I'm very happy about that.

Garry, for her part, presented the board with a sixteen-point assessment of how she felt "GLAAD and the community have benefited from the Schlessinger campaign" apart from getting Schlessinger off the air. On the organizational side, she mentioned the "unprecedented visibility" and "wonderful fundraising opportunity" the campaign had given GLAAD, which she said had become the "most visible" gay and lesbian movement organization. The campaign, she added, also became a rallying point and motivating force for GLAAD's staff and would give the organization "enormous leverage," i.e., increased access to media decision-makers, because it had demonstrated the power of the gay and lesbian community. Her analysis of the campaign's ramifications for the community, meanwhile, emphasized its success in "injecting" the notion of defamation against gays and lesbians into public discourse at a time when federal hate crimes legislation and the Boy Scouts' exclusionary policies were being discussed in media. The campaign also afforded GLAAD many "coalition-building" opportunities with organizations like the National Organization for Women, thereby demonstrating that "our issues" are "more universal." Finally, she said, it gave the community a chance to "flex its power" and get "fired up" about something, and community organizations "a big ol' ... platform" that "GLAAD built," a "hook [on which] to hang their work."

Garry's assessment of the campaign's success came in September 2000. By then, it was already clear that the combined efforts of GLAAD and SDL were having a major impact. GLAAD waited until the program's official cancellation to claim victory, even though its initial objective in the campaign – stemming the tide of Schlessinger's defamatory rhetoric – had been achieved some time earlier. For GLAAD to claim victory on that basis, however, would have left it vulnerable to the same accusations that had dogged its campaign from the time SDL had come on to the scene, namely that it was all too willing, in the name of good relations with media companies, to allow a bigot to have a national platform. Spurgeon foresaw the dilemma at the September 2000 board meeting when he asked: "When do we claim victory?" "I would hate," he said, "for this whole thing to be summarized by ... StopDrLaura.com."

SDL, by contrast, untainted by the suspicions that accompanied GLAAD's insider status, was free to redefine the meaning of stopping *Dr Laura* in terms oddly reminiscent of GLAAD's initial position. Already, in October 2000, Aravosis had claimed, in an article commissioned by the *New Republic* for an advertising supplement on new technologies, that "no matter when Schlessinger's TV show is finally canceled (the ratings are so bad that it's only a matter of time), StopDrLaura.com has already won. We've used the Internet to teach Paramount and Viacom a painful lesson about profiting from prejudice, and we've gotten Schlessinger to tone down her anti-gay rhetoric." Then, on 17 January 2001, he posted an article titled "We Stopped Dr Laura" to the widely read soc.motss Internet newsgroup in which he announced that the SDL website had been shut down. He wrote: "While Dr Laura's television show is still on the air in many US markets, and Paramount has yet to announce that the show won't be coming back next fall, 'Dr Laura' TV has been banished to the wee morning hours in all the top ten markets, her ratings are abysmal, and she can get few advertisers any better than that lady with the tarot cards. Face it folks, we all came together and we stopped Dr Laura." For Aravosis, it was "time to move on" and shift the community's attention to a new target: John Ashcroft, George W. Bush's then-nominee for attorney general.

Ironically, Aravosis's surprise announcement, based as it was on the criteria for victory that GLAAD had initially elaborated, left GLAAD with little choice than to occupy the space left by SDL's abrupt departure and wait for the actual cancellation of Schlessinger's TV program before it too could declare Dr Laura truly stopped. On 2 February 2001, GLAAD issued a "Laura Watch" arguing that Schlessinger appeared to be testing the waters to see if she could get away with anti-gay commentary. A recent episode, GLAAD said, had featured a segment on "what to do if your neighbor's mail is delivered to you by mistake and it contains child pornography" and "deliberately and exclusively chose to characterize pedophilia as men having sex with boys." In response, Renna, who had just been promoted to news media director, issued this statement: "What's clear is that even on the verge of cancellation, Schlessinger will not let go of her anti-gay agenda. And as Paramount's leverage evaporates, we're seeing a[n] emboldened Schlessinger go back on the offensive. Make no mistake, though: as long as she keeps making these kinds of remarks, this campaign is not over."

Seeing Schlessinger "putting up real flares," as Spurgeon put it during a conversation with me during this period, gave GLAAD real concern that Paramount and Schlessinger had concluded that SDL's departure from the campaign meant that the "dogs [were] off" and that it was time to "take off the handcuffs" to see if that might save the program. In this climate, Spurgeon said, SDL's unilateral declaration of victory was a "dangerous" and "irresponsible" signal to send. I asked him, given the circumstances, when GLAAD might be prepared to declare victory. "I wouldn't call it that," he answered, "but we will want to take as much credit as we can."

Taking credit, for GLAAD, proved to be much easier to do in mainstream media than it was in the gay and lesbian press. In his weekly column on Gay.com, Signorile attributed the campaign's success almost exclusively to the "tens of thousands of emails" and protests in over thirty cities initiated by SDL. In terms strikingly similar to how GLAAD had initially framed its objectives in the campaign, Signorile quoted Aravosis as saying: "We set out to inform America about the true nature of her rhetoric ... Through ratings and advertising clout, Americans said 'no' to Schlessinger." SDL had not, in fact, set out to inform America but to force Paramount to cancel the program. That SDL declared victory on the basis of GLAAD's definition of success, thus preventing GLAAD from doing the same with its own LGBT constituency, was a deeply frustrating situation for the GLAAD staffers who had worked on the campaign.

For GLAAD, recognition came from the people who were, from a professional perspective, in the best position to understand and evaluate the quality of its work: public relations professionals. Over the course of a weekend in October 2000, Spurgeon and Lund assembled a thick binder full of strategy documents, press clippings, internal emails, newsletters, etc., which constituted the evidence of GLAAD's efforts in the planning and execution of the Schlessinger campaign. They submitted the binder to the annual competition of public relations professionals sponsored by PR *Week*, which nominated GLAAD in the category of "non-profit PR team of the year." On 15 February 2001, Spurgeon travelled to New York City so that he could attend the awards ceremony, and he returned to the office the next day holding the award. In a voice mail he left for Garry, Spurgeon reportedly said: "Can you believe it? We even beat out the Center for Tobacco Free Kids!" The victory cake served in the office that afternoon had the GLAAD logo rendered in icing along with the words "Congratulations GLAAD Team." At the board meeting following the PR *Week* win, Garry said that Roseanne Siino, a GLAAD board member who is also a PR professional, had told her, as a measure of the importance placed on these awards, that "most [PR] agencies have a full-time staff person dedicated to PR *Week* submissions."

## The Balance Shifts

The foregoing account of the Schlessinger campaign makes clear that the leaders of both GLAAD and SDL, in making their strategic and tactical choices, were motivated by a wide variety of personal, institutional, professional, and political factors. This variety of factors cautions against framing the campaign's success too simply as the victory of so-called outsiders on behalf of a grassroots gay and lesbian constituency, as Signorile did when he wrote on Gay.com that "the majority of thanks and congratulations needs to go to the activists in StopDrLaura.com who weren't paid for their efforts, and who showed us all just how powerful we could be."¹⁸ SDL's efforts undeniably contributed to the campaign by mobilizing a large grassroots constituency, but the fact that SDL leaders were not paid did not, in itself, make them outsiders.

Whether directly or not, SDL leaders stood to benefit professionally from the campaign. Waybourn owned Window Media, which managed the largest group of gay and lesbian newspapers in the United States, and the LGBT press benefited from an ongoing and rousing story. Klein was a public relations consultant, and the campaign's success added to his resume. Aravosis was president of an Internet consulting group that developed web-based strategies for non-profit organizations, and SDL gave him national prominence. Lawson and Robbe were a television producer and public relations consultant, respectively, and SDL expanded their claims to professional expertise. The outsiders in the Schlessinger campaign were not really outsiders at all, but professionals cut from the same cloth as GLAAD leaders, and who, using the Internet in novel ways, stitched themselves into a competing banner.

Understanding the Schlessinger campaign as a contest for cultural authority among professionalized activists with extensive connections to media professionals better recognizes the possibilities, limits, and power relations of gay and lesbian media activism as it existed during my fieldwork. Despite an indisputable room "for a variety of tactics and objectives" in media activism, as Garry pointed out in one of her responses to Aravosis, the extent of media companies' power to "disarm, contain, and control" advocacy groups imposed structural constraints to which SDL and GLAAD were equally subjected (Montgomery 1989, 54). The media advocacy system is the historical product of network strategies designed to channel grievances into manageable forms, in part by compelling activists to become media insiders. In this system, as Streeter (2000, 80) argues, "not everyone is heard from, not all arguments are heard, and, even among those who do get a hearing, the power to influence the process is not evenly distributed." Getting heard at all requires the professional skills and connections that GLAAD and SDL both possessed. The advocacy system offers limited opportunities for democratic input, ranging from the cooperative to the moderately confrontational. It falls to those who possess the necessary capital to function within the system to select tactics from the available range and compete for the cultural authority to wield limited power and influence.

From the perspective of Bourdieu's field theory (Bourdieu and Wacquant 1992), SDL's deployment of itself as better representing the gay and lesbian community's interests functioned as a kind of social capital that lent the organization legitimacy within the LGBT movement and media fields and allowed it to chip away at GLAAD's professional authority. Although SDL mobilized thousands of people and injected tremendous momentum into the campaign, its success in doing so cannot be said to have been purely motivated by a righteous desire to "[show] us all just how powerful we could be," in Signorile's triumphalist formulation.[19] Looking at it from the perspective of field dynamics, SDL successfully exploited a vulnerability in GLAAD's propensity to "serve the community by working outside the community," namely that GLAAD's greater emphasis on working on the inside of powerful institutions obliged it to adopt narrower definitions of the community's interests and wishes than might otherwise have been the case. SDL's equally professionalized activists exploited this weakness to advance their own positions in the movement and media fields. SDL's leaders may have positioned themselves differently than GLAAD's did, but they were playing the same inside game.

SDL leaders probably never intended to supplant GLAAD. They did, however, demonstrate that GLAAD did not necessarily have a monopoly on gay and lesbian media activism and that it was possible, and perhaps desirable, to achieve a different balance between insider and outsider strategies in the age of mainstreaming. SDL forced GLAAD to shore up its cultural authority in the gay and lesbian movement by shifting the tenuous balance between its goals with media companies and its obligations to its gay and lesbian constituencies. In the next chapter, I explore how GLAAD's greater emphasis on serving the community in the wake of the Schlessinger campaign played out in relation to its attempts to represent a broader spectrum of its LGBT constituencies. As I show, it was around these issues that the contradictions inherent in the politics of mainstreaming became the most apparent.

## CHAPTER 4

# Sex, Race, and Representation

This film is not intended as an indictment of the homosexual world.
It is set in one small segment of that world which is not meant to
be representational of the whole.
Opening disclaimer, *Cruising*, 1980

Queer as Folk is a celebration of the lives and passions of a group
of gay friends. It is not meant to reflect all of gay society.
Opening disclaimer, *Queer as Folk*, 2000

We don't represent absolutely every gay and lesbian person on this planet, but
I'd like to think that we could represent ones that … are sexually active.
Scott Seomin, GLAAD Entertainment Media Director, 2000

On a wall in Scott Seomin's office was an original black and blood-red
poster for William Friedkin's *Cruising* (1980), which is widely considered one of the most homophobic films ever produced by Hollywood.
Starring Al Pacino as a cop investigating a string of grisly murders in
New York City's gay sadism and masochism scene, it portrayed gay men
as little more than victims or predators lurking in dark and depraved
sexual worlds. Seomin told me he bought the poster on eBay as a re-
minder of the importance of his work. On the opposite wall was *Cruising*'s photographic positive image, so to speak, a poster for Nicholas
Hytner's *The Object of My Affection* (1998), awash in soft whites and
baby blues. Whereas the *Cruising* poster depicted a kind of urban gay
inferno, its counterpart featured an airbrushed Manhattan skyline as

the backdrop to the romantic posturing of its lead actors, Jennifer Aniston and Paul Rudd. Underneath the title was a caption: "A love story that could only happen between best friends."

The dichotomy implied by Seomin's office decor might suggest nostalgia for simpler times. Yet, even by GLAAD's definitions of defamation, arriving at positions about cultural texts was never as simple as telling the difference between *Cruising* and *The Object of My Affection*. Positions are intrinsically matters of perspective. They are formed in the process of viewing the world in particular ways and, as such, always produce exclusions. They imply (and exclude) not merely their opposites, but all other possible positions not taken. The very act of taking up a position, therefore, brings up thorny questions of political representation. How and on what bases, then, did GLAAD's leaders arrive at positions? Whose perspectives did they take into account, whose did they exclude, and why?

As I discussed in chapter 3, questions of political representation became especially thorny for GLAAD in the context of the Schlessinger campaign; the campaign's intra-movement dynamics challenged GLAAD to refocus on activities that better represented the wishes and interests of a broader range of gay and lesbian constituencies than those its version of the politics of mainstreaming had initially served. These efforts at broader representation also manifested themselves in adjustments made to other communications activities during my fieldwork, and in this chapter I analyze how GLAAD's leaders grappled with the diversity of their constituencies in their responses to two especially complex cases: the Showtime Networks television series *Queer as Folk* and Eminem's *The Marshall Mathers LP*.

In both cases, GLAAD found itself in confrontation with corporate entities with which it had enjoyed good relations and a high level of access in the past, in part because of Joan Garry's previous employment at both Showtime and MTV. Like the Schlessinger campaign, both were test cases of the theory that significant access leads to significant political outcomes. Finally, both highlighted fundamental problems as to whom GLAAD could be said to represent, i.e., which parts of the amorphous entity called the "gay and lesbian community" GLAAD's leaders knit together to make wholes (or holes)? Exploring these questions reveals a host of tensions and contradictions, particularly around sexual and racial representation, as GLAAD's leaders struggled to reconcile their commitments to the politics of mainstreaming with media industry pressures; internal organizational differences; and their various personal, political, and professional investments.

In the first part of this chapter, I analyze GLAAD's responses to *Queer as Folk*, whose depictions of gay men leading promiscuous sexual lives challenged business-as-usual assumptions about positive versus negative images. I argue that GLAAD's leaders deflected this challenge by focusing criticism on the lack of representation of people of colour on the series at a time when the organization was coming under internal and external pressure to advocate more effectively on behalf of more diverse constituencies. In the second part of this chapter, I look at GLAAD's internal dynamics through its campaign against the homophobic and transphobic lyrics of Eminem's *The Marshall Mathers LP*. The Eminem campaign raised complex questions about the limits of GLAAD's willingness and ability to represent the views of people of colour on an issue of direct concern to the queer communities that form around hip-hop music. Ultimately, both cases illustrate sociologist Jane Ward's (2008, 132) argument that "lesbian and gay activists embrace racial, gender, socioeconomic, and sexual differences when they see them as predictable, profitable, rational, or respectable." As I also show, discourses of diversity in a neoliberal world selectively fail to represent those whose differences "are not easily professionalized, funded, or used for other institutional or financial gains."

## Desexualization and Diversity: GLAAD's Response to *Queer as Folk*

Cultural critic Michael Warner (1999) argues that queer identities are marked by a stigma whose origin lies in the sexual shame that pervades Western cultures. One approach to resolving this issue, which the post-Stonewall liberationists favoured, was to confront shame directly and attempt to dismantle its cultural foundations. Another approach, that of mainstreaming, is to symbolically distance gay and lesbian identities from the shame of sex, which leaves movement organizations confronting a schizophrenic divide: "On one side, the movement must appeal to its constituency – people who often have nothing in common

other than their search for a sexual world and the shame and stigma
that such a search entails ... On the other side, that movement attempts
to win recognition for these sorry sluts and outcasts, wringing a token
of dignity from the very culture that produces and sustains so much
shame and stigma in the first place" (Warner 1999, 49). According to
Warner (49), the gay and lesbian movement tends to "draw the curtain
over the sexual culture without which it could not exist" and "speaks
whatever language of respectability it thinks will translate." As a result,
it gets caught up in the "tension between these two standards, internal
and external," which "defines gay and lesbian politics, saddling its
spokespersons with difficult dilemmas" (49–50).

A little bit *Cruising* and a little bit *Object of My Affection*, *Queer as
Folk*, which was based on a British series by the same name, presented
GLAAD with a unique and challenging set of parameters. It was the first
dramatic series on US television to be set in a declaratively gay universe
(and to some extent a lesbian one, though lesbians were largely confined
to the domestic sphere). It featured abundant drug use and explicit sex
– some of it intergenerational, some of it performed in public spaces,
and some of it promiscuous. At its sexy centre was a more or less
amoral, unapologetic, defiantly proud egotist, Brian, whose relationship
with Justin, a few months shy of his eighteenth birthday in the first
episode, gave the show its narrative thrust. Far from condemning, or
pitying, or ridiculing its cast of gay types, the series, which was set in
Pittsburgh and filmed in Toronto, portrayed the soap operatic highs and
lows of the lives and loves of its blond ingénue, its lovable man-child, its
nerdy accountant, its funny and oh-so-sensitive queen, its PFLAG mom,
its femme lesbian mothers, and its adorable scoundrel. What was a gay
and lesbian media activist organization to do?

On 1 December 2000, two days before the US premiere of *Queer as
Folk*, a story appeared in the *New York Daily News* under the title:
"GLAAD to Be of Help to New Series." The lead paragraph read:
"Showtime's new drama 'Queer as Folk' may portray a segment of the
gay and lesbian community in an at times stereotypical way, but don't
expect an uproar from the folks at the Gay and Lesbian Alliance Against
Defamation." In the article, Seomin called the program "compelling, in-
triguing, graphic, humorous and, at times, disturbing." Admitting that
it might offend gays and lesbians concerned about its depiction of gay

men as "sexually unbridled," Seomin said: "We can't have it both ways. GLAAD's not here to say that every portrayal has to be picture-perfect ... Stereotypes are based in truth and humor, they're not invented out of thin air. And more than any minority, the gay and lesbian community can laugh at itself."[1]

That light mood proved short-lived, as GLAAD issued a public statement just six days later in which it criticized *Queer as Folk* as a depiction of a "subset of our community" that is "frank and honest" but "falls short of fair and inclusive." The statement noted the program's inclusion of "both positive and negative images." On the positive side, it mentioned the "camaraderie between the lead characters, a boy's intense coming out, a lesbian couple raising a child fathered by a gay man, and the men's supportive families." On the negative side, it bemoaned the "focus on the men's promiscuity, their narcissism and smugness, and the recreational use of drugs." It went on to criticize the core characters as "exclusive unto themselves" and offered a mix of faint praise and not-so-faint condemnation: "This stark and unapologetic depiction of their licentious egocentrism is a bold contrast to traditional media stereotypes of gay men as victims, amusing commentators, or assorted felons. For this core group to all share a shallow dedication to homogeneity is realistic. What is not realistic is how they can all apparently live in Pittsburgh without encountering any people of color – gay or straight ... There are numerous missed opportunities to responsibly represent diversity."

The criticism regarding racial diversity was unprecedented for GLAAD and could have been – but was not – made about virtually every other television program with gay or lesbian content in the then-history of television programs with gay or lesbian content. Even stranger than the ambivalent wording and the unusual (for GLAAD) criticism regarding lack of racial diversity was the fact that about one month after the statement was released, and for a period of about two weeks, an ad for *Queer as Folk* appeared on the GLAAD website. Clicking on it opened a window to the Showtime website. A few months after that, in a Los Angeles ceremony attended by no fewer than seven cast members (in addition to Showtime producers and executives), *Queer as Folk* received a GLAAD Media Award for outstanding drama series, beating out *Buffy the Vampire Slayer*, *Dawson's Creek*, *Felicity*, and MTV's *Undressed*.

How are we to understand this schizophrenic array of actions and positions? In this section, I explore three interconnected dimensions: (1) the personal convictions and politics of GLAAD's leadership; (2) the interplay between GLAAD's programs team and communications team; and (3) the chilling effect of economic sponsorship on advocacy.

Although I was not able to gain access to high-level discussions about *Queer as Folk*, the topic having been deemed too controversial to allow for my presence, I had the opportunity to conduct interviews about the series with the three staff members most directly responsible for developing GLAAD's position. I also observed mid-level staff meetings, public events, and meetings of the board of directors, and was given access to some documents like memos and emails. Together, these materials provide a good indication of the decision-making process about the series and of the positions taken by various individuals within GLAAD.

Steve Spurgeon, the director of communications, told me that the management team, which consisted of himself, Garry, Dilia Loe, deputy director of programs, and Julie Anderson, deputy director of development, had been unusually slow to take a position on *Queer as Folk*. Indeed, during a staff meeting in October 2000, Spurgeon reported that the issue simply "was not coming up" at the management team level and that he had finally felt obligated to force the discussion. As a result of this pressure, he told his staff, the management team had resolved to get behind the program as a "fair, accurate, and inclusive representation of a part of the community." The wording ("a part of the community") and the fact that it had taken so long to make a decision indicated that the endorsement was less than enthusiastic.

Spurgeon told me that the issue made him feel personally "uncomfortable" because he had a "hard time separating his personal from his professional responsibility." On a personal level, he told me, he would not have supported the program. On a professional level, however, he felt "obliged to give the program support" because GLAAD's mission advocates for "fair, accurate, and inclusive images," and not for "positive images." He added: "I don't see how we ... as an organization can be so wholeheartedly supportive of what I consider to be highly assimilationist programming such as *Will and Grace* and then not also embrace something that shows another segment of our community."

*Queer as Folk*, he elaborated, is "fair, accurate, and inclusive for some people ... A lot of people are out there making love, you know? I'm sorry, that is a part of what gay life is about. Okay, now here we have the other extreme where people are loving every bush that doesn't move ... Okay fine. But you know what? That happens. We know they're there." Spurgeon's comments exemplified the dynamic Warner describes, wherein movement leaders, despite attempts to distance themselves from the shame of sex, still feel an obligation to represent people whose sexual proclivities run counter to the dominant culture's definition of propriety. That definition, however, was not something Spurgeon was willing to question. He explained that he is a "middle-aged man from the conservative Midwest" who believes that in the fight for gay and lesbian equality, "everything's about the undecideds." That demographic, he told me, would have difficulty "embracing the sensibility of the characters on this show."

I asked him what in particular might offend, and Spurgeon listed the following: the characters call each other "faggots," "use each other for sex," and take drugs, and the series dramatizes what he called "every parent's worst fear: the gay predator as abductor of boys." The show, he said, depicts an "underage youth" engaged in a sexual relationship with a man twelve years his senior. For Spurgeon, the fact that the youth is depicted as a self-possessed and enthusiastic sexual being who is just months away from his eighteenth birthday is of little importance because such finer points would be lost on most people. The opinions of most people on these matters, he believed, are framed by the law, and, in many US states, the law considers the intergenerational relationship depicted on *Queer as Folk* to be illegal (although in fact, in Pennsylvania, where the show was set, the age of consent was sixteen).

Among GLAAD's senior staff, Seomin, who did not sit on the management team, was by far the most enthusiastic supporter of *Queer as Folk*. During a communications staff meeting held shortly before the premiere, he exclaimed, "Love it!" (in the style made famous by the Wayans brothers in their "Men On..." sketches) in response to Spurgeon's request for an update on how GLAAD would respond to the series. Despite that humorous expression of personal support, Seomin announced that GLAAD would distance itself from *Queer as Folk* somewhat by declining an offer to benefit financially from the Los Angeles premiere. With regards to media interviews, on the other hand, Seomin said that GLAAD would be "positive about it without a lot of qualifiers" and would congratulate Showtime for being "inclusive of one segment" of the gay population and "not being afraid of gay male sexuality." Other staff members expressed that this was a good way of putting "a positive spin on a tricky situation" and that this was a "smart" position for GLAAD to take.

The situation was tricky because GLAAD's leaders had been unable to agree on exactly what position to take. The compromise they arrived at was to distance the organization from the series by refusing to benefit from its premiere and at the same time give it a measured amount of support in interviews. The position was "smart," because, depending on how the series was received by mainstream and LGBT media and audiences, GLAAD could point to either aspect of its response as evidence that it had always been on the right side of the issue – whatever it turned out to be. The strategy illustrates the internal/external tension that defines much of GLAAD's work. On the one hand, the problem with being perceived as too supportive lay in explaining this support to mainstream reporters, especially if the series turned out to be controversial and alienating to straight viewers: why were representations of gay men as sexually promiscuous acceptable to GLAAD in this instance but condemned as stereotypical in others, reporters might ask? *Queer as Folk* is a fair and accurate representation of a segment of the gay population, GLAAD spokespeople might respond. On the other hand, Seomin warned in a memo distributed in mid-August 2000, if the program turned out to be highly popular among gays and lesbians, as he believed it would be, being perceived as not supportive enough would leave GLAAD vulnerable to "tirades" by the gay and lesbian press that could "easily spill over to the mainstream."

In retrospect, Seomin need not have been so concerned about the gay and lesbian press, which generally showed very little interest in GLAAD's position on *Queer as Folk*. For example, during a communications staff meeting held shortly before the management team arrived at its position, Spurgeon complained that the *Advocate* had not contacted GLAAD for its cover story on the series. "For all they knew," he quipped, "we had lots to say about it."

The ambivalent stance of the management team did not sit well with Seomin. In an interview, he singled out the decision not to benefit from the premiere as "ridiculous" and said he had been disappointed to learn of it from a reporter while on vacation. I asked him what he thought had motivated the management team to distance GLAAD from the series. He responded:

> This is a ... raw, nearly X-rated, certainly R-rated, view of gay men who do drugs and have a lot of promiscuous, meaningless sex ... You know, the gay men I know, frankly, they have sex ... There's so much in our world, gay and straight, when it comes to sex, it's shame-based, but certainly that's magnified for gay people because we're told that we're sick and wrong and all that. And I feel really bad because I see that here. I see a lot of shame-based decisions. We don't represent absolutely every gay and lesbian person on this planet, but I'd like to think that we could represent ones that ... are sexually active.

The contrast between Spurgeon's and Seomin's positions could not have been clearer: in the internal/external dichotomy that characterizes the movement's relationship to sex, Spurgeon came down on the side of mainstream respectability, while Seomin defended the dignity of the "sorry sluts and outcasts" of Warner's (1999, 49) formulation.

For Garry, meanwhile, the most challenging part of deciding how to respond to *Queer as Folk* was the question of whether there is a "sufficient quantity of images out there so that this becomes one of a variety of pictures that people see of gay and lesbian life." *Queer as Folk*, she told me in an interview, "in many ways represents ... a depiction of the kinds of stereotypes that GLAAD in its early days [was created] to fight against." "All the main character seems to think about is really his next trick," and another character, "who happens to be seventeen," "is equally as predatorial with anyone ... to whom he is attracted for that moment in time." One of GLAAD's roles, she added, "is to really get the word out that this is ... what some of us are, but ... there are many of us who are not like this." Ultimately, though, Garry said she recognized that the program is a fair "depiction of a segment of our community." "As a lesbian," she told me, "I don't have any interest in watching it ... It certainly feels ground-breaking and bold and absolutely a picture of who some of us are ... but I don't feel celebratory about it." Still, she concluded, it is fair for a media company to depict gay men in this way, "just as it is fair to show lesbians who live in New Jersey behind white picket fences." (In her public appearances, Garry often joked about being a mini-van-driving lesbian mother of three who lives in a house with a white picket fence in suburban New Jersey with a partner of more than twenty years.) "But you know," she added, "that's no more relevant to guys who go to sex clubs than ... films about sex clubs [are] to me."

In rereading the interviews I conducted with Spurgeon, Seomin, and Garry, the last of which occurred on 7 November 2000, I was struck by the fact that none contained a word about *Queer as Folk*'s lack of racial diversity. Nor did I record any mention of the topic in my field notes about the staff and board meetings I attended prior to the program's 3 December launch. What happened to make racial diversity one of GLAAD's top concerns in its 10 December 2000 statement about *Queer as Folk*?

I believe the answer lies in the interplay between two parts of GLAAD: the communications team and the programs team. The division between these teams came about as a result of the restructuring Garry implemented in 1999. Previously, communications had been conceptualized as being part of programs, which included activities oriented to both the LGBT community and mainstream media. With the restructuring, Garry separated out the external communications function from the internal community function, which exacerbated existing tensions. Given license to operate with relative disregard for how its decisions might be received in the LGBT community (as I discussed in the previous chapter), the communications department under Garry's leadership came to set the priorities for the entire organization. Those relegated to the programs team – i.e., those in charge of LGBT community media training, volunteer management, community relations, research and analysis, as well as programs serving LGBT communities of colour – were marginalized by the restructuring and struggled to assert their voices. This situation made for a tense organizational culture that divided programs staff from everyone else.

Many GLAAD staffers, for example, told me about a group exercise conducted during an all-staff weekend retreat in which everyone in attendance was asked to split into two groups according to whether they considered themselves primarily professionals or activists. Group facilitators presumably meant the exercise to help ease tensions by promoting open discussion, but it had precisely the opposite effect. Each group met in separate rooms to discuss how it felt about the other. Programs team members all gravitated to the activist group, while the communications and development team members, with a few exceptions, chose the professional group. One development staffer told me he would have preferred to align himself with the activists, but had felt compelled to join the professionals to preserve his standing with his colleagues. Overall, another staff person reported, there were only eight self-described activists among the couple dozen or so staff members at the retreat. The activist group, the staffer said, was made up exclusively of "people who had a certain kind of identity: people of colour or transgender [individuals] ... people who were in the regional offices ... people on the programs team ... There were these clear-cut things that bound us together. And all of us have felt disenfranchised in some way."

After meeting in separate rooms, the two groups reconvened and began their discussion. Anger quickly flared up among members of the communications team, some of whom felt personally targeted by comments made by members of the activist group. It did not help matters that these staffers were in the midst of the Schlessinger campaign and that StopDrLaura.com, GLAAD's rival organization in the campaign, had done a good job of exploiting professional/activist tensions in the LGBT movement at large to undermine GLAAD's standing within it. Seomin told me that he barely succeeded in not walking out on the retreat as a result of the exercise. Another communications staffer, who had been working around the clock on a draft op-ed for *Time*, became upset and had what he called a "public falling out" with one of the retreat facilitators. "Only activists label professionals professional," this staffer told me in an interview, and the underlying message of such labelling is that there are "too many professionals" in the organization and "not enough activists." This staffer objected to the exercise because it forced those in the professional group to choose a "loaded" label they had not selected themselves. The activist/professional division, he insisted, is "artificial" because it is based on "subjective measurements" as opposed to "real distinctions." He went on to argue that everyone who works at GLAAD is an activist by virtue of being involved in an organization with a "progressive" mission.

Of course, the staffer was right to point out that there is a subjective element to definitions of what constitutes an activist or a professional, and that one's position on these definitions is bound to affect one's feelings and perceptions. It is also true that almost all GLAAD staff, regardless of which group they chose during the exercise, considered themselves both activists and professionals. Therefore, forcing them to choose between one label or the other was indeed artificial. However, the defensive reactions on the part of certain members of the professional group indicated that the two poles existed in an uneasy tension at GLAAD, the source of which, I would argue, was the unacknowledged, or at least downplayed, dominance of an external orientation to LGBT activism within the organization. That GLAAD's leadership tended to value activities oriented toward swaying "public opinion" more than those oriented toward serving the needs and representing the interests of LGBT communities was abundantly clear. It was obvious in just about everything the organization did during my fieldwork: from the overwhelming institutional emphasis on the Media Awards; to the amount of time and energy devoted to celebrities, mainstream media professionals, and corporate executives; to the assumption – common in hiring decisions – that activism could be learned but that professional skills were an absolute prerequisite; to the resources allotted to communications compared to programs; to the things singled out as significant accomplishments during board and staff meetings. That the development staffer who had wanted to identify with the activist group felt compelled to join the professional group is also telling: it was clear to him which group he needed to profess his allegiance to if he was to maintain or advance his position in the organization.

The internal/external division between programs and communications, while generally operative at the level of organizational structure, did not always correspond to the attitudes and practices of individual staff members within each of these teams. In the case of *Queer as Folk*, GLAAD's communications leadership expressed a range of opinions: Seomin was an ardent defender of gay male sexual autonomy as against sexual shame, Spurgeon adopted an ambivalent position, and Garry preferred to distance GLAAD from what she saw as a stereotypical – and therefore harmful – depiction of gay male sexuality. Although she adopted an externally oriented position in that instance (notwithstanding the fact that many gays and lesbians would agree with her), Garry was instrumental in getting the board to approve funding for the internally oriented Cultural Interest Media Project, whose objective, according to a board report, was to "expand our work to promote fair, accurate and inclusive representation of LGBT people of color in mainstream, community and specialty media." So it was that, beginning in 2000, longtime staff member Loren Javier came to be cultural interest media manager. Garry also approved sensitivity training for staff, formed a committee to discuss and devise other diversity initiatives, and mandated an increase in the visibility of people of colour in GLAAD's publications.

By the time *Queer as Folk* premiered, Garry had begun to look for ways to integrate the new diversity focus into GLAAD's communications work. She told the June 2000 board meeting that to "harness the power of diversity" is not just about what GLAAD's staff and board look like, "it's about our work." "I don't see this as a separate thing that lives out here," she declared. That sentiment was put to the test when Javier received phone calls the day after the premiere from people concerned about the series's virtual whitewash. He relayed these concerns to his supervisor, Loe, who brought them to the management team, which decided to include them in the GLAAD statement about the show.

The GLAAD statement about *Queer as Folk*, and particularly its criticism of the lack of racial diversity, took Showtime by surprise, according to Gene Falk, who in addition to being a Showtime executive was a former co-chair of GLAAD's board of directors with over a decade of involvement in the organization. These twin roles led to some minor confusion during the interview I conducted with him as he used the collective pronoun "we" to refer sometimes to Showtime and sometimes to GLAAD. Falk told me that many of his colleagues felt "ambushed" because GLAAD had not honoured an implicit agreement to warn media companies that criticism was on the way. The organization's access to media executives, he explained, "works both ways" because "it gives you responsibility as well as giving you certain privileges. The good news is that Showtime wanted to know what GLAAD thought and let what GLAAD thought help shape the thinking about what should be happening with the show. But then GLAAD has an obligation that if you're gonna say 'well we got a problem with this,' to alert people to the fact that this is gonna come." Early in developing the show, he explained, Showtime executives had submitted a script to Seomin. They were concerned that the original British series had generated controversy because of its "stereotyped" (his word) view of the gay world and wanted to know if GLAAD would "take up arms." After hearing Seomin's feedback, Falk said, network executives were "not sure that the organization was gonna give it a big wide hug and say this is the best thing we've ever seen," but they came away satisfied that GLAAD would not oppose the series and would, at the very least, praise its ground-breaking nature. Instead, he said, what they got was "this lukewarm ... thing that made it sound like the only reaction was 'there were no people of colour on the show.'"

Falk's comments suggest that, whatever interactions Showtime producers had with GLAAD representatives prior to the premiere, concerns about a lack of racial diversity had not come to light. Furthermore, there is little evidence to suggest that GLAAD had much input into the program. In a mid-August 2000 memo to the management team, Seomin stated that, although he had spoken to the producers of *Queer as Folk* several times, he had not been able to meet with them in person. "They were not avoiding GLAAD," he wrote, "rather, our schedules conflicted and they are now in the middle of filming." Seomin also stated that they had "kept me in the loop along the way regarding casting, shooting schedules and headaches," such as the difficulty of getting advertisers to agree to product placements.

If Seomin was kept up to date as to casting, as he stated, there is nothing in the memo to suggest that he expressed any concerns about it Nor, as I noted above, did concerns about racial diversity come up in the communications team and board meetings I attended prior to the premiere. One area of concern that did come up during communications team meetings, by contrast, was a line in the first episode in which Brian makes a passing reference to Matthew Shepard's murder. In an interview, Spurgeon told me that the line had bothered him because "it's too soon to take Matthew Shepard's death and make it a flip retort. Not because ... it was or wasn't done well in this particular segment, but [because] that opens the floodgates for people who may not be as well-intentioned." Seomin asked the producers to change the line. It aired without modification.

In an interview I conducted with him shortly after the television premiere, Seomin told me he disagreed with the management team's decision to include diversity concerns in the GLAAD statement about *Queer as Folk*. He also insisted that he had discussed the issue of racial representation with one of the producers while the series was still in development. "I did bring it up," he said. "We did our complaining. We were heard." With a sigh denoting exasperation, he added: "Now is not the time to complain."

Seomin told me that his objections were professional in nature. He said that by "complaining" about the absence of people of colour in the series, "we make it look like we don't know what's going on ... we don't know how television is made." The statement, he elaborated, made GLAAD appear professionally naive:

> I feel as if ... Loren gets a phone call from some group of colour and he says "oh my gosh, you're right" and I'll make sure Scott gets right on this. You know, I think the whole idea of Cultural Interest Media could ultimately hurt us more than it's helping us. And I'm real concerned with that. We're setting ourselves up for failure, making promises that aren't realistic. It's our job, but our job is to be smart about what we do and I know ... I know the deadlines television makes, I know who has power and who doesn't have power, I know the development process and I was involved with *Queer as Folk*, so I know what's going on. It's ... disappointing.

Falk expressed a similar view: "I spent the last ten years [at GLAAD] getting us beyond this and I [was] completely furious that we [were] going to blow it all up now. You know, it was stupid. And it was stupid not just from Showtime's point of view but from [the point of view of] any media professional ... I got calls from friends saying, 'what are they thinking?' You know, is this back to the good ol' days of political correctness?"

For Falk and Seomin, raising the issue of racial diversity was ineffectual because it was unprofessional. To be "smart" (as opposed to "politically correct") is to be "realistic" about the limitations of "how television is made" and act in harmony with its decision-making processes. That means knowing how to address oneself to the right people at the right times and in the right ways. To behave otherwise is to risk losing the most valuable asset a professional media activist can possess: the respect of professional peers upon whom access depends.

Like Seomin, Falk was careful not to question the substance of the concerns about racial diversity: "I completely understand why people of colour were upset, and, you know ... the head of Showtime programming was equally upset ... That criticism was not something that bothered anyone. It was the way it was delivered." He suggested that a better way to deliver the criticism would have been to acknowledge and celebrate the more innovative aspects of the program and tone down the harsh criticism: "It was a question of balance. If it had been written the other way, if it had said: 'this is great Showtime is doing this and we don't even agree with all the things that are in it' ... and, by the way, we're also really concerned that there are no people of colour ... and you should write to Showtime and tell them that you think that. I think people at Showtime would have applauded." Falk did not say whether he believed such a neutered statement would have been more likely to convince Showtime executives to cast more people of colour (the history of media activist interactions with the networks suggests otherwise). He did, however, have at least two good reasons to feel invested in the proper etiquette for delivering criticism: (1) his concern about maintaining GLAAD's reputation for professionalism; and (2) the fact that GLAAD's rather harsh statement had the potential to derail Showtime's carefully calibrated advertising campaign targeting the gay and lesbian community. Showtime's marketing department had anticipated, and indeed probably welcomed, controversy about promiscuity, drug use, and intergenerational sex, but had not counted on being criticized for *Queer as Folk*'s racial homogeneity, a much less saleable object of controversy.

Showtime executives were very displeased. Falk told me that the chairman of the network, Matt Blank, had threatened to fire him. "I mean, he was joking," Falk added, "but it was like 'you were supposed to make sure this didn't happen.'" In turn, Falk said he spent forty-five minutes "just about yelling" at Spurgeon. Some at Showtime even wanted GLAAD to publish a public retraction, but, Falk says, "that had more to do with emotions."

All joking aside, Blank's threat of dismissal suggested the extent to which, from Showtime's perspective, maintaining good relations with advocacy groups was about containing criticism that might spill over into more costly forms of public debate. From GLAAD's perspective, the price of friendly, cooperative relationships is that criticism could only go so far and must be delivered at the right time to the right people, preferably behind the scenes. That a line had been crossed in this instance was made clear by Showtime's reaction, which, according to the minutes of an emergency GLAAD executive committee meeting, included "some threats, both clear and unclear." The minutes went on to reassure committee members that a meeting between Garry and Blank had been scheduled and that Garry hoped to use the occasion to "illustrate to Showtime just how important this relationship is to GLAAD."

Shortly after Garry's meeting with Blank, a banner advertising *Queer as Folk* appeared on the GLAAD website. One staffer told me that he expressed strong reservations to Garry about the appropriateness of a media activist organization advertising media content. In response, this staffer said, Garry explained that Showtime had been extremely upset by the critical statement about *Queer as Folk* and that it had become necessary for GLAAD to repair its relationship with the network if it was to have productive conversations with it in the future, including on the topic of racial diversity. Later that same year, cast members of *Queer as Folk* were present at all four GLAAD Media Awards ceremonies in New York, Los Angeles, Washington, and San Francisco. In addition to accepting the award for outstanding drama series, they helped raise over $100,000 for GLAAD by presiding over the auctions of walk-on parts on the program.

If GLAAD's leaders did, in fact, use their patched-up access to Showtime executives to pursue discussions about the absence of people of colour on *Queer as Folk*, it was not reflected in subsequent seasons of the series. In September 2002, a GLAAD media release deplored a sharp overall decline in the number of LGBT characters on network television relative to the previous year and a "total lack of people of color, bisexual and transgender portrayals on network television." According to the following year's media release on diversity in television, the situation had improved somewhat with the arrival of new programs that, "while groundbreaking, remained predominantly male, white, affluent and decidedly 'fabulous.'" The statement also noted, "shows like HBO's *The Wire* and *Six Feet Under* and Showtime's *Queer as Folk* feature lesbian and gay characters in complex romantic and sexual relationships. And *The Wire, Six Feet Under* and *The Shield* include gay and lesbian people of color who are more complex, more fully realized and more three-dimensional than most gay characters on broadcast television." GLAAD's leaders had circled back to the moderate position Seomin favoured. Any concerns that remained about the depiction of gay male sexuality on *Queer as Folk* were now subsumed within a carefully worded, vaguely neutral characterization of its romantic and sexual relationships as "complex." As for the continued absence of people of colour in significant roles, the media release could only be read as critical of *Queer as Folk* by implication. The series was simply, but perhaps pointedly, omitted from the list of those that included "complex, more fully-realized and more three-dimensional" people of colour.

I read GLAAD's criticism of the lack of racial diversity on *Queer as Folk* as a displacement of the anxieties some of the organization's leaders had about sex on the series onto arguments about racial representation. In the initial stages of forming a position on the series, the issue that most troubled GLAAD's leaders – with the exception of Seomin – was not so much the absence of people of colour as it was *Queer as Folk*'s display of queer difference from a phantasmatic mainstream ostensibly devoid of recreational drug use, sex for pleasure, or intergenerational sex. By foregrounding the issue of racial diversity, GLAAD's leaders took a potentially contentious emphasis on criticizing *Queer as Folk* for its disreputable sex and drugs and displaced it onto the unimpeachable morality of advocating for more racial diversity, which few people will take positions against. In the end, the fact that GLAAD's leadership worked so diligently to repair relations with Showtime at the first sign that advocating for greater racial diversity might land them in trouble with the network is another indication of the limits of professionalized media advocacy.

## The Deracialization/Reracialization of Eminem

GLAAD's public position on Eminem's *The Marshall Mathers LP*, in contrast to its position on *Queer as Folk*, systematically avoided any discussion of race. GLAAD's communications team tailored its message for the (imagined) white, middle-class mainstream by emphasizing the harm to kids that Eminem's lyrics could be said to inflict. The programs team, by contrast, pursued activities designed to explore and discuss the complex relationships among sexuality, race, class, and gender as depicted in Eminem's album. The division within GLAAD on the topic of Eminem provides one of the clearest illustrations of the problems for queer politics and culture of the dominance of an externally oriented mainstreaming politics at the organization.

## The Communications Team

GLAAD's involvement with Eminem began when Seomin received a copy of *The Marshall Mathers LP* prior to its 23 May 2000 release. The album, he found, contains no fewer than eighteen instances of the word "faggot" and various references to insulting or humiliating gays, lesbians, transgender people, or women. Among the most egregious and explicitly hateful lyrics was this passage from the song, "Criminal": "My words are like a dagger with a jagged edge / That'll stab you in the head / Whether you're a fag or lez / Or the homosex, hermaph or a trans-a-vest / Pants or dress – hate fags? The answer's 'yes.'" In another song, "Marshall Mathers," Eminem refers to rival rappers as "faggots" and boasts that he does not "need help from D-12," his posse of Detroit homeboys, to "beat up two females in make-up, who may try to scratch me with Lee Nails." The "females" in question turn out to be men in drag who taunt him with cries of "Slim Anus," a reference to Eminem's darker alter ego, Slim Shady. "You damn right," comes the retort, "Slim Anus. I don't get fucked in mine like you two little flaming faggots!"

On 25 May 2000, GLAAD released a GLAAD Alert that called on Eminem's label, Interscope Records, to "stop and think of the consequences of publishing such material" and to "raise its standards for what products it produces and what artists it promotes." It called on supporters to "let Eminem know how such disregard for others can lead to discrimination, physical abuse and even death." A few days later, GLAAD sent out a press release that called Eminem's lyrics "the most offensive homophobic lyrics" the organization "has seen in many years." Once again, the statement posited a link between the "hatred and hostility conveyed on this CD" and "violence against gay men and lesbians." Interscope Records, record retailers, and Eminem, the statement concluded, "have a responsibility" to "consider [the] impact" of Eminem's music on its "impressionable audience" of "easily influenced adolescents who emulate Eminem's dress, mannerisms, words and beliefs."

In the month following the album's release, GLAAD's leadership contacted representatives of the top twenty music retailers in the United States and received assurances from one company that it would allow buyers to return Eminem CDs if they found the lyrics objectionable. Another retailer agreed to curtail its promotion of the album. GLAAD leaders also contacted Interscope Records and Eminem's management, but were unsuccessful in meeting with them. The record company, Seomin told GLAAD's board in June 2000, was "hiding behind a statement made to Kurt Loder," host of MTV News, in which Eminem had said, "the lowest, most degrading thing that you can say to a man when you're battling him is call him a faggot and try to take away his manhood. Call him a sissy, call him a punk. 'Faggot' to me doesn't necessarily mean gay people. 'Faggot' to me just means taking away your manhood." "Oh! The subtle nuance!" Seomin sarcastically told the board.

By June 2000, the album had enjoyed the strongest ever *Billboard* debut by a solo artist, received widespread critical acclaim, and sold close to five million copies. MTV, a channel with which GLAAD had enjoyed good relations and a high level of access, was promoting Eminem heavily and had gone so far as to devote an entire weekend to him during which it had renamed itself EmTV. To make matters more complicated, Brian Graden, MTV's head of programming at the time, was an openly gay man and a major GLAAD donor.

Garry met with Graden in June and with Judy McGrath, MTV president, later that month. She requested, among other things, that MTV produce a news special devoted to the question of "hate lyrics" and that it limit its promotion of Eminem and not allow the rapper to participate in the network's upcoming Video Music Awards (VMAs). Graden and McGrath, although they reportedly expressed feeling conflicted about the matter, responded that their hands were tied because of Eminem's sales. They nonetheless went on to produce a news special.

The hour-long *When Lyrics Attack* aired in August 2000 and features clips of past interviews with Eminem, as well as commentary from fans, prominent music critics, advocacy organizations, celebrities, and musicians. Though highly edited (it appeared on MTV, after all), the program manages a thought-provoking, if not in-depth, discussion of many questions raised by Eminem's music, among them: Are protests of Eminem similar to past protests of musical acts by religious conservatives and/or puritanical parents' organizations? Does the artfulness of Eminem's music make a difference? Can his songs rightfully be considered parody or irony? If so, are young audiences sophisticated enough to understand this supposed intent? Do most audience members interpret Eminem's attacks on women and gay men as arising from little more than a desire to shock (rather than a deep-seated hatred of gays and women)? Does Eminem, as an artist, have the right to speak his mind without justifying himself, or does he bear responsibility for the harm his words might cause? Is Eminem a role model for kids? If so, is it morally wrong for a multinational record company to market Eminem's album to young audiences? Is there in fact a link, as Garry argues in the program, between hurtful lyrics and actual violence?

In interview clips, Eminem acknowledges that his lyrics are calculated to shock the sensibilities of critics but denies any violent intent. He tells Loder: "I know what I'm doing when I sit down to write … you know what I'm saying? It doesn't happen by accident." He urges his critics to "stop analyzing my shit too in-depth. Every single word that I say doesn't necessarily mean something." Besides, he tells another interviewer, "I'm not here to justify anything I say or do." And that, he says, is "one of the luxuries of being me."

In Eminem's defence, it is true that many of his lyrics begged listeners not to take him too literally. In the song, "Who Knew," Eminem indicates surprise at all the attention his lyrics attract: "Damn! How much damage can you do with a pen?" On "Criminal," he declares: "Shit, half the shit I say, I just make it up to make you mad. So kiss my white naked ass." In the chorus for "Kill You," a song about his mother, Eminem raps: "Bitch I'ma kill you! You don't wanna fuck with me. Girls neither – you ain't nothing but a slut to me." He concludes: "Ha ha ha! I'm just playin' ladies. You know I love you." On "Criminal," he follows up "Hate fags? The answer's 'yes,'" with "Relax guy, I like gay men."

These disclaimers tended to satisfy mainstream music critics, many of whom went out of their way to praise the ingenuity of Eminem's lyrics while lightly dismissing their excesses. In a column for *Salon*, Eric Boehlert noted that the critical reaction to *The Marshall Mathers LP* had been "wildly enthusiastic." The *Arizona Republic*, he reported, called the album "quite entertaining if not taken too seriously." VH 1.com, for its part, described it as "a bona fide masterpiece." *Newsweek* called Eminem "arguably the most compelling figure in all of pop music." The critics, Boehlert argued, "have been working overtime trying to soften [Eminem's] gruesome lyrics," trying to "convince readers (and perhaps themselves) that Eminem's odious tales are simply the latest in the grand tradition of shocking youthful rebellion." Reviewers, he wrote, employed "analogy after analogy" in the service of this argument. They compared Eminem's album to the Rolling Stones, Freddy Krueger movies, the wood-chipper scene from *Fargo*, Quentin Tarantino's *Pulp Fiction*, Howard Stern, Rodney Dangerfield, Alice Cooper, Richard Pryor, TV wrestling, *South Park*, and Jerry Springer. For Boehlert, how-ever, these comparisons simply did not hold up, given the extremes to which Eminem's music goes. Boehlert quotes from "Amityville": "My little sister's birthday, she'll remember me / For a gift I had ten of my boys take her virginity." Critics, Boehlert argued, are "so afraid ... to give an inch in their battle with the Bill Bennett moralists of the world that they're now championing an artist who raps nearly nonstop ... about sluts, guts, cocaine and getting 'more pussy than them dyke bitches total.'"[2]

Given the nearly nonstop stream of invectives on his albums, how was Eminem so successful in getting radio play and MTV exposure? The answer lay in withholding media-unfriendly lyrics on a few key tracks and cleaned up versions of a few songs. One, for example, eschewed rape and murder for edited-out swear words and amusing jibes at celebrities. Moreover, the videos for many of Eminem's songs featured comical, cartoonish elements that seemed designed to appeal to a broad cross-section of the kids, teens, and young adults who formed MTV's core audience.

So it was that despite GLAAD's request to the contrary, MTV made Eminem the centrepiece of its 2000 VMAS. He received awards for Best Video of the Year, Best Male Video, and Best Rap Video. In an inter-view, Spurgeon told me: "We were – I think the technical term is pissed – that they were having Eminem prominently featured that night at the awards because we had told them that was one of the things that we re-ally wanted them not to do. And they damn well went ahead and did it."

As with the early stages of the Schlessinger campaign, negotiations failed to produce the desired outcome. Unlike the Schlessinger campaign, however, GLAAD's leadership decided not to delay in employing public protest strategies. "It had to happen," Spurgeon told me, "because we'd already been through a lot of other stages with them."

GLAAD leaders decided to organize a protest of the VMAs, which were held on 7 September 2000 at New York City's Radio City Music Hall. To aid in their efforts, GLAAD representatives made calls to what Spurgeon called "like organizations" (such as the New York Gay and Lesbian Center, People for the American Way, and the National Organization for Women) and "our donor base." The turnout was, Spurgeon admitted, "pretty slim," about forty to fifty people, but "enough to make a pretty respectable showing on TV." Still, Spurgeon told me he believed the protest was "effective because it was a good visual" and "gave us the peg to play off other media." "The real benefit," Spurgeon concluded, was that it "allowed us to talk about the fact that we did it." It was, as Garry later put it to the board of directors, not so much a protest as a "media visibility opportunity."

In a sign that MTV executives may have thought it advantageous to cover (and thus help manufacture) the controversy, the network broadcast images of the protest during the VMA pre-show and interviewed Romaine Patterson, a junior employee of GLAAD's communications team, whom Spurgeon said "we used because she was young, in that demographic." At GLAAD's urging, MTV also agreed to broadcast a public service announcement produced for the Gay, Lesbian and Straight Education Network that features Shepard's mother talking about the violent impact of anti-gay rhetoric.

On 19 October 2000, a few weeks after the VMA protest, GLAAD held a Fairness Awards fundraising luncheon in Los Angeles – distinct from the Media Awards – that honoured both Bunim/Murray productions, which produces MTV's *The Real World*, and Mark Ordesky, New Line Cinema/Fine Line Features president. A few celebrities attended, including former cast members of *The Real World* and Tori Spelling, star of New Line's gay-themed romantic comedy, *Trick*. According to two GLAAD staffers I spoke to, a drag queen who appeared in the movie, Miss Coco Peru, was asked by New Line employees not to show up to the luncheon dressed in drag. She defied the order, thereby upstaging Spelling ever so slightly.

In the programme distributed to attendees, GLAAD described the Fairness Awards in the following manner: "Fairness Awards recognize long-term commitments made in the vital area of equal rights. In particular, [they] honor institutions and individuals from the profit and non-profit sectors who have taken active, front-line positions in the battle for fair, accurate and inclusive representation of lesbian, gay, bisexual, and transgender (LGBT) people." In practice, these award luncheons were highly lucrative fundraising opportunities for GLAAD, which charged attendees as much as $500 per seat, or $10,000 per table. The formula was simple: choose a chief executive officer or other high-ranking corporate executive (or, in one case, the executive director of a non-profit organization) to honour, book a hotel banquet room large enough to accommodate a few hundred people, secure the presence of a few celebrities, and hold a luncheon complete with speeches and packaged audio-visual material testifying to the accomplishments of the honoured executive and/or company. Past recipients of Fairness Awards included corporate executives from Pacific Bell, Sun Microsystems, Condé Nast, Warner Brothers, Bravo!, Time Inc, the Ford Motor Company, *Daily Variety*, Coca-Cola, and Sony Pictures Classics.

It was customary for the recipients of Fairness Awards to select someone to present their award to him or her. Bunim/Murray chose Graden. This raised the question: should someone with whom GLAAD was feuding be allowed to make the presentation? Garry decided no. Graden was still invited to attend the luncheon, and did so, but a former *Real World* cast member presented the award in his stead. In her remarks at the luncheon, Garry took the unusual step – in a forum normally devoted to (self-)congratulations – of making comments sharply critical of the corporate culture the event was meant to celebrate. MTV executives, she said, are "the good guys," but the network's refusal to put a damper on its promotion of Eminem had put her in the awkward position of picketing her former employer. Her "biggest surprise and disappointment" since taking GLAAD's helm, she stated, had been "how infrequently gay and lesbian people in positions of power actually use that power." According to a GLAAD staffer I spoke to afterwards, Graden "seemed displeased" and did not applaud after Garry's speech.

Coincidentally (or not?), just a few months later, MTV announced that it was launching a year-long campaign called "Fight for Your Rights: Take a Stand Against Discrimination," which began with the

10 January 2001 broadcast of an MTV-produced movie about Shepard's murder. The film was followed by a scrolling list of the names of hate crime victims, along with a description of the crimes committed against them. The list continued uninterrupted for 17.5 hours: not so long as to interfere with the airing of MTV's most popular program, *Total Request Live*, but still long enough to allow MTV to trumpet the fact that it had lost $2 million in ad revenue.

Interviewed in *Billboard*, Graden said that the campaign had been in the making for two years and was "not a response to the controversy."[3] In another interview, however, he stated: "We [MTV] began to feel in 2000 [that] there was a particular shift happening and a lot of pop culture was beginning to cross the line in a way that was dangerous. Can we protect the audience from everything? Probably not. But what we can do is get them to at least think about what they see and what the impact may be."[4] He added that MTV would continue to play Eminem videos that met the network's standards, but that it would stop inviting Eminem to its events because it had realized he "wasn't an artist we wanted to get behind." Had MTV executives suddenly had an epiphany? Were they changing their tune as a result of GLAAD's pressure? Or had they realized that after giving Eminem their maximum promotion ("The Real Slim Shady" was MTV's most played video in 2000), it was now more profitable to keep milking the controversy that GLAAD had helped them create than it was to continue promoting an album that had been out for more than six months?

After the Fairness Awards, GLAAD's leadership had turned its attention away from MTV and debated how to continue with the campaign, which themes to prioritize, and what tactics to privilege. Would it be about corporate responsibility for hate lyrics? Would it be about homophobia in hip hop more generally? Would it be specifically about Eminem? Would it include protests? Would it have local as well as national elements? These questions sometimes spilled over into communications team teleconferences to which I was privy. During one such call, in which Spurgeon sought input from his team, a junior staff member stated that she had been meeting with people to learn more about hip hop because, she admitted, "I don't know lots." She and another junior staff member then proposed to create a "music version of the style guide" that GLAAD distributes to journalists. The proposed style guide would have spelled out acceptable and unacceptable ways of referring to LGBT people in music and been distributed to DJs. As he heard his colleagues describe their idea, Seomin became increasingly animated and began shaking his head from side to side, but it was Nick Adams, a mid-level communications staffer, who spoke first. Adams stood out among the communications staff as one with a long history of involvement in progressive politics and as the only transgender person. He had initially joined GLAAD as a volunteer in the early days of GLAAD/LA and had been active in a variety of lesbian and gay, feminist, and transgender organizations ever since.

Adams made the case that a style guide would have to be careful not to single out Eminem and hip hop as the sole purveyors of hate lyrics in the music industry. To take aim at hip hop, which is rooted in the African American and Latino communities, and not, say, at hard rock, which appeals mainly to whites, would expose GLAAD to unwelcome criticism, he argued. It might make sense to focus on Eminem because he is the most "egregious" example, he said, but GLAAD would then run the risk of appearing "obsessed with the kid with blond hair." Whatever the approach, it would be important not to demonize all hip-hop music and artists, and to work from a well-researched position: "there's not a long history of hip-hop music at GLAAD," Adams cautioned.

Seomin jumped into the discussion and argued that, from a professional standpoint, a style guide made little sense. He explained that, although he often gets calls from entertainment industry professionals asking for the GLAAD "bible" of dos and don'ts, he opposed this way of doing things. The organization's function, he believed, was to apply its professional judgment to arrive at measured, context-dependent evaluations of content: "We're not censors and we're not standards and practices." He gave the example of how the producers of the short-lived sitcom, *Normal, Ohio*, had called him about the use of the word "fag" in a script, and had expected him to oppose its use as a matter of principle. He asked to read the script and concluded that it was appropriate to use the word in that instance. Eminem's use of the word, by contrast, constituted for Seomin a "blatant," "obvious," and "black and white" case of defamation. The appropriate way to respond, he concluded, is case by case: "We don't need to do a style guide."

The meeting did not produce a clear consensus about how to proceed. The junior staffer whose idea had been shot down lamented the lack of "any definitive decisions made of what we want to do." She expressed further disappointment that none of the local community leaders she had spoken with about the possibility of protesting Eminem concerts in their cities were "running with it," which led Seomin to argue against the very suggestion that GLAAD might sponsor local protests. He proposed instead that concert promoters might be compelled to make a donation to an organization like the Matthew Shepard Foundation. Cathy Renna countered that one of the lessons of the Dr Laura campaign had been that media were unlikely to cover the campaign without protests. Media, she said, "are going to want b-roll of people doing something."

Decisions about how to proceed, ultimately, rested not with GLAAD staffers, but with the management team and the board's executive committee. Those decisions finally came with the early January 2001 announcement that Eminem had been nominated for Grammy Awards in four categories, including Album of the Year. Anticipating the announcement, the communications team issued a press release the day before in which it urged journalists to "discuss issues of lyrical and corporate responsibility when reporting on Eminem." Within days, GLAAD spokespeople appeared on NBC's *Today*, ABC's *World News Tonight*, CNN, and *Access Hollywood*, among others.

With its Eminem campaign now attracting major media attention, GLAAD announced that it was organizing a protest of the Grammys in coalition with the National Organization for Women (NOW), the Gay, Lesbian and Straight Education Network, the LA Gay & Lesbian Center, and Parents and Friends of Lesbians and Gays, among other gay and lesbian, women's, anti-violence, and religious organizations. The protest was slated for the day of the Grammys, to be held on 21 February 2001 at the Los Angeles Staples Center.

GLAAD's leaders contacted the music industry group that organizes the Grammys, the National Academy of Recording Arts and Sciences (NARAS), to propose ways that the two organizations might cooperate. Spurgeon told his staff during a meeting in early February that "this is a make or break opportunity for the Academy. They either get behind the gun or in front of it." In a meeting with the head of NARAS, Michael Greene, Garry asked the Academy not to invite Eminem to perform at the Grammys and for help in securing a good location for the GLAAD protest. She also floated the idea of jointly organizing a televised town hall meeting to be held the day before. In addition to representatives from the two sponsoring organizations, GLAAD's plans for the event were to include a well-known hip-hop producer or artist (to be provided by NARAS) and youth on both sides of the Eminem debate. The audience would be made up of youth from the Los Angeles Unified School District.

On 9 February, Greene made good on one of GLAAD's requests by issuing a press release on NARAS letterhead announcing that he would participate in a jointly organized event entitled "Intolerance in Music: Town Hall Meeting." However, his cooperation with GLAAD ended there. Later the same day, NARAS confirmed that Eminem had accepted its invitation to perform at the Grammys. From that point on, Greene put up one roadblock after another. During a staff meeting, Adams reported that Greene had decided not to support a protest near the red carpet because it would, in his words, "carnivalize" the Grammys. Spurgeon told his staff that Greene's proposed locations for the protest appeared "designed to put us in Inglewood" (a predominantly African American neighbourhood considerably south of the Grammys venue). Greene also did not come through with a hip-hop recording artist or producer for the town hall meeting. Finally, he communicated that the Academy would agree to distribute a pin or ribbon to artists who supported GLAAD's campaign only on the condition that it be "couture" (in Spurgeon's words), which left too little time to produce something adequate. Finally, Greene said that NARAS and CBS, the Grammys broadcaster, would air an anti-violence public service announcement only if it met their high production standards. When Spurgeon suggested that NARAS and CBS produce one, he was told that they "don't have the production facilities." Noting the irony, Spurgeon summed up GLAAD's production capabilities relative to those of NARAS and CBS: "Maybe we can get some vinegar and some baking soda and make a volcano."

To make matters worse, rumours had begun to circulate that Elton John had been approached to join Eminem on stage at the Grammys. Seomin had already learned that the Academy's initial invitation to Eminem was conditional upon his performing the song "Stan," an artful ballad that features an epistolary exchange between Eminem and the obsessed fan of the title, who, in a desperate bid to catch Eminem's attention, drives his car off a bridge with his pregnant girlfriend stuffed in the trunk. Ironically, the song is not without homoerotic overtones as

Stan tells Eminem: "I love you Slim, we coulda been together, think about it." In addition to the song's two characters, both performed by Eminem, the album version of "Stan" features a melancholy chorus sung by the British female singer, Dido. It was to sing this chorus that John's services were reportedly being sought by the Academy.

As the communications team prepared a response to the announcement that Eminem would perform at the Grammys, Spurgeon wondered whether the GLAAD statement should address the rumours about John's possible involvement. His gut instinct told him no: "I don't put out subjective media statements," he told me. On the other hand, he recognized that an Eminem-John duet had the potential to derail the campaign in a major way, in no small part because GLAAD had, just the previous year, given John a Media Award for his achievements in combating homophobia. As a result, Spurgeon felt it was his responsibility to do everything in his power to stop the duet. He decided to call "one of our media friends" at a national outlet to ask for advice and feedback on how media professionals would respond to various scenarios. He told me that he explained his predicament thus: either GLAAD staffers could seem like "complete weenies" if they put out a statement that reads, "if they do this, then we'll do this," or they could "look asleep at the wheel." The media friend reportedly agreed that putting out a hypothetical statement was "down on the list of things to do, but not off the list" if there were "no other options." The advice, Spurgeon told me, was to try to get to John by more direct means.

After working unsuccessfully to get either Judy Shepard, Matthew's mother, or Matilda Krim, the founder of the American Foundation for AIDS Research to which John has given generously, to call John directly, Spurgeon turned to someone he referred to as "my old friend Fran," John's publicist. As had also been the case with Laura Schlessinger's main public relations person, Fran was a former colleague of Spurgeon's. Because he had not spoken to her since 1989, however, Spurgeon had to place a cold call and, he told me, "got the harridan at the front desk." He left a message and figured "either it'll ring a bell or not," meaning he was unsure whether or not Fran would remember him.

Shortly thereafter, as it turned out, Fran rang and informed Spurgeon that "Elton hasn't made his decision yet." She suggested that he send her "the statement you would release" if John were to confirm his participation. Minutes after receiving the draft statement in question, she called Spurgeon back and reportedly exclaimed: "Wow! This is strong, Steve." Spurgeon told me that he shot back: "Have you listened to Eminem's lyrics?" Fran then asked Spurgeon to provide additional information about why John should decline the invitation. The communications team hurriedly assembled a package that included copies of hate mail GLAAD had received in connection with the Eminem campaign. Spurgeon told me he decided to include the hate mail because he wanted John "to see who he's appealing to." It was all to no avail however, as GLAAD's entreaties fell on deaf ears. Late on Friday, 10 February 2001, John released a statement announcing he would perform "Stan" with Eminem at the Grammys. The GLAAD response read, in part: "GLAAD is appalled that John would share a stage with Eminem, whose words and actions promote hate and violence against gays and lesbians. Last year, GLAAD bestowed upon John one of our most prestigious honors, named in honor of GLAAD founder Vito Russo, for outstanding contributions to combating homophobia. We believe John's actions today violate the spirit of this award."

In an interview conducted with the *Los Angeles Times*, John stated that his reasons for doing the duet included his respect for Eminem as an artist and his perception that Eminem was extending an olive branch to the gay and lesbian community: "If I thought for one minute that he was a hateful bastard, I wouldn't do it."[5] Meanwhile, Greene appeared to be speaking from the same talking points: "If Elton John believed that Eminem was really homophobic, he wouldn't be doing it. Or, if Eminem really meant what he was doing, he wouldn't perform with Elton John."[6] Ironically, Eminem, who was not quoted in any of the articles, later claimed that he had no idea John was gay. As communications scholar Bethany Klein (2003) writes: "Eminem is either the only person on the planet to not know John is gay or an artist adept at constructing his persona as a polysemic text, a text from which his own beliefs and attitudes are difficult to decipher."

John, too, is no stranger to the periodic use of controversy to refresh a polysemic public persona. Along with Frank Sinatra, Shirley Bassey, and Liza Minnelli, he was among the artists who accepted an invitation to perform in Sun City, the segregated South African resort that flourished under apartheid. In 1992, he had performed Queen's "Bohemian

Rhapsody" with Axl Rose at an AIDS benefit. The duet might have been unremarkable except for the fact that the Guns N' Roses front man had been under criticism for "One in a Million," which featured the following lyrics: "Immigrants and faggots / They make no sense to me / They come to our country / And think they'll do as they please / Like start some mini Iran / Or spread some fuckin' disease." As would now be the case with Eminem, John had helped to rehabilitate a popular music figure accused of homophobia (among other things) and provided cover for the corporate entities associated with that figure.

Indeed, the Eminem/John Grammys duet, which was masterminded by Jimmy Iovine, the head of Eminem's label, and Doug Morris, chairman of the Universal Music Group, was a public relations coup for the music companies. With one brief announcement about a five-minute performance to come, they had neutralized GLAAD's campaign and fuelled media interest in Eminem, the Grammys, and John.

GLAAD's leadership faced a difficult choice: either try to isolate the latest recipient of the Vito Russo GLAAD Media Award as a traitor to the community, or acknowledge a difference of opinion and attempt to refocus the media coverage on Eminem's hate lyrics and their alleged links to violence. It soon became clear that they could not sustain an attack on John without also distancing themselves from a good many other gay and lesbian activists and organizations. On 13 February 2001, the *New York Post* reported that the Eminem/John duet "has opened a raging rift among gay activist groups." The article contrasted GLAAD's position with that of three other carefully selected activists. Near the beginning of the article, Seomin stated that John "should be disgusted and ashamed of himself." Independent activist Bill Dobbs, well-known as a thorn in GLAAD's side, countered with an anti-censorship message: "GLAAD is more interested in selling tickets to its fund-raisers than advancing gay people. They don't want to confront messages anymore, they just want to shut things off, and I've got a problem with that." Ex-journalist-turned-activist Ann Northrop declared: "I like Eminem. I think he's too smart to be homophobic and what he's doing is more of a cultural analysis. I think GLAAD has been misguided." Only Dan Wilson, the most institutionally bound of the three (he was the director of the New York Lesbian and Gay Community Services Center), struck a more diplomatic note. The decision to perform at the Grammys, he said, is "Elton's choice. We're not going to argue with different tactics on how to destroy ignorance."[7]

Also institutionally bound, but differently positioned, was David Smith, the communications director for the Human Rights Campaign (HRC). Asked to comment about the duet, Smith opted to give John the benefit of the doubt. He told the *San Francisco Chronicle*: "We have the highest regard for Elton John and we believe he must be doing this for a well thought out reason. Hopefully his reason for doing it will be clear before, during or after the performance. Obviously, Elton John cares deeply for his fellow gay people. His advocacy, activism and philanthropy all underscore that."[8] Interestingly, given the choice between endorsing GLAAD's position, saying nothing, or supporting John, HRC chose the latter. As the dominant organization of the gay and lesbian movement, HRC could probably afford to distance itself from GLAAD, just as it had when Smith (reportedly) approved funding for StopDrLaura.com's rival anti-Schlessinger campaign. GLAAD's leaders, by contrast, showed little desire to engage HRC in an internecine battle. A few months later, at the 2001 Washington Media Awards, GLAAD gave HRC a special recognition award for the latter's Equality Rocks concert, which had been held the previous year in conjunction with HRC's Millennium March on Washington, which GLAAD had decided not to endorse. For the GLAAD board, recognizing the concert constituted a way to appease tensions between the organizations.

Smith's decision to side with John infuriated Spurgeon. During an informal chat in his office, Spurgeon told me: "My counterpart at HRC has no idea what we're doing ... He never called me. It's a cavalier, disrespectful thing to do." I asked him why he thought Smith had taken a position that undermined GLAAD's efforts. Spurgeon answered: "He just likes to see his name in print." A few months earlier, I had asked another GLAAD staffer why she thought Smith had decided to give money to StopDrLaura.com. She responded that Smith was "green" and "just likes to have his name in the papers."

I asked Spurgeon if he had spoken to Smith since becoming GLAAD communications director. He answered that he had called him three times, on one occasion because he knew that Smith was in Los Angeles; and that only one of those phone calls had been returned, and only to say that Smith could not "make time" to meet. Spurgeon said that he

considers it "a disservice to the community when the two communications directors of the two most visible organizations don't even talk to
each other," and added that he had worked in a highly competitive environment during his corporate career and had never encountered such
treatment. In the corporate world, he said, he "would expect a call from
his competitors" every so often, and even have lunch with them once in
a while. Why is it, he asked, that people who are "not competitors" cannot talk to each other "colleague to colleague"?

If Spurgeon insisted that he and Smith were not competitors, it was
because he recognized that GLAAD and HRC are both LGBT movement
organizations. They were also not competitors in the sense that each of
the major movement organizations have carved out areas of expertise to
which they are devoted more or less exclusively: national politics, state
politics, local community services, media, legal issues, education, etc.
Despite this high degree of specialization, however, issues rarely stay
contained within a single area and organizations still compete for the
same resources, one of which is media visibility.

That HRC and GLAAD were competitors for the rewards made available by the LGBT movement game was also clear from the way David
Steward, the co-chair of the board, introduced me jokingly at a board
meeting as a "spy from HRC." Steward's joke initially struck me as
strange: would it not have made more sense to say I was spy from a conservative Christian organization like the Family Research Council? But
then I realized that in the movement field, the spies one really worries
about are from like-minded competitors for donors and visibility, not
ideological opponents. This struck me as significant because, throughout my fieldwork, GLAAD's leaders were so careful to try to safeguard
the fiction that sister movement organizations were allies and not competitors. The most frequent reason they gave for denying me access to
particular meetings, besides that "personnel issues" might be discussed,
was that "comments about other organizations might come up."

In his comments to me about his tense relationship with Smith, Spurgeon insisted that GLAAD and HRC were the "two most visible organizations" of the movement. By pointing to GLAAD's visibility, as they
often did, GLAAD leaders could imagine that they occupied positions
comparable to those of HRC's leaders, despite the fact that HRC was
a larger, wealthier, and more politically influential organization. To the

extent that GLAAD was as visible as HRC during this period of my field-work, GLAAD found itself attracting much more media attention than it normally "should" have. That HRC may have wanted to bring GLAAD down a peg follows from this observation.

A survey of GLAAD's membership conducted in 2000 offers further insight into this competitive relationship. The survey found that fully 75 per cent of GLAAD members also made financial contributions to HRC. As a whole, GLAAD's members were 75 per cent male, 93 per cent white, and 28 per cent had incomes over $100,000 a year; 58 per cent claimed to read a newspaper every single day, including on weekends. The two organizations were competing for the same white, male, often wealthy, newspaper-reading funding base. No wonder, then, that GLAAD communications staffers were quick to dismiss Smith for liking to see his name in the papers. His ability to intervene in, and get quoted on, "their" issues with impunity was a thorn in their side and a hindrance to their mandate to advance GLAAD's institutional positioning.

In the field of professional activism, cultural authority tends to accrue where it has already taken root. The more dominant one is, the more likely one is to "see one's name in the papers" and the less it is to one's advantage to have very much to do with the smaller players, lest such as-sociations heighten their profiles. In this sense, as an organization whose visibility was growing in the mainstream, GLAAD represented something of an emerging threat to HRC's cultural authority. This might explain, in part, why Spurgeon had so much trouble getting Smith to return his phone calls, and why Smith was less than supportive of GLAAD's Dr Laura and Eminem campaigns. This dynamic, whereby the leaders of a large movement organization defend their cultural authority against emerging threats by less-dominant actors, might also explain why Spur-geon himself was often reluctant to deal with, and sometimes dismis-sive of, the movement's smaller organizations.

I sat one day in Spurgeon's office in early February 2001 as he spoke with Loe, who was returning his phone call. He told Loe that Seomin had received a pilot tape of a new sitcom based on the movie *Kiss Me Guido*. He explained that Seomin had been involved with the show from the very beginning and had "kept pushing" the producers for "diver-sity, diversity," given that the program is set in New York City. The "good news," he said, is that the producers cast an "Asian guy as the

main character's sidekick." The bad news, Spurgeon told Loe, is that
the character is the "nelliest, gayest" character imaginable, just as he
was in the movie, "except that now he's Asian." Could Javier run this
tape through his "sensitivity filter," Spurgeon asked? (Since Loe was
Javier's supervisor, such requests had to go through her.) After Loe
agreed, Spurgeon added the proviso that the tapes not be shared with
anyone else: "We get these tapes on the good graces of production companies," he said, "we wouldn't want Loren to shop this tape around to
this and that small interest group like the American Chinese yada,
yada, yada." This was, he said, to be "fair to producers." Although
Spurgeon was right to point out that it was not in producers' best interests to have multiple "interest groups" involved in shaping the content of productions, it was also true that it was not in GLAAD's best
interests to provide other organizations with opportunities to give input
into Hollywood productions. Movement organizations wield the most
cultural authority when they act as the lone, or at least leading, spokespersons on any given topic.

Thus, John's participation in the Grammys was, from GLAAD's perspective, an unwelcome development not simply because it undermined
GLAAD's campaign messages, but also because it opened the door to a
number of other gay and lesbian positions being publically expressed on
the topic of Eminem. Ironically, then, the reporting of a wider range of
gay and lesbian opinion was perceived, from a public relations standpoint, not as a welcome expansion of discourse representing a broader
cross-section of GLAAD's LGBT constituency, but as a loss of strategic
efficacy. In a public relations campaign, success means limiting the
debate as much as possible to what can be controlled, keeping a lid on
too many complicating issues, sticking to strategic simplifications, and
getting media to cover favoured angles to the exclusion of all others. In
other words, success meant winning the competition to have one's position (and one's name) dominate in media.

It follows that media discussions of issues that deviated from the preferred message were perceived as threats to be neutralized. The most
complicated issue in this regard was Greene's incendiary charge, repeated in various media outlets, that GLAAD's Eminem campaign was
evidence of a politically correct double standard: "Hip-hop music has
been delving very explicitly into homophobia and misogynistic themes

for years. So all of these groups that are so liberal – GLAAD and women's groups or whatever – where the hell have they been all of these years? They didn't feel it was politically correct to come after African Americans. Now there's a white, blond punk running around pointing his middle finger at everybody, but his themes are nothing new."[9] Never mind that NARAS itself had been infamously slow to recognize hip hop at the Grammys: for years, for as long as rap music was primarily the domain of African American and other racial and ethnic minorities, the Grammys had been content to largely ignore its existence. Greene's statement was rife with the hypocrisy of one who felt confident that such claims would go unchallenged and allow NARAS to score public relations points at GLAAD's expense.

Greene's accusation infuriated communications staffers, one of whom referred to Greene as a "fucker" during a team meeting. In an interview, Spurgeon called Greene "a duplicitous character" who played "the race card" as a "dodge and divert tactic." He added that Eminem's "origin," i.e., his racial or ethnic identity, "had no bearing on our decision." Besides, Spurgeon pointed out, Dr Dre is African American and "the driving force behind Eminem." The problem was that Greene's accusation "wasn't something you could respond to really neatly," Spurgeon told me, and therefore was not something he felt comfortable responding to at all. Everyone knows, Spurgeon told his staff, that Eminem is a way for "Dr Dre to crossover into a bigger market," but addressing that issue was a "whole Pandora's box that's too big to open." "We've avoided talking race," he told them, because "it's too uncomfortable." He instructed his staff to "bring it back to high schools."

Spurgeon's comments suggested that the key to understanding why GLAAD took on Eminem, even though it had not tended to address past homophobic hip-hop lyrics, was not Eminem's whiteness per se but the fact that he was reaching "a bigger market" than had other hip-hop artists to that point. The implication in Greene's statement, then, despite its evident hypocrisy, was not without merit. GLAAD was only interested in Eminem insofar as his popularity extended to millions of white teenagers, a position consistent with its primary concern with mainstream media representation. So while the fact of Eminem's whiteness might have had "no bearing" on GLAAD's decision to mount a campaign against him, his massive popularity among white audiences most certainly did. That popularity was itself partly a function of Eminem's whiteness, which provided a point of identification for millions of white male teenagers. MTV producers implicitly recognized this when they began the 2000 VMAs broadcast with literally dozens of Eminem look-alikes flooding the aisles of Radio City Music Hall. It was as though MTV had decided to play up GLAAD's (and others') fears about "easily influenced adolescents who emulate Eminem's dress, mannerisms, words and beliefs."

As GLAAD's communications team struggled to refocus the campaign on its preferred message about the threat posed by Eminem to kids in high school – and away from "Elton John is a traitor," "the gay community is divided," or "GLAAD is racist" – the mood in the Los Angeles office began to grow tense. I arrived around 12:15 p.m. on 13 February 2001 to find that the door was locked. Hearing voices on the other side, I knocked softly, then loudly, and was let in. I asked Eric Wilks, who was the executive assistant/receptionist/office manager for the office, why the door was locked. He explained that an all-staff call had just been held to discuss security issues following the reception of an unusual amount of hate mail. Wilks informed me that the office door would remain locked until the situation had calmed down. He joked with Bill Pryor, the finance manager, that they should come up with a password like "'Shirley Temple is divine,' or something." Pryor, not missing a beat, turned on his heels and headed toward his office. "'Divine *is* Shirley Temple' would be better," came the repartee.

Later that afternoon, Spurgeon told me that he had wanted to release the hate messages to media as evidence of the potentially violent impact of Eminem's lyrics. On the advice of the Los Angeles Police Department, however, he decided not to disseminate the messages because they might spawn imitators. One in particular raised concerns: "By the way i'd [*sic*] be careful when you [*sic*] mail arrives. Not everything in a small box is nice." Later that day, just as Spurgeon was about to leave the office, a suspicious-looking old box covered in packing tape arrived via courier, causing a bit of a stir. It turned out to contain an extra-large white T-shirt with "GLAAD" printed on it. Spurgeon told me that the shirt had been specially ordered in response to a tip from a GLAAD-friendly industry insider who had been present during a Grammys production meeting when Eminem had reportedly blurted out: "I want to wear a fucking GLAAD T-shirt." In response to the tip, the communications team had decided to make one and send it to Eminem on the off chance that he might actually wear it during his performance. One GLAAD staffer even speculated during a meeting that Eminem might reveal the T-shirt when speaking in the voice of Stan, the "obsessed fan" with a "romantic crush" on Eminem.

Meanwhile, the controversy about Eminem had become *the* story of that year's Grammys. On 12 February 2001 alone, Seomin gave fourteen interviews on the topic. He told one reporter that he might as well have organized a "junket at the Four Seasons." Despite the intense media interest, many communications staffers were growing concerned that their two main events, the town hall meeting with NARAS and the protest on the day of the Grammys, might be poorly attended. During a meeting, Spurgeon anxiously told his staff: "I think we'll need no less than 250 [people] to be taken seriously." Seomin accused other organizations of not supporting the protest sufficiently. He said during a staff meeting that he had spent the last two years at GLAAD listening to people on the programs team talk about "coalition-building," but "when we call on them to produce bodies, they don't come through." Be that as it may, this way of referring to gay and lesbian community members as bodies, which was common in communications team discussions about the Grammys events (often in the form of "we need all the bodies we can get"), was perhaps symptomatic of another set of reasons why the protest was not attracting the wished-for level of community support: it appeared that some GLAAD staffers thought of protesters not as agents voicing their concerns, but as human props in a stage-managed media spectacle, like a studio audience at a television taping or movie extras answering a casting call.

Both the communications team events held in conjunction with the Grammys were scheduled to accommodate media crews rather than protesters. The town hall meeting, which GLAAD staff hoped would be attended by high school students, was scheduled for 3:30 p.m. on a Tuesday at the downtown library. Not only would most students still be in school, but the downtown location meant that it would be difficult to get to because of Los Angeles's peculiar geography. As for the protest, it was scheduled for 3 p.m. the following day. That decision had been arrived at after an end-of-day brainstorming session between Spurgeon and Lund. Unsure as to when to schedule the protest, Spurgeon told Lund that he would "put a call ... to our friends in the media" and ask them, "When would you expect us to be there?"

If the communications team could count on one thing, it was support from an unlikely (and somewhat unwelcome) source: Lynne Cheney, wife of then vice president Dick Cheney. Asked by CNN to comment on the Eminem-John duet, Cheney said: "Elton John has been so good in the past speaking out on issues of equality for gay people, on issues of being against violent language against gay people ... I am quite amazed and dismayed that he would choose to perform with Eminem."[10] Cheney might as well have been using GLAAD's talking points. Had she suddenly developed a compulsion to defend gay and lesbian people (perhaps, given her openly lesbian daughter) or was something else going on?

Cheney's testimony to a September 2000 hearing of a Senate committee about marketing violence to children provides some additional context. Cheney, who is the former chair of the National Endowment for Humanities, told committee chair John McCain: "I have lately been very disturbed by the lyrics of the rap singer Eminem." The lyrics, she said, "could not be more despicable. They could not be more hateful in their attitudes toward women in particular. There are many groups that Eminem is quite despicable toward. But he is a violent misogynist." Not especially known for her feminism or advocacy on behalf of the groups targeted by Eminem's lyrics, Cheney's concerns made more sense in light of other statements in her testimony in which she paraphrased her "good friend" Peggy Noonan, a cultural conservative known for her efforts to sanitize popular culture. Children, Cheney stated, are like "intelligent fish swimming in a deep ocean" whose "waves are more and more about sex and violence." Quoting Noonan directly, Cheney added that the danger is that, unlike their parents, today's children "never had a normal culture against which to balance the newer, sicker one ... The water in which they swim is the only water that they have ever known."[11]

As Richard Kim pointed out in the *Nation*, the parallels between the rhetoric of GLAAD and Cheney on the topic of Eminem recalled the "unholy alliance" between cultural conservatives and anti-porn feminists. These parallels made some GLAAD staffers uneasy. One day, I sat in Renna's office as she was interviewed on Baltimore public radio. "I'm not Lynne Cheney," she said, "but we oddly agree on some things now, which is weird." Spurgeon, in an interview with me, summed up the reaction of GLAAD's leadership to Cheney's public comments as: "That's frighteningly close to what we're saying." He told me that GLAAD had sent Cheney a letter that offered to "share our information" regarding Eminem "if that will help you in formulating your opinion." "The thinking there," Spurgeon explained, "was [that] this may be the one and only chance in four years that she would acknowledge, maybe I have something to learn from the gay community." Cheney declined to meet or talk.

Spurgeon was quick to distance himself from this effort at rapprochement and to minimize its potential ramifications. He told me: "I can't imagine we'd have anything in common with Lynne Cheney, so this was pretty surprising. So it was like, it was almost like the poem 'Convergence of the Twain.' You know, there was this brief, brief nanosecond in time when Lynne Cheney and GLAAD's messages intersected and we thought, well, for this nanosecond, let's at least acknowledge that." The motivations may have been different, but the shared framing of the issue as being about nothing more (or less) than the impact of lyrics on children and teenagers had led both GLAAD and Cheney down the same narrow path. This position, because it abstracted the lyrics from any social context, advanced the view that certain words set to music were simply unacceptable under any circumstances. Eminem's lyrics, in short, were simply indecent and therefore offensive, a way of framing the debate that had GLAAD climbing into bed with conservative culture warriors like Cheney and Noonan.

If GLAAD's leaders chose this position, I would argue, it was not because they were unaware that the cultural impact of Eminem's music and lyrics was a complex issue, but because it was a position that played well to media frames for covering cultural controversies. In an interview with me, Spurgeon expressed his conviction that GLAAD had been responsible for making the debate about the impact of Eminem's lyrics on children into an important national news story. "GLAAD really did tip this one," he told me, using the language of Malcolm Gladwell's (2000) book, *The Tipping Point*. "We had to do so little," he said, because US culture was ready to have this conversation. He added that for years his job was to have a sense of "where the marketplace is" and that the communication team's success in tipping the Eminem story "really is where my marketing background comes into play."

Spurgeon's comments about the marketplace made clear the extent to which GLAAD's messages in the Eminem campaign, with their emphasis on the presumed impact of decontextualized lyrics on children and teenagers, were tailored to reach the mass of worried middle-class parents that populate the United States suburbs. They were tailored, in other words, for maximum dissemination within mainstream media. From the standpoint of the amount of media coverage devoted to the controversy, the strategy worked wonders. The GLAAD and NARAS town hall meeting was broadcast by MSNBC in its entirety and covered by the *Today Show* and literally dozens of other media outlets. The rally received even broader coverage, including on MSNBC, the *Today Show*, *Good Morning America*, and CNN. As Spurgeon told the GLAAD board, the rally received coverage from "every major outlet you can think of with the exception of the *Advocate*."

The scope and intensity of this media coverage stood in sharp contrast to the striking lack of participation by GLAAD's gay and lesbian constituencies. In its coverage of the town hall meeting, the *Minneapolis Star-Tribune* noted, "about 125 people attended the forum at the Los Angeles Public Library, but half were media."[12] An article in the *Boston Globe* about the rally stated that "the protest outside the Grammys yesterday was as dull as the music awards show is often accused of being" and that "TV cameras almost outnumbered demonstrators."[13] In an interview with me, Spurgeon admitted that the turnout for both events had been disappointing: between one hundred and 150 people for the rally, and less than half of that for the town hall meeting. Among the reasons for this lack of participation, he cited the downtown location of both events, the lack of an "industry heavy-hitter," the difficulty of getting young people to attend the town hall meeting, and "urban phobia," namely white people's fears about venturing into predominantly non-white neighbourhoods (downtown Los Angeles borders on predominantly black and Latino areas). Ultimately, Spurgeon said he recognized that "the issue was a little remote for people and there was so much division on the topic." Unlike the Schlessinger campaign, he said, "a lot of folks didn't necessarily see this as their issue, so I don't think there was a lot of motivation to go through the many hurdles ... to be down there to attend."

Kristen Schilt, a doctoral student in sociology who was interning at GLAAD as part of an ethnographic methods class, attended the rally and shared her field notes with me (I was in New York at the time). Her impression was that there were only about one hundred people there, including media: about twenty people in their late teens and early twenties; about twenty middle-aged men; and the rest GLAAD staff, media, and representatives from NOW and the other participating organizations. Schilt's account goes on to describe how participants at the rally invoked race to support their arguments about the unacceptability of Eminem's lyrics. NOW's Patricia Ireland, she noted, argued that Eminem's label would not have released a record by a Ku Klux Klan grand dragon that contained racial invective. A demonstrator whom Schilt described as looking "like a stereotype of a gay muscle man" (huge arms, goatee, leather vest and cap, Gold's Gym T-shirt, and denim shorts) handed out lyrics to a rap song parody whose lyrics posed the question, why is Eminem free to spout homophobia when he would never be allowed to use "the N-word"? Invited speaker Robin Tyler pulled out a sheet of paper, apologized for what she was about to read, and explained that she had taken the slurs about gays, lesbians, and transgender people in an excerpt of Eminem's lyrics and replaced them with racial insults. Tyler's new version blared over the loudspeakers: "My words are like a dagger with a jagged edge, stab you in the head whether you're a nigger or a kike, a wop or a chink. Hate niggers, the answer's yes." Schilt, who described feeling extremely uncomfortable, wrote in her notes that "a few people from the sides started booing." For all the care GLAAD's communications team had taken not to discuss race with media in connection with Eminem, they could not prevent rally participants from doing so. The manner in which they did so, furthermore, was illustrative of African American lesbian feminist scholar Barbara Smith's (1999, 651) argument that white feminists and gay and lesbian activists often use race to draw analogies to their own struggles when doing so helps advance their objectives, and then almost always in the absence of substantive anti-racist analysis or practice.

I returned to New York about a week before the Grammys after I had attended a GLAAD board meeting and spent a few days observing rally preparations in the Los Angeles office. I watched the Grammys broadcast in the basement lounge of Splash!, a popular gay bar in the Chelsea district that had advertised its lounge as a good place to watch the show. I paid particular attention to the reactions of the bar's patrons as Eminem won every award for which he was nominated with the exception of record of the year. Those reactions were, to say the least, mixed: some cheered as Eminem walked on stage to accept his awards, a few booed, and those who had cheered when he won screamed in outrage when he was denied record of the year. The Eminem-John duet really caught the attention of these patrons, most of whom ceased conversation and appeared riveted to the screen during the performance. Afterwards, as Eminem and John hugged on stage, most of them cheered.

I shared these observations with Spurgeon, who said he was not surprised by what I described. He immediately pointed out that my sample was "not our audience." "It doesn't really matter what the boys at Splash! think," he said. Who exactly was the intended audience of GLAAD's Eminem campaign, then, I asked him. Steve responded: "Kids … kids in school who are held hostage in this environment for hours a day and if you're the victim there's nowhere to run, nowhere to hide. I truly, truly, truly believe it is about victimization and the permission that these lyrics give some kids to make other kids feel worthless. And to me, in my head, that was always where the audience was and then, secondarily, the parents who allow the allowances to be spent for that." His eyes literally teared up as he said this and I did not doubt for a moment the sincerity of his response.

Still, Spurgeon's comments begged a question: if all that mattered was what kids and their parents thought about Eminem, then what could be said of GLAAD's claim to represent a gay and lesbian constituency, let alone a gay and lesbian constituency that includes people of colour? Spurgeon appeared little concerned about such considerations. The important thing, he told me, is to adopt a clear position: "You can't say 'a lot of folks think this, and a lot of folks think that.' You have to put a stake in the ground." GLAAD's position on any given issue, he argued, does not claim to represent what everyone in the gay and lesbian community thinks. A position expresses "how this organization, which has a charter about defamation, believes these words have impact." When HRC comes out with a position about a candidate, he analogized, it does not represent every gay and lesbian person in the United States, but "a politically savvy opinion that represents a gay point of view."

No matter, then, that the savvy gay point of view happened to correspond to a Christian conservative point of view, as long as it got the right kind of mainstream media coverage. The parallel with HRC is striking, given that organization's infamous 1998 endorsement of then New York governor Alfonse d'Amato, an anti-abortion Republican who had supported modest anti-discrimination legislation protecting gays and lesbians but whose Democratic challenger was far more progressive overall. The supposedly "politically savvy" endorsement, in any case, backfired completely as d'Amato's Democratic rival won the election. Similarly, GLAAD's framing of the Eminem issue as about little more than the presumed direct links between words and violence raised serious questions about just whose gay point of view the organization could claim to represent in an Eminem campaign based on equating offensive lyrics and anti-gay violence. That particular framing did manifestly little to elicit the participation of a gay and lesbian constituency, and particularly of gays and lesbians of colour, whose relationships to Eminem and hip hop were considered too complicated to warrant public discussion.

### The Programs Team

Another part of GLAAD, the programs team, devised a radically different, if much more modest, way to address the Eminem controversy. It organized a panel discussion in New York City, "Homie-Sexual Hip-Hop," that highlighted the relationships between hip hop, race, place, class, gender, and sexuality. This event garnered almost no media coverage outside of student and community-based newspapers, but attracted dozens of people – many of them young, many of them African American, many of them active participants in hip-hop culture – to GLAAD's New York office. The panellists were James Earl Hardy, author of the popular B-boy Blues novel series about life "on the down low"; Karter Louis, a gay hip-hop and R&B artist; Shanté Smalls, a fellow of Amnesty International's Outfront program; Jason King, an adjunct professor at New York University who teaches a class about hip hop; and Star Perkins, a lesbian feminist activist and hip-hop DJ.

The panel was held at GLAAD's midtown headquarters and was organized by two programs team staffers: Javier, who flew out from San Francisco to moderate the panel, and Jay Plum, a staffer for GLAAD's Research and Analysis Program who helped find the panellists. When I arrived, I found the conference room absolutely packed, with some people spilling out into the hallway. I estimated the crowd at about seventy, and well over half were people of colour. Audience members were also younger on average than was typical for any other GLAAD events I attended. The average age, it looked to me, was somewhere in the mid-twenties, with a few participants in their late thirties or early forties.

The conference room was so full, in fact, that a number of staff, including Loe and junior members of the programs, development, and operations teams, had gathered in Loe's office, located beside the conference room, to make room for the guests. I found everyone assembled around Loe's computer screen, and Loe surfing the website of Good Vibrations, a woman-owned sex-toy store based in San Francisco. An animated, light-hearted discussion ensued about the pros and cons of various toys, why so many dildos were shaped like animals, the need for lube in anal sex, and other such sexual trivia. One visibly anxious staffer wondered out loud whether discussing such matters at work was appropriate and was told by another: "What's the problem? We're sex positive here." Suddenly, a junior communications staffer who had been in the conference room listening to the panel discussion burst into Loe's office and announced excitedly: "Okay! I just need to say that, from a communications standpoint, I have a real problem with them talking about race when we've been trying so hard to stay away from race. I have a real problem with that." An awkward silence fell over the room as everyone looked to Loe, the only senior staffer in the room, for a response. Loe, impassive, remained silent and waited for the realization to dawn on the communications staffer that the comment was not welcome. She then gently redirected the conversation back to Good Vibrations.

The junior staffer's outburst and Loe's refusal to dignify it with an answer was an indication that the programs team had organized the "Homie-Sexual Hip-Hop" panel precisely *because* the communications team had "been trying so hard to stay away from race." The point of the panel was to gather people knowledgeable about hip hop to discuss how not only race, but also gender, sexuality, and class, structured the white mainstream's reactions to Eminem and GLAAD's approach to its campaign. One panellist, King, said:

> There's never a moment when we're outside of race, or outside of sexuality or outside of class. Because of the nature of the society in which we live we're always in those modes. And so, it's never convenient to suddenly disassociate yourself from race to talk about homophobia ... It's also part of the way in which heterosexism gets consolidated, is around white supremacy ... You have to read [Eminem] in terms of race and in terms of sexuality in order to figure that out. I think if you're willing to discard one or the other, you don't understand his power, his claim to authenticity.

Eminem's appeal, the panellists asserted, is in large part based on his ability, as an ostensibly heterosexual white male, to claim authenticity in relation to black performance traditions. They differed as to the validity of this claim to authenticity, but all agreed with Smalls that "if Eminem were black we wouldn't be having this discussion," because, Hardy added, "no one would have heard of him." He continued: "There's definitely a really crazy kind of reverse racism going on with Eminem. You know, this white boy who is selling millions of copies of records to other disaffected and angry and angst-ridden white youth ... And quite frankly, Caucasian, white queer America is scared because now a face has been put on rap music that looks exactly like them."

Hardy went on to point out that until Eminem came along, mainstream journalism had devoted lots of attention to anti-police, anti-white, and anti-Semitic elements of hip hop and virtually ignored its homophobic, heterosexist, or even sexist and misogynistic elements. Yet these sexist and homophobic elements have been present in hip hop for years. Where was "white queer America," Hardy asked, when rap music's reach had not yet extended to the white suburbs? Hardy made this point even more explicitly in an interview published in the (short-lived) journal of GLAAD's Center for the Study of Media and Society, *Images*. Asked why Eminem had "become such a lightening rod," Hardy said: "Because he is white. And given that the majority of gay bashings are committed by white males and they make up the bulk of Eminem's audience, it was no surprise that there was such a loud outcry from white queers. Such a response also points to just how racist the gay activist movement and media are. Homophobia in rap wasn't worthy of being vigilantly challenged when it had a black face and, as such, only directly impacted African American and other same-gender-loving people of color."[14]

Hardy explained that many African American men "on the down-low" see the gay identity promulgated by movement organizations like GLAAD as a white construction that "has nothing to do with affirming me as a black person." Expanding on this theme, the panellists pointed out that the national gay and lesbian magazines, driven by profit, feature virtually no people of colour and do little to support gay and lesbian artists, let alone gay and lesbian artists of colour. An audience member who had once been the only person of colour on the editorial board of a gay and lesbian publication said that he was told time and time again that putting a person of colour on the cover was "economic suicide." Unless the organizations and media of the gay and lesbian movement start supporting queer-affirmative cultural forms that are of value and interest to people of colour, this audience member said, the only alternative will be to create "our own separate community."

Another audience member, an African American gay man in his early twenties, stated, "Eminem is closer to my culture and my interests than the GLAAD protest is." This sentiment was widely shared among the panellists, all of whom noted the existence of gay, lesbian, and feminist hip-hop communities and the importance of hip-hop music in their own lives. In addition to being a "space of aggression," King said, hip hop is a "space of expansion" that holds the promise of contributing to what he called "critical social diversity." In fact, he argued, hip hop may be the most homosocial and homoerotic music ever made. "It's so homo-erotic," Hardy piped in, "because there are so many homosexuals [in hip hop]!" Noting how "different the discourse in this room is from the dis-course I get in my [inbox] from GLAAD," the young audience member expressed his hope that the evening's discussions might inform GLAAD's positions in the future.

After the panel, Javier invited audience members to stay and interact informally with GLAAD staff, the panellists, and one another. Unlike al-most every other GLAAD event I attended during my fieldwork, this one did not include Absolut-sponsored vodka drinks. There was, however, a modest spread of Middle Eastern food: hummus, baba ghanoush, lentil salad, and pita bread presented in large Tupperware containers, as well as cans of soda that had been brought over from the staff room. As I moved about the room, I heard the young man who had spoken toward the end of the panel discussion reiterate his reservations about the Eminem protest. He and his friends, he told Loe and Plum, did not agree with the protest and wondered how GLAAD, which, he said, is supposed to represent the community, had decided to go ahead with it. "I mean," he said, "I was never polled." GLAAD's public stance on Eminem, he continued, "makes it sound as though the entire community is irate." His own feeling, however, was that "people who don't know hip hop are irate," and as for the rest, "some like Eminem, some don't." That said, he thought it was "fine to protest," although he did not recognize himself or his views in GLAAD's position. "Thanks for the panel, though," he said as he turned toward the door. As he left the GLAAD office, a development staffer handed him an invitation to an upcoming Media Awards kick-off party. As many exiting attendees pointed out to GLAAD staffers, it was ironic that the party they were being invited to was at a Chelsea bar called g, which had a well-deserved reputation for catering almost exclusively to upscale, professional, gay white men.

The panellists posed for photos with Javier before they left the GLAAD office. Two group shots were taken, the respective merits of which I heard a handful of staffers discuss a few days later. Everyone taking part in the discussion agreed that the picture in which the panellists were playfully adopting hip-hop poses was more interesting and reflective of the spirit of the event than the one in which they were standing conservatively in an orderly row. However, a communications staffer said that she thought GLAAD's publications manager would prefer the more conservative pose for the newsletter sent out to members. The hip-hop pose, she pointed out, featured one of the female panellists grabbing her crotch. "That will never fly," she said, adding, "it's too bad, though."

I noticed that many audience members from the hip-hop panel did indeed show up at the Media Awards kick-off party at g a few days later. Instead of hummus and pita bread, they were treated to a catering spread with an elaborate French country theme: fancy cheeses, crackers, and artichokes artfully distributed around a giant hock of ham. A decorative basket of hard-boiled quail and chicken eggs completed the arrangement.

Feeling adventurous, and having never before eaten a quail egg, I could not help but carefully peel one and pop it into my mouth. "Like chicken egg but with a more delicate flavour," I told a GLAAD staffer.

g, enveloped in elegant light-tan wood with a large circular bar as its centrepiece, gradually filled up with as many as eighty to 120 people. At the height of the evening's attendance, one of the New York Media Awards co-chairs got up on a small stage. He was flanked on either side by giant Absolut bottles: one made out of Plexiglas, the other projected onto the wall. He was wearing a dark business suit and appeared to be in his early forties, tanned (in February in New York), with well-groomed, jet-black hair. He talked about the importance of the Media Awards for GLAAD's fundraising and encouraged all table hosts – people who had made commitments to recruit a certain number of paid attendees – to keep selling tickets. This should not be too difficult, he emphasized, because the tickets are a tax write-off. He then described the event as "one of the four best husband-hunting events in New York City." Then, as though realizing for the first time that there were also women present – most of whom were not likely to be looking for husbands – he added, sheepishly, "and hopefully soon there will be more women also."

A few weeks later, the Spring 2001 issue of GLAAD's newsletter arrived in the mailboxes of GLAAD members. It featured a two-page spread about the Eminem campaign that included a paragraph touting "Homie-Sexual Hip-Hop" as one of "three high-profile events on the two coasts to keep a focus on hate lyrics." The panel was described thus: "A standing-room-only audience engaged in a lively discussion that once again placed GLAAD as a community leader." The accompanying photo showed the panellists standing in an orderly row, smiling broadly, their hands a respectable distance from their crotches.

## Virtual Diversity

During the February 2001 GLAAD board meeting, as Garry left to be interviewed about Eminem by an NBC *News* crew, board members split up into three groups and were asked to rank the following organizational priorities: (1) expanding GLAAD's Internet presence and online activism; (2) diversifying to include so-called ethnic and non-English speaking media; and (3) investing in GLAAD's regional offices to make them more functional. When Garry returned, each group reported about the priorities it had identified for the organization. The first group said that regional offices had emerged as the first priority, closely followed by Internet advocacy. Diversification, it said, came third because the group felt the "impact" GLAAD could have in this area is "not immense." The second group ranked Internet advocacy as its first priority, followed by diversification and regional offices. This group reasoned that "digital online media is here to stay" and that investing in it provides opportunities to incorporate "multiple languages," address "diversity" concerns, and create mechanisms for "giving online." The third group, finally, reported that "emotionally," it felt that the "most important was diversity," but that when it came down to the actual voting, "digital got more points." Regional offices, it said, was the "lowest on our list by far." By the end of the discussion, a weak consensus had emerged that investing in digital media might also contribute to addressing regional and diversity goals and was therefore the most desirable option.

Advertising executive Howard Buford, whose last board meeting this was, raised his hand and asked to speak. In a cool tone of voice, he pled the case that diversifying the communities GLAAD serves is "the one most" important thing GLAAD could do as an organization. Diversity, he said, "affects every issue" and goes to the core of "who we are and who we are working for." "I hope," he stated, "that we are not choosing not to do this because it is harder than the others." "Is this then going to be the total diversity of the organization?" he asked, as a pall descended upon the room. (There was only one other person of colour in attendance besides Buford, a Los Angeles lawyer by the name of Richard Kim whose first and last board meeting this was. By the time of the following board meeting in June, he had resigned, leaving no people of colour on the GLAAD board.) Buford's tone then became more insistent as he declared: "Even the most white-shoe firms in America get it ... For God's sake, even American Express gets it!" "We have to mean something to a larger base of people," Buford said. "Don't not choose it because it's the hardest, most transforming, most difficult thing you can do."

In the weeks that followed the board meeting, Garry and the rest of the management team developed an analysis of GLAAD's organizational priorities. It emphasized digital media as GLAAD's "number 1 priority."

"A strong position in digital media," Garry wrote in a report, "will establish GLAAD as the 'cutting edge' queer non-profit (a niche that will be available only until the void is filled)." Large investments in GLAAD's Internet capabilities, the management team argued, would also serve the organization's regional and diversity objectives by making it possible to use the Internet to "engage, recruit, train and communicate with … an army of volunteer media monitors all across the country." "A virtual team covering Spanish language television or Korean American print," the management team concluded, "can be easily set up using the same basic model we might use in Minneapolis to cover key electronic and print outlets there."

Rather than invest in adequate staffing and infrastructure for GLAAD's regional offices – the cost of which the management team evaluated at $200,000 annually per office – or develop a range of programs targeted at the needs and interests of racial, ethnic, and linguistic minorities, then, GLAAD's leaders proposed to invest in technology. This priority offered one major advantage over the others: "Funding opportunities abound with an aggressive plan to use technology to drive our work forward. A thoughtful plan can be presented to corporations in Silicon Valley, to foundations and to individuals. A new kind of development 'campaign' can be created around it."

Accordingly, in February 2002, Garry announced that GLAAD was closing its offices in Atlanta, Kansas City, and Washington, DC; further centralizing its operations in New York City and Los Angeles; and investing in its Internet capabilities. The San Francisco office would remain open for a short time but was later quietly shut down. In a letter to GLAAD's membership, Garry described the decision to close GLAAD's regional offices as a "new regional strategy" designed to "create a smarter, more effective approach to regional and local media outreach." The organization would hire five "regional media managers," based in New York City and Los Angeles, "to support regional initiatives in key cities" and "make a six-figure investment in the re-engineering of glaad.org to create a place in which members like you can feel a part of GLAAD where you can get involved, interact with us and with one another, where your voice can be heard." This was not a "move to 'close' offices," she claimed, so much as an "increased commitment to our work in local and regional media." "Regional media is our #1 priority this year," Garry declared in the letter.

Writing in the *Washington Blade* about the decision to close offices and invest in GLAAD's website, executive editor (and former GLAAD board member) Chris Crain argued, "unfortunately, GLAAD is engaging in the sort of media spin that it specializes in training other gay activists to employ when the press starts calling. The truth is that, whatever GLAAD's recent success in the entertainment media capitals of New York and Los Angeles, the organization has been MIA in its lobbying efforts elsewhere."[15] The decision to invest in technology was also criticized by Buford, who, in an interview with me, expressed the view that investing in digital media was far from the best way for GLAAD to reach African American and Spanish-speaking populations. Investing in Internet technology as a way to reach minority ethnic populations, Buford said, is not an idea "that would come from someone who lived in those communities, you would not land on digital as the answer." The decision, he said, was "not about reaching those people" but about "never hav[ing] to interact with them."

With the closing of the San Francisco office, Javier decided to leave the organization. Monica Taher, who was given the title of people of colour media director, replaced him. With her arrival, GLAAD began to monitor Spanish-language media and hand out Spanish-language Media Awards. In assessing what future "cultural interest media" initiatives should prioritize, a GLAAD management team report proposed that a focus on Spanish-language media, perhaps combined with the opening of a new GLAAD office in Miami, where all major Spanish language networks are located, would affirm "GLAAD's brand positioning as the forward-thinking, cutting-edge non-profit in the lgbt community" and, unlike other kinds of diversity initiatives, present significant "development opportunities."

Loe said in an interview with me that she believed GLAAD had "misplaced priorities." The organization, she said, had become highly responsive to donors, media professionals, and celebrities, but was paying comparatively little attention to serving its gay and lesbian constituencies or to taking what she called the temperature of the community. In early April 2001, Loe announced that she was resigning from her position at GLAAD to become the executive director of the Arizona Human Rights Fund. The announcement came during an all-staff meeting during which Garry explained that Loe was heeding "the call of the land" and returning to her first love, local and state-level organizing.

Plum also left shortly after I ended my fieldwork. In an interview, Plum told me that the centre he directed had been conceived as an autonomous think tank, much like the National Gay and Lesbian Task Force Policy Institute. In practice, he said, there was little "respect for academic pursuits or for intellectual pursuits" in many parts of GLAAD, and corporate values of efficiency, productivity, and "applicability to mission" had come to dominate over time. The Research and Analysis program was eventually disbanded without a formal announcement.

The communications team also underwent a near-complete staff turnover within a few years of my departure. Spurgeon left the organization under hushed circumstances. Seomin – who told me he had never intended to stay on as entertainment media director for more than five years – left in 2003. Renna left in 2004 after just over two years as news media director, to become a public relations consultant. Garry announced that she was leaving in June 2005, after eight years at the helm. When Garry arrived at GLAAD, the organization had an annual budget of $1.5 million and was struggling to meet its payroll. When she left, it had an annual budget of over $7 million.

# Mainstreaming's Ambivalent Embrace

Many of the hoped-for gains of mainstreaming have come to pass since my fieldwork at GLAAD ended in June 2001. The US Supreme Court has endorsed marriage equality; openly gay, lesbian, and bisexual people are serving in the military; opinion surveys in the United States are showing unprecedented levels of support for LGBT rights and causes; and LGBT visibility in entertainment and news media, by GLAAD's own accounting, has generally improved in both quantity and quality, especially on television.[1] Consider also that when Apple's chief executive officer, Tim Cook, came out in 2014, he was leading the largest publically traded company in the world; one could be forgiven for thinking that gay people had taken up residence at or near the centre of dominant institutions.

In this context, the moment is ripe to assess how and why we got here, what has been won and lost in the process, and what comes next as GLAAD – and the US LGBT movement more broadly – likely enter a period of self-redefinition. Has the battle for inclusion been won? And if so, does GLAAD still have a purpose? The successes of mainstreaming have led some on the conservative end of the LGBT movement to begin to write GLAAD's obituary. For example, James Kirchick, a young gay conservative reporter and columnist, claimed in the *Atlantic* in 2013 that GLAAD has won the culture war and "lost its reason to exist." "Not only are media representations of gays plentiful," Kirchick wrote, "they are almost overwhelmingly positive." "The best thing the organization could do is dissolve," he concluded, "not because it is actively harmful, but rather because it is a victim of its own success."[2]

Coming to the defence of GLAAD in the pages of the *American Prospect* a few weeks later, Gabriel Arana pointed out that to declare the culture war over, as Kirchick had, "is to write a huge number of people out of the movement" and ignore the fact that "about half of Americans oppose same-sex marriage, over 40 percent think gay relationships are immoral, and you can still be fired for being gay in 29 states." What Arana recognized is that the gains of mainstreaming, measured in terms of inclusion, have been distributed unevenly, a situation that "does raise an existential question for organizations like GLAAD, and for the movement: Once gays and lesbians achieve legal equality and the most privileged among us can live and work without fear or discrimination, are we done?"[3] For GLAAD, whose institutional survival depends on making a case for its continued relevance, the answer is a clear no.

In February 2015, GLAAD released *Accelerating Acceptance*, a report which outlined the results of a public opinion survey the organization commissioned in 2014. According to this report, recent victories at the legislative and judicial levels belie "a layer of uneasiness and discomfort" with LGBT people. The survey asked self-identified heterosexuals in the United States how they would feel if they saw a same-sex couple holding hands: 36 per cent said they would be uncomfortable. Similarly, 34 per cent stated they would feel uncomfortable attending a same-sex wedding. When asked if they would feel uncomfortable bringing a child to such a wedding, 43 per cent answered yes. Finally, asked if "they would be uncomfortable if they learned that their child was dating a transgender person," the percentage of uncomfortable heterosexuals shot up to 59 per cent. The latter two measures suggest that an observation Gayle Rubin (1993, 6) made decades ago still holds true: "The current wave of erotic terror has reached deepest," she wrote, "into those areas bordered in some way, if only symbolically, by the sexuality of the young." GLAAD's survey suggests that heterosexuals in the United States, by and large, still feel the need to protect children from queer difference and queer sexual knowledge. The gay and lesbian movement's emphasis since the 1990s on the "full inclusion of homosexuals in the

core institutions of American society" has brought us to a deeply ambivalent place (D'Emilio 2000, 49).

The rate of social change has been dramatic since the 1990s, but
mainstream attitudes toward LGBT people still run the gamut from affection to insult. If these ambivalent feelings are mutual, as I suspect
they are, they have the potential to positively reshape the relationships
between LGBT people and the dominant culture. Like lovers entering a
new phase of a relationship, we as LGBT people might claim more space
for ourselves by embracing mainstreaming more ambivalently, just as
the mainstream has ambivalently embraced us. In other words, we might
acknowledge the gains of mainstreaming for what they have made possible without fooling ourselves into thinking that the dominant culture's
extension of respectability to some of us has solved – or can solve – the
most intractable issues we face as a collectivity.

The queer critique of the politics of respectability bears repeating: the
gains that mainstreaming makes possible – inclusion for some in the dominant institutions of society – come at the cost of reinforcing exclusions
on the basis of race, class, and gender. But even those who benefit the
most from mainstreaming pay a price for entering into the gated community that respectability makes. When we draw lines between good and
bad LGBT subjects on the basis of heteronormative assumptions, we cut
ourselves off from our movement's histories of resistance to dominant
norms and participate in a process of diminishing our own present and
future possibilities for self-definition and community building. As much
as I would love an articulated politics of difference that could replace the
existing politics of sameness, I think a more plausible alternative would
consist of a politics conducted on multiple fronts across fields of sameness and difference: a politics of ambivalence.[4] In response to the dominant culture's ambivalent embrace of selected aspects of our lives, we
might tap into and expand upon our own ambivalent responses to the
partiality of our relative inclusion. Against the normalizing force of mainstreaming, we might deploy a politics that builds upon the sense of
heightened personal and political possibility that comes from occupying
cultural spaces that are simultaneously inside and out. We might refuse
the implicit mandate to decide between inclusion or exclusion, sameness
or difference, respectability or marginalization, by staking our claim to

the mainstream and, at the same time, cultivating the ground that sustains queer alternatives. To imagine such an ambivalent cultural politics is also to imagine a role for GLAAD in mediating between the mainstream and the margins and promoting dialogue at the interstices of public life.

My view, in sum, is not that GLAAD has outlived its usefulness, but that GLAAD and the LGBT movement more broadly have much to gain from adopting more ambivalent positions toward mainstreaming's politics of respectability. Such positions could be derived on the basis of reflecting critically about the past, learning from tensions and contradictions in the present, and thinking imaginatively about the future. I conclude this book, therefore, with some thoughts about the past, present, and future of LGBT media activism formulated in dialogue with GLAAD chief executive officer and president since 2014, Sarah Kate Ellis, whom I interviewed in February 2015, and four of the protagonists of the preceding chapters, all of whom agreed to a final round of interviews conducted in late 2014 to early 2015: Cathy Renna, former director of community relations and national news media director, Dilia Loe, former deputy director of programs and operations; Steve Spurgeon, former director of communication; and Joan Garry, GLAAD's executive director from 1997 to 2005.[5]

### Reflecting on the Past, Present, and Future of LGBT Media Activism

In this book, I have sought to describe and analyze how GLAAD, during a key period of its history, negotiated the historical tensions in the LGBT movement, most notably between assimilation versus liberation, accommodation versus confrontation, and single-issue organizing versus progressive coalition building. In so doing, my objective was to provide an empirical basis from which to chart a course beyond the politics of mainstreaming and the neoliberal realignments of the 1990s. This study has lent support to the queer critique of mainstreaming developed by authors like Urvashi Vaid (1995), Michael Warner (1999), Alexandra Chasin (2000), and Lisa Duggan (2003), among others, but it has also shown that many of the debates that have animated queer critics of LGBT movement politics since the 1990s simmered beneath the visible surface of GLAAD's mainstreaming agenda. GLAAD's embrace of mainstreaming, like that of many other queer subjects in neoliberal times, was not without its ambivalences. These pervasive, structuring ambivalences, insofar as they suggest aspects of mainstreaming that did not always sit well with its own subjects, are a good starting point for imagining new possibilities for the unfolding present and future of LGBT media activism.

*Ambivalence 1: The field of LGBT media activism is structured by a persistent activist/professional tension that tends to be resolved in the direction of corporatization.*

As I showed in chapter 2, GLAAD's leaders in 2000–01 were primarily oriented to the media field, which is to say that their perspectives on what constituted effective media activist strategies were shaped by structures of belief and action that emanated from corporate media settings rather than from within the gay and lesbian movement. Their stated motivations for engaging in movement work often stemmed from a strongly felt dissatisfaction with aspects of their corporate jobs, even as the corporate skills and experiences they had amassed became the model for their activism. They wanted to give more meaning to their lives by helping others and "giving something back to the community" by putting their corporate and professional expertise to better use. Their model for action, the 1999 strategic plan that mandated "We Want In!" as its rallying cry, led them to de-emphasize confrontation with dominant institutions and prioritize the marketing and publicity needs of corporate funders in the interests of organizational fundraising objectives. In sum, the importation of corporate models for thought and action into the media activist field, however much it may have been motivated by a desire to put business skills to more socially progressive uses, tended to reproduce the field in the image of the approaches and priorities favoured by the corporate world.

Since leaving GLAAD, both Garry, who came from the corporate media world, and Renna, who came from an activist background, have parlayed the mix of skills, connections, and expertise they acquired over the course of their careers into consultancies directed at the not-for-profit sector. Garry, who insisted in a 2015 interview with me that her stated reason for leaving GLAAD in 2005 (to spend more time with her kids) was the real reason she left, said that she initially drew up a seven-year plan for herself with the goal of making a play for "one last big really cool job." Instead, she ended up becoming what she termed "an accidental consultant," in addition to teaching classes on media and social change and non-profit communications strategy at the University of Pennsylvania's Annenberg School for Communication. "GLAAD changed me in a lot of ways," she told me, because the organization helped her "realize the power of my voice." She co-chaired the LGBT finance committee for Obama in 2008 and said that she "could have gone to Washington," but "never cashed in a chit for the money that I raised" because she "realized that in Washington you don't get to have your own voice." She told me that the "tipping point" was when she launched a blog in 2012, which became a way for her to have an "impact on a broad, diverse constellation of non-profit organizations to help them become more effective." The blog, she said, is "my way of evangelizing to non-profit leaders and is as close to evangelical as I will ever get." By building an audience for her blog – she mentioned a monthly figure of 45,000 unique visitors – she has also been able to attract clients for her consulting business, which specializes in providing "strategic advisory services" and "organizational diagnostics" to the leaders of non-profit organizations who are experiencing difficulties with things like crisis management, fundraising, board management, strategic planning, social media strategy, leadership transitions, and financial disarray.

Renna, for her part, left GLAAD in 2004 after fourteen years, and spent a couple years working for a public relations firm that specializes in advising not-for-profit organizations. She then founded her own specialized consultancy, which she described to me as "a public relations firm for the LGBT community." In an interview I conducted with her in late 2014, she said her work as a communications consultant is not so different from many of the things she was doing at GLAAD, except that she does not do "the watchdoggy part" and gets "to choose who I work with." She emphasized that she continues to see herself as an activist and her work as expression of that activism. Her clients, she said, are people "who are interested in getting coverage for issues that they're working on," as opposed to people seeking publicity for its own sake. "I don't have clients who just want to get their name in the paper," she said. Since leaving GLAAD, she told me, she has learned how to run a business and how to raise funds, which, combined with her existing strengths in media, community, and public relations, add up to a mix of skills that resembles Garry's cumulative professional profile, although Renna does not claim to have Garry's level of corporate experience.

Taken together, the trajectories of Garry and Renna both add up to an important role in spreading a model of activism that articulates the methods and professional ideologies of corporate and public relations work to the social change objectives of non-profit work. Both have succeeded in converting the cultural, social, and symbolic capital they accumulated at GLAAD into start-up businesses that extend the reach of corporatized and privatized forms of activism to new social locations, helping to produce an increasingly hybridized corporate/movement field in the process. Garry's focus on "evangelizing to non-profit leaders" and having an "impact on a broad, diverse constellation of non-profit organizations to help them become more effective," further extends her influence, which is clearly tied to the reputation she built as one of the movement's most successful leaders. She shared with me that someone had recently told her that she had "created the HR department for the movement as a result of the people that I [referring to herself] mentored and managed and shaped." Among these "rock star hires," as she put it, are Rashad Robinson, now the executive director of Color of Change – an organization whose mission is to "strengthen the political voice of black America" – and Glennda Testone, who became the executive director of the New York City LGBT Center in 2009.

Garry's continuing influence on GLAAD and the broader movement field can also be discerned in the 2014 appointment of Ellis as GLAAD's president and CEO (a more corporate-sounding position title that encompasses the functions previously designated by the title of executive director). Like Garry, Ellis is Irish American and comes out of a corporate media background, having worked in publishing for Time Inc. as the vice president of marketing for a variety of lifestyle brands, most notably the magazine *Real Simple*. Whereas Garry arrived at GLAAD with expertise in new business development, Ellis arrived with a reputation for launching, relaunching, or "turning around" media properties. Also like Garry, Ellis is partnered with children and her pre-GLAAD activism was rhetorically centred on her family. When I asked Ellis in an interview if she had been an activist before coming to GLAAD, she immediately brought up the memoir she co-wrote with her wife, Kristen Ellis-Henderson, entitled *Times Two: Two Women in Love and the Happy Family They Made*. She told me that the book, which was published by Simon & Schuster in 2011, is "about being pregnant at the exact same time" and what "the modern family looks like" (the book explains that Ellis and her partner became pregnant on the same day).[6] Ellis and her partner were also featured in the Style section of the *New York Times* in 2011 in conjunction with the legalization of same-sex marriage in New York State (their participation in that article was arranged by GLAAD staffers, who are often contacted by journalists working on stories).[7] Finally, Ellis and her wife, who is a member of the all-female country rock band Antigone Rising, were depicted kissing on the cover of *Time* in March 2013 as part of a feature story entitled "Gay Marriage Already Won." (Ellis was the vice president of marketing for the "lifestyle group" division of Time Inc.)[8]

It would be difficult to devise a more literal example of making out in the mainstream than the image of a corporate media marketing executive and her rock star wife sharing a tastefully photographed kiss on the cover of one of the most iconic news magazines in the United States. The image of the kiss, shot against a white background by photographer Peter Hapak, is made intimate through tight cropping, inviting a voyeuristic gaze. Strong shadows accentuate the jawlines of both participants, further lending the image a slight sexual frisson that recalls the famous photographs of Bruce Weber for fashion labels like Calvin Klein or Abercrombie & Fitch. That Ellis would later be appointed GLAAD's president and also happened to be promoting a book about family life co-written with someone promoting a band further illustrates my argument in this book: whereas earlier coming out strategies were oriented to the creation of a mass movement to advocate for civil rights, making out in neoliberal times tends toward a winner-take-all culture that favours specific personal, political, and economic interests as individuals and organizations compete to produce the most profitable and marketable versions of LGBT identity. And since the market is the principal mechanism by which the value of making out is produced, much of that value ends up benefitting corporations and their owners – although, when conditions are right, some of it can also end up in the coffers of a movement organization like GLAAD.

Given the similarities between the personal and professional profiles of Garry and Ellis, it would be difficult not to interpret Ellis's hiring as an attempt by the GLAAD board to recapture some of the success the organization had under Garry, especially in light of the financial and other difficulties GLAAD experienced after Garry left in 2005. Garry's first successor was the four-term former Republican mayor of Tempe, Arizona, Neil Giulano, who inherited an organization with revenues of $7.3 million in 2005 and left it in 2009 with $5.3 million in revenues and a shortfall of over $1.2 million for the year. GLAAD's next president was a former Massachusetts Democratic state senator by the name of Jarrett Barrios, who was forced to resign in 2011 following allegations that GLAAD had taken donations from AT&T in exchange for lending its support to a proposed corporate merger (see introduction). When all was said and done, eight board members followed Barrios out the door (one of them a lobbyist for AT&T), along with about a quarter of GLAAD's staff. The next president, appointed in April 2012, was Herndon Graddick, who had been at GLAAD since 2010 as vice president of programs and communications and was promoted from within the ranks. Prior to GLAAD, he had been a climate change activist and a television producer at CNN, E!, and Current TV – the failed attempt by Al Gore and other investors to build a progressive Fox News alternative. Graddick resigned from GLAAD in 2013 after just thirteen months at the helm, which included a long leave of absence. GLAAD's annual report for 2013 listed revenues of $3.7 million and a shortfall for the year of $1.2 million. In other words, GLAAD's annual revenues had fallen to roughly half of what they had been under Garry in 2005, not to mention that the organization had been accumulating deficits for years.

Ellis told me that she spent the first year of her tenure doing what she could to rescue GLAAD from imminent financial ruin, just as Garry had in 1997–98. "When I was being brought on," she said, "it was: she's either closing the organization down or she's turning it around." When she first arrived, she was unsure whether or not the organization was even "turnaround-able" because, she added, "I hadn't been in the movement and I didn't know what the donors would think, what the funders would think, the foundations, and the major players – if they were even willing to take another look at us." She described spending 90 per cent of her time on development in the first year and telling the board that it

would take eighteen months to get GLAAD back on sound financial footing. What happened instead was that "we were able to turn it around
in twelve months, which was pretty unheard of, actually." Or perhaps
not completely unheard of: Garry had accomplished more or less the
same thing in 1997–98, also by focusing almost all of her first-year efforts on development, putting her team in place, and making a bid for
greater visibility for the organization, as Ellis also began doing in 2015
by launching two major initiatives: the previously mentioned Accelerating Acceptance survey, which Ellis is planning to repeat every year as
a way to measure progress, and a bus tour of six Southern states planned
in conjunction with a high-profile country music concert and web-based
mini-documentaries featuring, Ellis told me, "positive stories to elevate
everyday LGBT people who are doing great things" to promote the cause
of LGBT acceptance in the South.

When I asked Ellis what she thought of how her predecessors had
performed, she volunteered the following: "Joan's days are the golden
era and people talk about them with such reverence and admiration of
the work that was done here." She attributed this success to the fact
that, unlike the two politicians who were appointed to lead GLAAD after
Garry left the organization, Garry was "media savvy." "Because GLAAD
is so specific," she said, "and because what we do is so nuanced, it's really important to get someone who has the inner workings of media in
their blood." "You need a media expert there," she stated, "and Joan
was." This sense that GLAAD had faltered post-Garry because the men
appointed to lead the organization were politicians and not media
experts was echoed in almost identical terms by Garry herself, who told
me: "The two executive directors who followed me were politicians and
I think that as a result of that, whether they were good, bad, or indif-
ferent at their jobs, they didn't have a keen understanding of the media
that the job requires in my mind. And the newest person [Ellis] does
indeed have that."

As research employing Bourdieu's "cultural intermediaries" approach has suggested, workers in semi-professionalized fields like
advertising, branding, and marketing are especially invested in their own
claims to professional expertise because their jobs (and often elevated
salaries) depend less on obtaining credentials like degrees or professional
certifications than on making the case that they possess special abilities

and knowledge that allow them to "influence others' perceptions and attachments" (Maguire et al. 2014, 2). When Spurgeon discussed with me what he brought to the movement that traditional activists did not, he pointed to his years of corporate public relations experience and said: "I know how to market to America." Similarly, the first two words of Ellis's LinkedIn profile in March 2015 were: "Media virtuoso." She told me that her years of marketing experience had turned her into "somebody that understood media and knew that you could use it to advance culture" and "shape a narrative." In sum, media professionals like Spurgeon and Ellis make "claims to professional expertise in taste and value" on the basis of the kind of corporate media experience that only they possess (Maguire et al. 2014, 2). A politician or movement activist might, over time, develop a good understanding of how media work, but they will never be *of* media and therefore will never possess the unique expertise and abilities that supposedly come from having "the inner workings of media in their blood," as Ellis put it. Whatever else may be required or desirable, Garry, Spurgeon, and Ellis all suggested, being an effective leader of GLAAD means belonging to – and, by implication, playing by the rules of – the world of corporate media professionals. When I asked Ellis how she had convinced major donors to renew their commitments to GLAAD, she told me that, apart from discussing the continuing importance of media for the LGBT movement, she said to them: "I'm here now. I understand business. I have a business background. I have a media background. I understand how an organization or a company needs to be run." As this last statement suggests, the claim that GLAAD needs leaders who understand the media is not just about knowing how to shape a narrative or talk to media professionals but about knowing the media *business* and convincing donors that GLAAD is run like one.

Ellis's immediate predecessor, Graddick, was not a politician, but a television producer. The public record is unclear about why he resigned after only thirteen months on the job, but the rhetoric he employed during his short tenure suggests that he played the media activist game as both a "traditional" activist and as the media professional he also was (Graddick did not figure in the narratives of GLAAD's troubles that Garry, Renna, or Ellis offered). One of Graddick's most important initiatives, the Commentator Accountability Project, took direct aim at re-

ligious conservative activists who are often given license to spread hateful nonsense in the news. In an interview with the *Windy City Times*, an
LGBT outlet, Graddick indicated that GLAAD would be taking a more
confrontational direction: "I think that we should not pussyfoot around
certain issues. I think there are certain issues where we have to really
have backbone about. There should be no watered-down version of who
these people are."[9] In a blog post for the Bilerico Project about Graddick's first Media Awards in Los Angeles in April 2012, long-time
GLAAD observer and veteran journalist Karen Ocamb enthused: "It was
as if the prodigal son of the LGBT movement who had 'gone Hollywood'
was returning home to work and fight on behalf of all LGBT people. The
real take-away message from that GLAAD gala night was GLAAD *is
back!*" In the wake of the Barrios/AT&T controversy, Ocamb suggested,
Graddick had returned GLAAD "to its roots as a watchdog of news and
entertainment coverage, rather than a media sycophant." Indeed, as
Ocamb pointed out, Graddick's speech at the Media Awards was reminiscent of the kind of activist rhetoric favoured by GLAAD founder Vito
Russo. "Kids across the country," Graddick said, "are making themselves miserable, and frankly leading themselves to the brink of suicide
because of the bullshit they learn from a bigoted society. And it's the
role of GLAAD to fix that."[10]

Under Ellis's leadership since 2014, GLAAD also appears to be back,
but in a form closer to Garry's corporate media approach than to Russo's
confrontational activism. Ellis estimated that "the watchdog piece of
GLAAD's work" represents maybe 20 per cent of what the organization
does versus "probably closer to 50 per cent in the past" because, she said,
"everybody who has an account on Facebook or Twitter or YouTube or
Instagram can now be an activist and hold people accountable" so that
"people don't rely as heavily on GLAAD for that piece of it any longer."
Be that as it may, GLAAD's retreat from confrontational activism does
not mean that the organization is entirely doing the bidding of media
companies, just as it was not entirely subordinated to corporate interests
in Garry's time. The organization's recent history speaks to a continuing
professional/activist tension born of its deeply structured position as a
mediating force between the cultural industries and diverse LGBT constituencies. GLAAD's leaders will continue to contend with these tensions
and resolve them as best they can. That said, the trend in the direction of

more corporatization is unmistakeable and extends to social movements throughout the world. As Dauvergne and LeBaron (2014, 1–2) argue convincingly, the influence of corporations on social movements, which was already evident at GLAAD in 2000–01, has been spreading: "Over the last two decades activist organizations have increasingly come to look, think, and act like corporations ... Not only are more and more corporations financing and partnering with activist groups, but activists are increasingly communicating, arguing, and situating goals within a corporatized frame. And more and more activists are seeing corporate-friendly options as logical and effective strategies for achieving their goals." Although joining forces has win-win implications for corporations and movement organizations, an (unintended?) consequence of these alliances is that activists are forced into "moderating goals and methods to pay salaries and run projects," thus "legitimizing an unequal and unsustainable world order while simultaneously decreasing the power of activism to transform capitalism in any real and meaningful way" (25). Applied to the micro level of LGBT media activism, these conclusions suggest that, whatever its successes might be in financial terms, GLAAD's ability to transform media industries significantly will also remain limited as long as its leaders remain primarily oriented to winning and maintaining legitimacy in corporate media.

*Ambivalence 2: The activist/professional tension at GLAAD obligates the organization to compete for legitimacy in both the movement and media fields, opening the door for rival agents to exert some influence.*

As I showed in chapters 3 and 4, GLAAD's leaders often came into conflict with agents whose participation in the movement was primarily oriented toward increasing LGBT autonomy. These agents had been shaped by traditions of activism that have evolved relatively autonomous ways of perceiving, expressing, and advocating for a wide range of sexualities, gender expressions, relationship forms, and politics (including race and class politics). They embodied what might be termed (after Bourdieu) an activist habitus whose influence was waning with the arrival of powerful new agents. Many of these traditional activists left GLAAD over the course of my fieldwork – sometimes by choice, sometimes not. But those who stayed behind retained some measure of non-dominant influence in the organization, in part by virtue of the fact that they could legitimately claim to represent constituents whose interests were not well-served by mainstreaming approaches. Within the movement field, this real or perceived capacity to represent under-represented constituencies functioned as a kind of social capital. It remained in GLAAD's best interests to maintain links to a broad LGBT constituency, lest they lose support and legitimacy in the movement field, get criticized by activists and academics, or get lambasted in the LGBT press (the latter a frequent cause for concern).

The desire to avoid angering specific LGBT constituencies explains, in part, why GLAAD's leaders were initially so hesitant to criticize *Queer as Folk*'s "promiscuous" sexuality and took up advocating for more racial diversity in the series instead (as discussed in chapter 4). However, just as artists who "want to fulfill a function other than that assigned to them by the artistic field" soon "rediscover the limits of their autonomy" (Bourdieu and Wacquant 1992, 110), GLAAD's would-be advocates of racial diversity in media soon discovered the consequences of their attempts to stray outside the usual parameters and procedures of media activism as established by media companies. Subsequent events were a clear illustration of the primary importance of economic capital on the LGBT media activist field as GLAAD moved furiously to embrace *Queer as Folk* in public and repair its relationship with Showtime in private.

The dominance of economic capital on media activism was not absolute, however, as certain forms of social and symbolic capital also entered into play. They did so most strikingly in the Schlessinger campaign, in which GLAAD found itself competing with an entrepreneurial group of Internet-based activists calling themselves StopDrLaura.com (SDL). The dynamics of the campaign pushed GLAAD's leaders to take more aggressive action against Paramount Television or risk being further embarrassed in LGBT and mainstream media. GLAAD's leaders consistently disavowed the campaign's competitive dynamics and thought it in their interests to present a united public front. They were fond of saying that GLAAD "plays well with others," but in reality, the organization tended to collaborate only with organizations with a similarly dominant position in the movement field, and only to the extent that doing so was likely to advance GLAAD's own standing. As Vaid (1995, 302) explains, this is typical of a movement field that has proven itself largely incapable of producing meaningful coalitions: "Instead, the coalitions that get built are paper structures, involving the exchange of signatures rather than the exchange of ideas, bodies, energies, and commitment." If a meaningful coalition (however strained) did in fact emerge in this instance, arguably contributing to – if not causing – the campaign's success, it was as the result of the tactical manoeuvrings of activists who, as Garry told me in 2015, seized an "opportunity to paint me as a corporate insider" and managed to mobilize segments of the LGBT community in opposition to both Schlessinger's television show and GLAAD's backroom deals with Paramount Television.

The competition that drove much of GLAAD's participation in the movement also meant that decisions about how best to represent LGBT constituencies were often counterbalanced with considerations about how best to advance the organization's institutional standing, which sometimes made for a difficult equilibrium between competing interests. This dual aspect of decision-making was built into the language used to describe the mandate given to GLAAD's communication team: to design and execute strategies in the service of GLAAD's mission *"as well as* to raise the organizational profile of GLAAD as the leading force working to insure fair, accurate and inclusive images in all media" (board member training manual, emphasis added). The requirement that the communication team's actions contribute to raising GLAAD's organizational profile meant that issues tended to be framed to appeal to how media tend to cover controversial topics, thus further limiting GLAAD's potential field of action.

Nowhere was the importance to GLAAD of maintaining its own institutional standing more strikingly in evidence than in the Schlessinger campaign, which saw new entrants (or, more accurately, newly reconfigured agents of the media activist field) challenge GLAAD's dominance. SDL's arrival suggested ways in which the Internet has perhaps lowered the threshold for effective action in the movement field, making it possible for agents with the right kinds of social, cultural, and symbolic capital to challenge the dominance of powerful players even in the absence of large amounts of economic capital. The founders of SDL possessed not only the media skills and professional networks that were necessary to have an impact with media, but also the know-how to mobilize an activist constituency. With their Internet skills, activist and professional competencies, and, it was rumoured among GLAAD staff, economic support from the Human Rights Campaign, SDL leaders were able to launch a high-impact national campaign with relatively modest means. In so doing, they sent a message that GLAAD's dominant position in LGBT media activism could not be taken for granted. At the close of the Schlessinger campaign, the GLAAD board immediately moved to shore up the organization's Internet capabilities.

Ultimately, and perhaps counter-intuitively, the Schlessinger campaign was an illustration of the extent to which the media advocacy process often works to maintain the status quo. Both SDL and GLAAD, despite their differences, employed the same arsenal of media activist tactics, derived from the structure originally set up by media companies in the 1970s to deal with the growing number of media pressure groups that sprang up amid debates about homosexuality, abortion, feminism, and racial and ethnic representation (Montgomery 1989). The tactics used in the Schlessinger campaign, conventional as they were, were unusually successful in achieving a near-total advertiser pull out, igniting a public discussion about homophobic rhetoric, and mobilizing thousands of people. Schlessinger herself emerged from the campaign greatly diminished, her reputation tarnished, her radio listenership down significantly. However, while the campaign was extremely successful on its own terms, it did nothing to alter the massive structural imbalance between the multibillion-dollar media industry and the advocacy groups, GLAAD included, that struggle to be heard within the system (Streeter 2000).

From the perspective of those who led the Schlessinger campaign, however, it appeared as though its success had fundamentally altered the gay and lesbian community's relationship with media companies and advertisers. During a board discussion, Garry listed sixteen ways in which she believed the campaign had benefitted GLAAD and the gay and lesbian community, including the "unprecedented visibility" it had brought to the organization, the "enormous leverage" GLAAD now enjoyed with media companies, and the "wonderful fundraising" opportunities it had created. Board co-chair David Steward declared that the campaign had taught media that "there's a price to pay" for defamation and that companies who advertise on defamatory programs "won't get away with this kind of crap." Spurgeon went one rhetorical step further, announcing that the campaign had "changed the face of how advertisers link conscience to economics."

The campaign's very success contributed to what is at core a flawed assumption about the media advocacy system, namely that it constitutes an exemplary model of US-style democracy applied to business practices. As Thomas Streeter (2000, 80) persuasively argues, what the advocacy process actually produces is the illusion of a democratic system, as though "this *specific* set of interests and procedures was in fact the *totality* of possible concerns and forms of democratic action." The reality is that "in this system not everyone is heard from, not all arguments are heard, and, even among those who do get a hearing, the power to influence the process is not evenly distributed" (80). Most saliently, Streeter (80–1) insists, "questions of fundamental industry structure are not considered ... [and] the long-term imbalance of power that provides much of the motivation for the advocacy groups in the first place is thus taken as a given."

As Swartz (1997, 126) describes, the competitive dynamics of fields "help create the conditions for the 'misrecognition' of power relations and thereby contribute to the maintenance of the social order." Agents who engage in field competition "misrecognize the arbitrary character of their social worlds" because "they take for granted the definition of rewards and of ways of obtaining them as given by fields" (126). Thus, although agents may struggle to improve their positions within fields, they "nonetheless reproduce the structure of fields" (126). The result is that the advocacy process tends to work in the interests of the most privileged because it requires a filtering process that dispenses with arguments and forms of contestation that might upset established power. If engaging in media activism depends on competing for the organizational prestige, visibility, and standing that only media companies can grant, for example, then media companies will always maintain the upper hand, no matter what victories might be fought and won on this uneven terrain.

Given the lopsided structure of these power relations, it is not surprising that as GLAAD has gained prominence in the LGBT media activist field, raking in more and more of the rewards this field makes available, it has tended to act more and more as a service provider to corporations and media professionals and less and less as a troublemaking watchdog. Over time, the major focus of its activity became serving media professionals' needs and interests by acting as a "resource" to them, and, in periods of conflict, to fulfill GLAAD's mission through what the organization's 1999 strategic plan called "constructive engagement." GLAAD's continued pre-eminence came to depend on a way of doing things that was as undisruptive to media producers as possible and a protocol for activism that tended to value good relations with "our friends in the media" above all.

Like the journalists Tuchman studied in the 1970s, GLAAD staffers evolved highly routine ways of interacting with representatives of dominant institutions whose ideological framework regarding what constitutes proper professional behaviour and legitimate sources of authority they also shared. This had the effect of channelling responses to issues in particular directions, making it likely, for example, that Garry would give more weight to input by *Frasier* producer (and Paramount employee) David Lee about how to respond to Schlessinger than to the perspectives of LGBT activists who were calling for a more forceful response (quite apart from Lee's importance as a major donor to GLAAD). These professional routines also meant that GLAAD was largely constrained to adopt moderate, non-confrontational approaches to issues as a way of preserving its legitimacy among media professionals. To be perceived as too radical in the professional world of media producers is to be condemned, if not to invisibility then to the status of troublemaker. A sign of GLAAD's success in positioning itself as a moderate voice for the movement – despite the more confrontational stance that movement competition forced it to take – was the PR *Week* award the organization received for its Schlessinger campaign, which further reinforced the sense that corporate media professionals were an important, if not the most important, audience for the organization.

The GLAAD staffers I re-interviewed in 2014–15 remembered the activist/professional tensions in ways that reveal the organization's need to play to a variety of professional and activist audiences and reveal also, by extension, the structurally hybrid nature of the LGBT media activist field. Spurgeon, who came to the organization with a corporate public relations background, gave this assessment of his time there: "I fell short in my appreciation of the visceral part of the gay community," he said, explaining that he "was never comfortable with the kind of rabid emotional aspect" he described as typical of some approaches to activism. He added: "I never quite coped with that, which was to my detriment I think in my position. I would've been better if I had, but I didn't have exposure with that." After leaving GLAAD in 2002, Spurgeon returned to agency work in public relations before retiring in 2009.

Garry told me that she chose a corporate communications strategist like Spurgeon as GLAAD's communications director because she felt "there weren't … sufficient skill levels in the non-profit space around advocacy communications" in 1998. She said her choice "served me very well" but acknowledged that it also created difficulties because "a person with that kind of training didn't come naturally with this notion of constituents and stakeholders, they come as the protector of the brand." The problem, she said, is that "you need to create a balance between that [the corporate strategist approach] and the people who are really boots on the ground and really understand the constituents so that you're hearing both things in your ears." "I think the single biggest piece of advice that I would give myself in 1998," she told me, "is remember that you serve a large group of stakeholders, of constituents, that you represent … The work is in the service of your stakeholders."

The dynamic tensions in the LGBT media activist field among various stakeholders explain why Garry appointed people with activist backgrounds, such as Renna and Loe, to high-profile (though non-dominant) positions. Renna was something of a bridging figure; someone Spurgeon said "had a foot in both camps, if you will, so she was a terrific guide and translator for me." In addition to Renna, Garry said she relied on Kerry Lobel, head of the National Gay and Lesbian Task Force at the time, to provide advice whenever she found herself "in the throes of things." She said she would reach out to Lobel to say: "Okay, here's what I'm thinking about sending out. How do you think this will play?" Such reaching out may have helped Garry avoid angering certain groups of people, but it failed to provide a mechanism for democratic consultation of – or accountability to – GLAAD's diverse constituencies and stakeholders.

Similarly, Loe's position in the organization fell short of ensuring a strong activist voice on GLAAD's management team. As discussed in chapter 1, Loe was put in charge of operations, as well as overseeing programs oriented to serving the LGBT community, such as media trainings. When she left GLAAD in 2001, she said, "I was an administrator … I was supervising staff in the field and had lost my connection to what I felt was very important work to me, which was community organizing and working with people one on one." She described tensions in the management team: "Culturally, it wasn't a very good fit ... It felt like we weren't really focusing on ... work that we thought was a priority, there were just these little turf battles going on and it felt like, well, it just didn't feel like good work." Her most positive memories of working for the national office were of thoughtful discussions had with her small programs team, one of which, she told me, "was a healthy conversation around the marriage issue" that emerged when her team began doing media trainings for marriage activists on the front lines of what would emerge as the defining issue of the gay and lesbian movement in the 2000s. She explained, "there were some people on staff who really weren't sure about – not high level staff, program staff – who really didn't want to engage on that level and support an institution that they really weren't fond of anyway." These conversations were occurring at GLAAD just as they were in the broader LGBT movement, something no one would have known from consulting GLAAD's website or from the mainstream media coverage of the issue. After leaving GLAAD, Loe worked for a few years in LGBT movement politics at the state level in Arizona, a context she called even more conservative than GLAAD. When I reached her in 2014, she had moved to California and was teaching university courses in what she termed the "macro part of social work." She described her ongoing activism as mainly focused on economic justice issues.

### Ambivalence 3: Playing to the mainstream will only get you so far (inside the tent).

As discussed in the previous two sections, the LGBT media activist field was characterized by pervasive tensions between a dominant professional pole and a non-dominant activist pole that obligated GLAAD to compete for legitimacy in both the corporate media and the social movement fields. The dominance of the pole formed by the influence of corporate media professionals had a further implication: GLAAD communications staffers, like (other) corporate media professionals, consistently sought ways of framing issues that would "play well" with mainstream audiences, which were imagined implicitly as white, middle-class, and heterosexual. Being "smart" about reaching those audiences meant being "realistic" about what they would or would not tolerate. Hence, for ex-

ample, GLAAD's leaders decided to criticize the intergenerational relationship depicted in *Queer as Folk*, despite its face-value legality in Pennsylvania, where the series took place. Spurgeon, for example, told me he
worried that the storyline dramatized "every parent's worst fear: the gay
predator as abductor of boys," despite the fact that the younger participant in the relationship was clearly depicted as both consenting and
capable of giving consent. The promiscuous sexuality on the series and
its depiction of drug use among gay men was also seen as problematic.
Unable to argue that these representations were unfair or inaccurate, and
unwilling to engage in a debate that might have placed the issues raised
by *Queer as Folk* in a broader context (a debate that, to be fair, would
have been difficult to conduct in mainstream media), GLAAD's leaders
devised a communications strategy that cast harsh judgment on the gay
men depicted in the program. *Queer as Folk*, they suggested, might be accurate for *some*, but certainly was not representative of all. The problem
with such rhetoric, as Cathy Cohen (1999, 341) argues in the case of
black community responses to the AIDS crisis, is that they engage in a
"process of secondary marginalization, where dominant discourses which
[seek] to stratify and distinguish between "worthy" and "unworthy"
marginal group members [are] replicated and in some cases adjusted to
similarly mark and divide" segments of a community. As Scott Seomin,
GLAAD's director of entertainment media, said to me in response to
GLAAD's criticism of the promiscuousness of the characters on *Queer as
Folk*: "We don't represent absolutely every gay and lesbian person on
this planet, but I'd like to think that we could represent ones that ... are
sexually active."

GLAAD's construction of its primary audience in its Eminem campaign was also problematic, insofar as its public messages about the rapper's music mimicked those that right-wing religious conservative
organizations might direct at anxious white suburban parents. Instead
of engaging with the construction and reception of Eminem's persona
and his complex relationships to questions of race, class, gender, and
sexuality, GLAAD's communications team insisted on the media-friendly
frame that Eminem's lyrics had the potential to harm kids. This reduc-
tive argument cast those who listen to Eminem as cultural dupes, in addition to perpetuating a long-discredited direct effects model of media
reception. This may have played well to media's frames for covering

controversies about popular culture (and indeed, it generated massive coverage), but it contributed little to building support for GLAAD's campaign among LGBT people, many of whom were people of colour and/or teenagers with mixed feelings about the music. More insidiously, by insisting as a matter of strategy that race not figure in GLAAD's public communications about Eminem, the organization further marginalized the voices of many LGBT people of colour. The rich debates that were occurring among LGBT hip-hop fans were thus silenced in favour of a set of talking points implicitly designed to excite the passions of white, middle-class, mainstream adults.

A final vexing consequence of GLAAD's emphasis on directing its appeals to media professionals and/or mainstream audiences was that the organization often used its public relations skills to manage negative reactions to its own strategies and tactics from within LGBT activist circles. Obligated by the structure of the LGBT media activist field to find a balance between competing strategies and tactics oriented to one or more of three poles – movement, media, and/or mainstream – GLAAD's leaders were constantly called upon to resolve tensions and contradictions at the personal, professional, institutional, and political levels. With the notable exception of the Schlessinger campaign, in which activist pressure caused GLAAD to take stronger action against a media company, these tensions tended to be resolved in favour of maintaining good relations with media professionals and media companies. In sum, GLAAD operated within a multipolar, hybrid field whose structure allowed for limited kinds of politically inflected advocacy to take place on behalf of diverse LGBT constituencies, but whose prevailing fiction, which could be summed up as "media are our friends," did not allow for the power relations that gave the field its shape to be named and addressed. But like the ideological framework studied by Lutz and Collins (1993, 282) in a different context, the media-as-friend narrative "falls apart in situations of conflict" and is revealed to be a self-serving fiction: media are friends to political constituencies when it is in their self-interest to be so and/or in a movement organization's institutional self-interest to say that they are.

Caught in the tension between representing LGBT difference and highlighting sameness, and unable or unwilling to combat or articulate the consequences of media power over itself, GLAAD was often reduced to taking mainstream-friendly positions at the cost of an "autonomous carving-out of political space" (Gamson 1998, 216). Yet, as Gamson argues in *Freaks Talk Back*, the LGBT movement needs to promote both the kinds of representations that favour mainstream integration and those that challenge the heteronormative status quo. Both strategies are necessary because they do different kinds of political work. The problem is that the emphasis since the 1990s on strategies designed to lead to greater inclusion in dominant institutions has meant that only one side of the political equation between sameness and difference has been well served. Advocates of an ostensibly pragmatic, incremental approach to social change, like Kirk and Madsen (whose early influence on GLAAD I documented in the introduction), might respond that this is just as it should be: "When you're very different, and people hate you for it, this is what you do: *first* you get your foot in the door, by being as *similar* as possible; then, and only then – when your one little difference is finally accepted – can you start dragging in your other peculiarities, one by one. You hammer in the wedge narrow end first. As the saying goes, Allow the camel's nose beneath your tent, and his whole body will soon follow" (Kirk and Madsen 1989, 146). This gay version of wedge politics resembles the ideology of the so-called trickle-down economics of the Reagan era: the extension of privileges to the few is justified by the promise that they will eventually benefit the many. Moreover, it presumes that those who are closest to the centres of power but still excluded on account of their "one little difference" (who they have sex with) are entitled to the bulk of the resources for which all movement actors compete; others need only stand back and wait their turn. If indeed there are signs that the camel's nose has made its way beneath the tent, there are also signs that the body is getting restless. At the risk of taking the analogy too far: does the camel's nose even realize what lies behind it? If life is good for the nose, what interest does it have in letting any other part of the camel in, especially the parts that might – from the perspective of a sensitive nose – stink up the tent? Assuming that movement organizations are even interested in further hammering in the wedge, would it not be preferable, from the value standpoint of promoting a fuller range of political possibilities, to endeavour to make the

tent bigger by working to dismantle the assumptions about respectability that restrict entry to it in the first place? A larger tent with a larger
opening would also attenuate the sharp distinctions between inside and
outside, and perhaps allow more back and forth between the two.

## A Politics of Ambivalence

In 2007, I attended the Minneapolis Pride march, which consisted of a
familiar procession of church groups, sports teams, high school marching bands, community organizations, politicians, drag queens, leather
folk, lesbian mothers, gay fathers, and corporate floats (the Minneapo-
lis-based Target Corporation led the parade and distributed thousands
of rainbow-coloured Target-branded temporary tattoos). But amid the
predictable was something I did not expect: a group of young people
marching behind a banner announcing the arrival of the Revolting Queers,
who appeared as a series of couples in wedding outfits. At first glance,
they seemed to be making a conventional statement about marriage
equality, but something about their self-presentation and political performance did not quite fit the bill. Some of the marchers in white wedding dresses were genderqueer – like the "bride" whose dress, worn off
the shoulder and cut up, drew attention to the absence of breasts and revealed a pair of shapely masculine legs. In their wake, in lieu of the expected wedding party, marched mourners in black forming a funeral
procession and carrying coffins inscribed to the memory of some of the
issues that marriage equality forgot: queer homeless youth, transgender
rights, universal healthcare, women's rights, welfare reform, body image
politics, and racism. Amid the largely uncritical celebration of visibility
and consumerism that Pride everywhere tends to produce, the Revolting
Queers stood – and stood out – for something else.

Groups like the Revolting Queers speak to possibility that a queer
movement might define itself more broadly across lines of gender, sexuality, class, and race. They point to the possibility, in the words of Lisa
Duggan (2003, 41), that a "sustainable opposition" to the cultural
politics of neoliberalism might be articulated, one that could "connect
culture, politics, and economics; identity politics and class politics;
universalist rhetoric and particular issues and interests; intellectual and
material resources." Duggan looks for ways to transcend the schisms in
left politics between political economic approaches and identitarian

strategies that have been criticized for their recuperability within a consumerist ethos. She recognizes that the popular appeal of neoliberal discourses cannot be countered via disciplining strategies designed to bring the left into alignment with any "pure" model of politics within which differences can be subsumed in the name of some fictitious unity. Against the tendency to "admonish and advise" potential allies on the left to get behind a particular program, Duggan (2003, 81) writes, it would be more productive "to *locate*, *engage*, and *expand* productive political moments for future elaboration."

The advent of activist formations like the Revolting Queers is only one among many potentially productive political moments that might be engaged and elaborated upon, but among the things that strike me as especially notable about this group is its deployment of a serious, yet playful, even pleasurable politics. It does not appear to be repudiating the consumer culture of the gay and lesbian mainstream so much as simultaneously engaging and colliding with it in an attempt to shift it in more progressive and critical directions. The Revolting Queers actively took part in the orgy of consumerist Pride it denounced, becoming part of its spectacle in the process, but in doing so, it made visible, for a time, its embedded absences. More importantly, in terms of my argument, the group exemplified that an ambivalent performance can generate a cultural politics of either/or, neither/both that refuses the false choice between assimilation or revolution, consumerism or anti-capitalism. More than an attempt to incite revolution in any usual sense of the word, its was a revolt against the authority of the gay and lesbian mainstream to define queer politics narrowly in consumerist terms and an assertion of the possibility that mainstream forms like Pride could be made to also mean something else, something more, perhaps even something queer. Like mainstreaming strategies, such carnivalesque political theatre might not, by itself, fundamentally transform the balance of power, but it at least has the virtue of keeping multiple political possibilities in view. As I read it, the Revolting Queers issued an invitation to cultural citizenship and democratic participation that tentatively exceeded neoliberalism's narrow interpellation of queers as little more than privatized gay consumers.[11]

Thinking about the Revolting Queers' *détournement* of Pride, I wondered if similar tactics might be feasible on a larger scale. What if GLAAD had used its media platform to amplify a fuller range of the discussions that were going on about Eminem within the organization and in the LGBT community at large? What if the more complex discussions that GLAAD was allowing to take place on a local basis in New York City had substantially informed the work of its communications team in Los Angeles? And what if GLAAD didn't hold itself to just one (media-friendly) position on each issue when the reality is that, on some issues more than others, the constituencies it ostensibly represents hold a variety of defensible (and potentially politically useful) opinions?

Spurgeon acknowledged to me that the issues around Eminem were much more complicated than the official message would allow, but a campaign conducted in mainstream media, he argued, needs to play to media's inherent biases in covering issues in certain ways and not others. This is a valid argument, but I think it fails to recognize a fuller range of possible ways to conduct LGBT media activism. To understand why, it is perhaps helpful to look at Michel de Certeau's (2011) *The Practice of Everyday Life*, in which he develops a distinction between "strategies" and "tactics" via an analogy to the space of the city. He argues that strategies are like the physical roads, buildings, and traffic signs that govern the city's use. Strategies, he argues, are controlled by powerful institutions like governments and corporations and there is little any individual can do to change them. Tactics, on the other hand, are analogous to the multifarious ways in which people move about the city, adapt it to their purposes, and exercise a certain freedom to choose among possible trajectories. "The place of the tactic belongs to the other," but since it emerges only in relation to a more dominant power, its place is never secured: "It has at its disposal no base where it can capitalize on its advantages, prepare its expansions, and secure independence with respect to circumstances ... On the contrary, because it does not have a place, a tactic depends on time – it is always on the watch for opportunities that must be seized 'on the wing.' Whatever it wins, it does not keep. It must constantly manipulate events in order to turn them into 'opportunities.' The weak must continually turn to their own ends forces alien to them" (xix).

By nature, the field of LGBT media activism occupies the shifting space of the tactic because it forms in relation to the strategies established by dominant power. The public relations approaches favoured by GLAAD's professionalized activists are just one set of tactics among the many that can potentially be deployed within the tactical field of LGBT media activism, but this choice tends to amplify the perspectives of elites to the relative exclusion of the perspectives of other constituencies because, as corporate communications scholar Lee Edwards (2011, 61) explains: "Public relations is not a free-floating, neutral occupation, isolated from its social context. On the contrary, it is loaded with value judgements: PR itself is a 'culture' with its own mores, standards and value judgements of what is and is not good 'PR.'" Moreover, public relations practitioners tend to have "patterns of cultural taste, knowledge and activity ... consistent with those observed among dominant social groups from higher classes" (70). Prestige in public relations tends to be measured in terms of closeness to power: the more powerful the client, the more prestigious the public relations firm or practitioner. In practice, this means that practitioners have "a stake in the existing economic and political status quo, from which they benefit" and that neoliberal ideas of "consumer choice, the supremacy of the market and individualism, which define the wider economic and political field, are less likely to be questioned" (70). Public relations practitioners, Edwards (71) argues, "exercise 'symbolic violence' – perpetuating the dominance of an elite group of individuals over less powerful groups in society through their discursive work."

I began this book by suggesting that making out in the mainstream could refer both to the attempts made to make LGBT people more visible in the majority heterosexual culture and to the ways in which various individuals and organizations attempt to profit from that visibility. The neoliberal strategies to these ends cannot be so easily dislodged, but I hope this ethnographic study of GLAAD's struggles to exert influence over media, movement, and mainstream has made clear that there were more tactics at the disposal of GLAAD's leaders than they often realized. The preceding analyses of the Media Awards, the Schlessinger campaign, and GLAAD's responses to *Queer as Folk* and Eminem, as well as the summary above of the structuring ambivalences in the LGBT movement field, all reveal some queer possibilities in the roads not taken, if only GLAAD's leaders had perceived and exercised their limited autonomy differently.

During my fieldwork, GLAAD's leaders often spoke of how constant the organization's mission had remained despite the magnitude of the

changes it has undergone over the years. During the inauguration party
for the new GLAAD office in New York City, for example, one outgoing
board member (who had been responsible for raising more than $3 mil-
lion over the course of his tenure) spoke of GLAAD's mission as the rud-
der that had kept the organization on course through difficult times. His
statement asserted continuity in the face of dramatic change and almost
unbelievable growth. It also suggested that the new, beautifully designed
office was a reward for the board's steadfast adherence to the organization's core principles. It occurred to me at that moment that the board
member's tribute to the clarity of the GLAAD mission was in fact a declaration of ownership over it. I thought of all the people not invited to
the party: those who had left GLAAD over disagreements, who had been
forced out, or who might have wanted to take part but did not feel (or
were not in fact) welcomed. And as I thought about these absent others,
many of whom probably believed in the GLAAD mission just as much as,
if not more than, the people assembled in the new office, I looked
around and saw, with few exceptions, white, middle-aged, politically
connected, upper-middle-class people with high-profile jobs, many of
them in the media industries. I also saw talented, skilled, intelligent, and
hard-working people who were deeply committed, in both their personal and professional lives, to the idea of improving the lives of gays
and lesbians.

However one might feel about it, the large organizations of the LGBT
movement are increasingly led by people like Garry and Ellis – professionally accomplished, often charismatic people who hail from corporate backgrounds. If there is no returning to the movement field as it was
before the neoliberal shift of the 1990s, is there a chance that today's
leaders, endowed as they are with greater political-economic capital than
ever before, might be convinced to steer the movement toward greater
democratic participation and representation, i.e., a more ambivalent embrace of mainstreaming and of its politics of respectability?

On balance, the preceding analysis of GLAAD's media advocacy work
does not hold out much hope for those who, like me, would wish for the
LGBT movement to "move" in more autonomous directions. But having
recognized the structural limits of the media advocacy system, it is still
possible to imagine that GLAAD and other movement organizations
might do more to promote an "autonomous carving-out of political

space" in which to debate the future of the LGBT movement beyond mainstreaming (Gamson 1998, 216). Movement leaders can, within the set of conditions under which they operate, exercise their limited agency differently, i.e., make different choices that better exploit possibilities for movement autonomy within the fields in which they compete for resources. My proposal for a more ambivalent embrace of mainstreaming strategies will undoubtedly strike some as insufficiently radical. Be that as it may, it recognizes the structural and symbolic limits to queer involvement in hegemonic systems at the same time as it asserts that those limits are not set in stone. The tent of which Kirk and Madsen (1989) spoke, which symbolizes all that the LGBT movement might aspire to, need not be conceptualized as a static structure, but as something that can be packed up and moved on, torn apart, sewn back up, expanded, and rebuilt again and again. Our energies as a movement might be directed less at entering into the tent as it exists, and more at helping to make a different kind of tent whose conditions for entry are not predicated on the dominant culture's criteria for respectability.

A politics of ambivalence in relation to mainstreaming would represent a necessarily temporary tactical gambit – a conjunctural and contingent *realpolitiks* of sexual representation adapted to the mainstream's partial embrace of those aspects of our lives that most resemble its normative fantasies about itself. This is a not a time for great refusals, but a moment to be on the lookout for the emergent possibilities that might disrupt the hegemony of neoliberalism. These attempts to engage with queer possibilities in the present also need to be attentive to common sense understandings of what mainstreaming has made possible. I agree with Steven Seidman (2002, 6), who writes: "The very real and significant improvement in gay people's lives that have been made possible by recent social reforms should not be discounted." The gains of mainstreaming are not merely "virtual" (as Vaid and other queer critics might say), even if they fall far short of full civic equality for all LGBT people. But just as we should not discount the gains of mainstreaming, we should not discount its limits. We should, as Duggan suggests, endeavour to identify, engage with and expand upon what is politically valuable about these profoundly ambivalent times.

A necessary first step toward a more ambivalent embrace of mainstreaming would be for movement leaders to consciously come to terms with the structural positioning of the organizations they lead. On this point, Bourdieu scholar Rodney Benson (1999, 477) suggests the importance of making visible the power relations that structure what social agents are able to accomplish in the world: "The first step toward change is to bring to consciousness the invisible structures of belief and practice that lead actors to unwittingly reproduce the system, even as they struggle within it." Movement leaders will also need to be convinced to democratize decision-making processes, render themselves more accountable to diverse LGBT constituencies, and reduce their dependence on a small number of wealthy donors and the legitimating sanction of dominant institutions. None of these things will be easy, given the deeply engrained corporate/professional habitus of today's movement leaders, who are predisposed to react defensively to the criticisms levelled against them. However, as Bourdieu might remind us, habitus is not fixed for all time, it is, rather, a "kind of deeply structured cultural grammar for action" that, just as grammar organizes speech, "can generate an infinity of possible practices" (Swartz 1997, 102). This conception of the relationship between agency and structure does not make all cultural practices equally possible or likely, of course, but it does point to the extent to which the habitus of social agents, their "cultural grammar for action," is conditioned by the resources, forms of struggle, and power relations that are specific to the fields they cultivate and that cultivate them. As I have shown in this book, the media activist field that GLAAD's leaders inhabited during my fieldwork in 2000–01, however dominated it was by the politics of mainstreaming, was also changed as a result of activists' efforts – many of them operating from within GLAAD – who seized the opportunities created by the structuring ambivalences described above to make the organization more responsive and accountable to the constituencies on whose behalf it claimed to speak. These ambivalences concerning GLAAD's relationships to media, movement, and mainstream still exert a structuring influence over the field today, as the choice of Ellis as leader makes clear. I believe they are the best starting point from which to elaborate a new and more inclusive, responsive, and effective politics of LGBT representation.

Those of us who care about the future of the movement beyond mainstreaming must help foster, through struggle and dialogue, new dispositions in our leaders that might result in more diverse, more transformative kinds of cultural and political representation. The stakes of such struggle and dialogue are nothing less than the future of queer autonomy: the future of our relative capacity as non-dominant sexual and gender iconoclasts living in a hyper-mediated, hyper-consumerist world to think for ourselves and form alliances with others. I hope the readers of this book will share my sense that expanding this sense of queer possibility is something worth fighting for.

# Notes

## Introduction

1 My ethnographic work – mainly involving participant observation, over thirty-five in-depth interviews, and archival research –
was carried out over a period of eighteen months in 2000 and
2001, with five additional interviews conducted in late 2014 and
early 2015. I began part-time fieldwork in late January 2000, and
spent an average of two days a week in the GLAAD/NY office, in
addition to attending board meetings and GLAAD Media Awards
in both Los Angeles and New York. In September 2000, I travelled to Los Angeles to begin full-time fieldwork and stayed there
until mid- December. Finally, in January 2001, I moved to New
York City to carry out another five months of full-time fieldwork.
My last day in New York, 1 June 2001, was my last official day
in the field (although I attended one last board meeting and Media
Awards show in San Francisco shortly thereafter). At various
moments during my fieldwork, I consulted document archives
housed in the New York and Los Angeles offices, the San Francisco Public Library, and the GLAAD collection at the Cornell
University library.
2 Note on terminology: I often use "gay and lesbian" in lieu of the
more inclusive "LGBT." This choice is intended to reflect and

describe (rather than endorse or reproduce) the marginalization of bisexuals and transgender individuals by the "dominant strains of the movement" (Chasin 2000, xviii). GLAAD has increasingly advocated on behalf of bisexuals and transgender people, which is why I sometimes refer to it as an organization of the LGBT movement, particularly when discussing its more recent activities.

3 Phil Reese, "GLAAD's Communication Breakdown; Barrios Voted Out," *Washington Blade*, 18 June 2011, http://www.washington blade.com/2011/06/18/glaads-communication-breakdown.

4 Eliza Krigman, "AT&T Gave Cash to Merger Backers," *Politico*, 10 June 2011, http://www.politico.com/news/stories/0611/56660.html.

5 Reese, "GLAAD's Communication Breakdown."

6 Editorial, "Is Backing AT&T a Civil Right? GLAAD Should Know Better," *Boston.com*, 25 June 2011, http://www.boston.com/bostonglobe/editorial_opinion/editorials/articles/2011/06/25/is_backing_att_a_civil_right_glaad_should_know_better/.

7 According to Albert F. Moe (1966, 96–107), the contemporary sexual connotations of "making out" as kissing or necking developed from the earlier meaning of "to succeed." For young men of the 1930s and 1940s, for example, to "make out" was to persuade a woman to consent to sex.

8 See, for example, Danielle Riendeau's 7 August 2007 review of *Basic Instinct* on *After Ellen*, which stated:

> As for Catherine, she certainly doesn't buck any trends in terms of bisexual stereotypes. She is promiscuous and – if the infamous ending is to be believed – a killer herself. However, many have read the character of Catherine in a different light. She is powerful, sexual, smarter than the male protagonist and by no means owned by him. According to the director's commentary, this was the characterization Verhoeven intended: a strong, liberated woman. She might be a killer, but she's still the most powerful, most dynamic force in the movie.

"Review of 'Basic Instinct,'" http://www.afterellen.com/movies/20958-review-of-basic-instinct.

## Chapter One

1 According to his biographer, Vito Russo felt similarly about Darrell Yates Rist as Rist felt about the GLAAD board's purported deference to straight sensibilities. Schiavi (2011, 240) writes:
"Darrell's brand of timidity, straight out of Mattachine 1965, infuriated Vito." Russo's biographer describes a "massive protest"
held in New York after the 1986 *Bowers v. Hardwick* US Supreme
Court decision that upheld sodomy laws. "On behalf of GLAAD,"
Schiavi (239) describes, "Darrell Yates Rist cautioned the crowd
not to ruin tourists' fun and prejudice them against the cause." In
contrast, "Vito blasted the Supreme Court's sanction of bigotry
and energized exhausted marchers with a stirring defense of gay
and lesbian rights" (240).

2 The "culture war" rhetoric culminated with Patrick Buchanan's
(quoted in Chapman 2009, xxix) speech to the Republican National Convention, in which he stated: "There is a religious war
going on in our country for the soul of America. It is a cultural
war, as critical to the kind of nation we will one day be as was the
Cold War itself."

3 The issue of marriage gained prominence in 1996 when a Hawaii
court ruled that the prohibition against same-sex marriage was
unconstitutional. This decision reignited what had been a relatively dormant debate and led to the passage of a federal law,
named the Defense of Marriage Act, to define marriage as the
union of one man and one woman. The US Supreme Court struck
down a key portion of the law in 2013. See Moscowitz (2013) for
an account of how the same-sex marriage debate played out in
media.

4 Dave Cullen, "All in the Family: Dick Cheney's Lesbian Daughter,
Mary, Is Expected to Stump for the GOP Ticket," *Salon*, 30 July
2000.

5 Ibid.

6 Bruce Mirken, "The Coors Cunundrum: Is the Colorado Brewer
Our Friend?" *Frontiers*, 25 May 2001.

7 Cullen, "All in the Family."

8 Ibid.

9 Quoted in Mirken, "The Coors Cunundrum."

10 The tensions between Heffner and Garry created some difficulties for my research because Heffner had a key role in securing my entrée to GLAAD. Garry confessed to me that some members of her staff had wanted her to expel me from the organization after his departure. She told me that she ultimately decided to let me stay because she understood that my work was "not about us [GLAAD]," but "about Us [the movement]."

## Chapter Two

1 Joan Garry, "Sexual Orientation Is a State of Being, Not Just a Sex Act," USA Today, 16 June 2003.

2 Joan Garry, "Yes, America: You Do Know a Mother Who Is Gay," USA Today, 6 March 2002.

3 GLAAD's new CEO, Sarah Kate Ellis, reportedly earned $225,000 in 2014. Chuck Colbert, "GLAAD CEO Ushers in New Day at Media Advocacy Group," Bay Area Reporter, 29 May 2014.

4 The board had to make a similar decision concerning whether or not to nominate Normal, Ohio, the short-lived sitcom starring John Goodman as an openly gay man who moves back to his hometown in the Midwest. Again, the film and television subcommittee did not recommend the show's nomination and, in this case, GLAAD's board concurred with the decision.

5 According to a GLAAD survey of its major donors, 37 per cent were employed in the media industries (with 18 per cent "media," 14 per cent "entertainment," and 5 per cent "publishing"), and 75 per cent were male. Many major donors were recruited through parties (I attended about a half dozen of these) usually held in the well-appointed homes of existing major donors who would arrange for catering and ambience. Invitations were sent out to prospects, many of whom were friends or acquaintances of current major donors, or people identified by development staffers as potential GLAAD supporters. Absolut Vodka drinks were served, and after about an hour of cocktail party conversation, Garry would make a pitch that emphasized her professional credentials and those of her staff, described GLAAD's accomplish-

ments, and argued the need for more resources. Here, as with the
Media Awards, humour and sentiment were key, and Garry was
masterful at both. After her speech, development staff and board
members fanned out, talked up prospects, and handed out pledge
cards.

6 Meetings of the 2001 LA Media Awards committee often included
discussions about improving the quality of silent auction items,
i.e., offering more luxury items like Cartier watches and Gucci
handbags and fewer items like "baskets of lube," which was a recurring example of what not to include. Although I never saw any
baskets of lube at any of the silent auctions I witnessed, there was
certainly a healthy mix of luxury items and gay kitsch on offer.

7 There were also Propecia-branded disposable cameras at every
table. Guests who used the cameras and paid to get the film developed later found that each picture came back with a prominent
Propecia watermark.

8 According to Spurgeon, who told me the anecdote, Taylor had
been in her dressing room getting ready to go on stage when she
declared: "My hair is ready, I'm ready." The Media Awards producers rushed to reorganize the schedule to accommodate Taylor's
wish to speak ahead of schedule, and thereby delayed the presentation to *Will and Grace* of the award for Outstanding TV Comedy Series. The unintended consequence was that *Will and Grace*
received minimal media coverage because most reporters, many of
them under deadline, left immediately after Taylor's speech. In apparent retribution, no one from the cast or crew of *Will and Grace*
appeared on stage the following year to accept that year's Media
Award. A befuddled Ellen DeGeneres was left to hand the trophy
to a hotel lighting technician who had been hurriedly dispatched
by someone on the production crew to accept the award on behalf
of NBC.

9 Alex Donohue, "WPP's Enterprise IG Rebrands as the The Brand
Union," *Brand Republic*, 6 November 2007, available from Fac-
tiva.

10 Pamela Buxton, "Top 20 Design Agencies – Designers Go for a
Brand Overhaul," *Marketing*, 1 December 2000.

11 A leaflet produced by Enterprise IG to help GLAAD introduce its

new brand image suggests that the organization's "unique selling proposition" was distilled as a "media-focused organization that informs, influences, and educates." "As a voice for human rights," the leaflet continues, "glaad represents something special: a group with the focus and force to keep fighting for accurate images and perceptions."

12 GLAAD was rebranded again in 2010 by the brand consultancy, Lippincott, a direct competitor of Enterprise IG. The original press release announcing the rebranding included a postscript (since removed from the version of the release on GLAAD's website but preserved in my research files) titled "The back story." Apparently written by someone at Lippincott, the addendum appeared to make sly reference to humorous interpretations of GLAAD's logo that I had heard whispered during my fieldwork: that it looked like a "sperm and egg" coming together, or even more sophomorically, like semen splattered on a wall. "The existing mark," the unnamed writer declared, "thought to symbolize 'entities coming together' (not my choice of words) was poorly understood and uncomfortably biomorphic, memorable perhaps but otherwise not clearly a branding asset." It is hard to read "uncomfortably biomorphic" and not think that the author was referring to bodily fluids.

13 The Rand Corporation is a non-profit research organization with important ties to the US military-industrial complex, which, in the words of its mission statement, provides "objective analysis and effective solutions that address the challenges facing the public and private sectors around the world."

### Chapter Three

1 GLAAD's preferred way to refer to this campaign was "the Schlessinger campaign," though "the Dr Laura campaign" was more widely recognizable. Schlessinger's doctorate is in physiology, which means she had no particular expertise in counselling/psychology. Referring to her by her last name rather than "doctor" or her brand name "Dr Laura" was a way to try to

delegitimize her and highlight her dubious expertise. In this book, I follow GLAAD's usage.

2 Michelangelo Signorile, "Takin' It to the Streets," *Advocate*, 9 May 2000, 29–31.

3 Brian Lowry, "Dr Laura: All Is Fair in Syndication," *Los Angeles Times*, 11 January 2000. Joe Keenan, an openly gay writer-producer on *Frasier*, is quoted by Lowry: "What gay person working for Paramount could be happy about this? ... We feel the way the Von Trapp children would feel if Dad decided to divorce Maria and marry Joan Crawford. She's not a happy addition to the family."

4 Lowry, "Dr Laura: All Is Fair in Syndication."

5 Joyce Howard Price, "Paramount Allays Fears of Gays: Dr Laura to Offer 'Many Points of View' on Homosexuals," *Washington Times*, 17 February 2000.

6 *Hollywood Reporter*, 29 February 2000, 89; *Daily Variety*, 29 February 2000, 20.

7 SDL's page view statistics were given by the group itself. GLAAD did not release figures about website traffic.

8 Don Feder, "Sham from GLAAD Won't Fly on Main St," *Boston Herald*, 15 March 2000, 33.

9 The ad also ran later in business journals in Atlanta, Washington, DC, Boston, and Dallas in an effort to discourage local businesses from buying advertising time on Dr Laura.

10 Historically, GLAAD has not had close relationships with the National Association for the Advancement of Colored People or the Anti-Defamation League, despite attempts to engage these organizations in coalition work. One might speculate that GLAAD holds a less dominant position in the movement field and therefore pulls less weight than these much larger organizations, which tend to associate only with organizations of like size and purpose. It is also true that GLAAD has not historically had many programs oriented to the specific mandates of the National Association for the Advancement of Colored People and the Anti-Defamation League and that these organizations have their own histories of homophobia.

11  "P&G Opts out of Ad Crossfire," *Advertising Age*, 29 May 2000.

12  Debra Goldman, "Art & Commerce: Debra Goldman's Consumer Republic," *Adweek*, 29 May 2000.

13  Tom Shales, "A Case of the Creeps: 'Dr Laura' on UPN Looks Better on Radio," *Washington Post*, 15 September 2000, C1.

14  Aimee Grove, "Dr Laura Issues Apology, GLAAD Fires back Missive," PR *Week*, 16 October 2000.

15  Brian Lowry, "It Must Be the Neighbors Who Watch These Shows," *Los Angeles Times*, 6 December 2000.

16  David Hinckley, "Stations Consider Song Ads," *New York Daily News*, 13 March 2001, 8.

17  Melissa Grego, "TV's Gay Pride Parade," *Variety*, 11–17 December 2000.

18  Michelangelo Signorile, "The Fall of Dr. Laura and the Rise of Internet Activism," *Gay.com*, 4 April 2001.

19  Signorile, "The Fall of Dr. Laura."

### Chapter Four

1  Richard Huff, "GLAAD to be of help to new series," *New York Daily News*, 1 December 2000.

2  Eric Boehlert, "Invisible Man: Eminem May Be the Most Violent, Woman-Hating, Homophobic Rapper Ever. Why Are Critics Giving Him a Pass?," *Salon*, 7 June 2000, http://dir.salon.com/ent/music/feature/2000/06/07/eminem/index.html.

3  Carla Hay, "Is Anti-hate Campaign Contradictory to MTV?" *Billboard*, 20 January 2001.

4  Steven J. Stark, "MTV to Battle Hate with Silence," *Hollywood Reporter*, 5 January 2001.

5  Christopher Heredia, "Elton, Eminem Duet Irks Gays," *San Francisco Chronicle*, 12 February 2001, A1.

6  Dave Walker, "Bum Rap: Grammy Chief Says Eminem's Act Is Just Showbiz, Folks," *Times-Picayune*, 21 February 2001.

7  Richard Johnson, Paula Froelich, and Chris Wilson, "Gays Split on Elton-Eminem Act," *New York Post*, 13 February 2001, 6.

8  Christopher Heredia, "Elton, Eminem Duet Irks Gays," *San Francisco Chronicle*, 12 February 2001, A1.

9 Dave Walker, "Bum Rap." *Times-Picayune*, 21 February 2001.

10 Jill Serjeant, "Elton John Slammed for Performing with Eminem," *Yahoo News* (Reuters), 20 February 2001.

11 *Marketing Violence to Children: Hearing Before the Committee on Commerce, Science, and Transportation*, 106th Cong. (2000) (statement of Lynne Cheney, former chairman, National Endowment for the Humanities).

12 Jon Bream, "Rapper's Lyrics Spawn Discussion of Tolerance; Eminem's Grammy-Nominated CD has People Talking about the Line between Art and Hate Speech," *Star Tribune*, 21 February 2001, 4B.

13 Linda Gorov, "Protest Fails to Make Noise," *Boston Globe*, 22 February 2001.

14 "Keeping It Real: A Conversation about Race, Sexuality and Hip Hop," *Images*, Summer (2001): 22–7.

   The editor-in-chief of *Images*, GLAAD programs staffer Jay Plum, told me in an interview that he had intended the publication to be an accessible, irreverent journal of queer media cultural studies that is not afraid to ruffle some feathers and perhaps also "subvert the mission" of GLAAD a little by questioning some of its fundamental assumptions. At times, he said, GLAAD's leadership – particularly Garry – had embraced this vision for the publication, and at other times had feared it. Comments like Hardy's in the hip-hop issue of the journal were a particular challenge, he said, because they presented a very different point of view than what the institutional one had been. "That has been a struggle that I've had with Joan and Steve," Plum told me.

15 Chris Crain, "Mad at GLAAD," *Washington Blade*, 15 February 2002, 15.

## Conclusion

1 As measured by GLAAD's annual reports, the *Network Responsibility Index*, the *Where We Are on TV Report*, and the *Studio Responsibility Index*, all of which are available on glaad.org. The *2014 Studio Responsibility Index* notes: "GLAAD found that LGBT

representations in contemporary Hollywood films tend to be far more scarce and regressive than those on television."

2 James Kirchick, "How GLAAD Won the Culture War and Lost Its Reason to Exist," *Atlantic*, 3 May 2013, http://www.theatlantic.com/politics/archive/2013/05/how-glaad-won-the-culture-war-and-lost-its-reason-to-exist/275533.

3 Gabriel Arana, "Why We Still Need GLAAD," *American Prospect*, 7 May 2013, http://prospect.org/article/why-we-still-need-glaad.

4 I am indebted to Sarah Banet-Weiser (2012) for the formulation "the politics of ambivalence," which in her book about brand culture refers to the generative tensions between how brands circulate idealized normative meanings, on the one hand, and how these meanings are taken up variously by neoliberal subjects, on the other, leading her to conclude that brands "are ultimately precarious, and are subject to cultural misunderstanding" and therefore potentially "generative" of new political possibilities and ideals (218). She warns, however, "connecting ambivalence to actual praxis is a difficult thing and has no guarantees," while insisting throughout, as I also do, on the "*potential* of ambivalence, its generative power."

5 The semi-structured, in-depth interviews to which I refer in this concluding chapter were conducted in late 2014 and early 2015. Each interview lasted about one hour and asked participants to reflect on the past, present, and future of LGBT media.

6 According to an article on *After Ellen*, the book was spawned from a *Real Simple* magazine feature on Ellis and Henderson. In the article, Henderson states: "I think it's important to keep stories about families like mine in the spotlight. The more people read about my average, everyday, mundane life, the more they realize we're no different than they are. The sooner society gets that, the better off my kids' lives will be." Trish Bendix, "Sarah Ellis and Kristen Henderson Share their Stories in 'Times Two,'" *After Ellen*, 31 March 2011, http://www.afterellen.com/people/86481-sarah-ellis-and-kristen-henderson-share-their-stories-in-times-two/3.

7 Lisa Belkin, "For the Sake of the Children," *New York Times*, 22 July 2011, http://www.nytimes.com/2011/07/24/fashion/weddings/

gay-marriage-for-the-sake-of-the-children.html?pagewanted=all
&_r=4&.

8 David Von Drehle, "How Gay Marriage Won," *Time*, 28 March
2013, http://swampland.time.com/2013/03/28/how-gay-marriage-
won/print. I came up with the title of this book, *Making Out in
the Mainstream*, years before Sarah Kate Ellis, the woman who
would become GLAAD's president and chief executive officer in
2014, was featured kissing her wife on the cover of *Time*. As an
illustration of the book's argument, it could not have been more
a propos.

9 Kate Sosin, "Herndon Graddick Talks of a New GLAAD," *Windy
City Times*, 14 November 2012, http://www.windycitymedia
group.com/lgbt/Herndon-Graddick-talks-of-a-new-GLAAD/
40392.html. Showing backbone did not extend to former President Bill Clinton, who was given the Advocate for Change award
at the 2013 GLAAD Media Awards in Los Angeles while Graddick
was still in charge. Clinton, as a few hecklers reminded the audience, was responsible for signing the Defense of Marriage Act in
1996. He had since declared his opposition to the act and changed
his views on marriage equality.

10 Karen Ocamb, "GLAAD Is Back!" *Bilerico Project*, 13 July 2012,
http://www.bilerico.com/2012/07/glaad_is_back.php.

11 It is interesting to note that the oldest and one of the largest organizations of the gay and lesbian movement changed its name
from the National Gay and Lesbian Task Force to the National
LGBTQ Task Force. In the op-ed published in the *Advocate* on 8
October 2014 to make the announcement, executive director Rea
Carey listed homelessness, health care, workplace discrimination,
housing, education, bullying, adoption rights, immigration, aging,
transgender rights, and the additional burdens faced by LGBT people of colour as the issues the task force would tackle. It was the
clearest expression to date that a "post-marriage" agenda, which
looked very similar to the Revolting Queers's agenda in 2007,
was beginning to take root among the large organizations of the
LGBT movement.

# Bibliography

Alwood, Edward. 1996. *Straight News: Gays, Lesbians, and the News Media*. New York: Columbia University Press.

Ang, Ien. 2005. "Difference." In *New Keywords: A Revised Vocabulary of Culture and Society*, edited by Tony Bennett, Lawrence Grossberg, and Meaghan Morris. Malden, MA: Blackwell Publishing.

Banet-Weiser, Sarah. 2012. *Authentic(TM): The Politics of Ambivalence in a Brand Culture*. New York: New York University Press. Kindle edition.

Banks, Miranda. 2009. "Gender below-the-Line: Defining Feminist Production Studies." In *Production Studies: Cultural Studies of Media Industries*, edited by Vicki Mayer, Miranda J. Banks, and John T. Caldwell. New York: Routledge.

Barnhurst, Kevin G. 2007. "Visibility as Paradox: Representation and Simultaneous Contrast." In *Media Queered: Visibility and Its Discontents*, edited by Kevin G. Barnhurst. New York: Peter Lang Publishing.

Bawer, Bruce. 1994. *A Place at the Table: The Gay Individual in American Society*. New York: Simon & Schuster.

Becker, Ron. 2006. *Gay TV and Straight America*. New Brunswick, NJ: Rutgers University Press.

Bellant, Russ. 1991. *The Coors Connection*. Boston: South End Press.

Benson, Rodney. 1999. "Field Theory in Comparative Context: A New Paradigm for Media Studies." *Theory and Society* 28 (3): 463–98.

Berlant, Lauren. 1997. *The Queen of America Goes to Washington City: Essays on Sex and Citizenship*. Durham, NC: Duke University Press Books.

Berlant, Lauren, and Michael Warner. 1998. "Sex in Public." *Critical Inquiry* 24 (2): 547–66.

Bourdieu, Pierre. 1971. "Intellectual Field and Creative Project." In *Knowledge and Control: New Directions for the Sociology of Education*, edited by Michael F.D. Young. London: Collier-Macmillan.

Bourdieu, Pierre, and Loïc J.D. Wacquant. 1992. *An Invitation to Reflexive Sociology*. Chicago: University of Chicago Press.

Brown, Wendy. 2005. *Edgework: Critical Essays on Knowledge and Politics*. Princeton, NJ: Princeton University Press.

Cagle, Van. 2007. "Academia Meets LGBT Activism: The Challenges Incurred in Utilizing Multimethodological Research." In *Communication Activism*, edited by Lawrence R. Frey and Kevin M. Carragee, 155–94. Cresskill, NJ: Hampton Press.

Capsuto, Steven. 2000. *Alternate Channels: The Uncensored Story of Gay and Lesbian Images on Radio and Television, 1930s to the Present*. New York: Ballantine Books.

Chapman, Roger. 2009. *Culture Wars: An Encyclopedia of Issues, Voices, and Viewpoints*. Armonk, NY: M.E. Sharpe.

Chasin, Alexandra. 2000. *Selling Out: The Gay and Lesbian Movement Goes to Market*. New York: Palgrave Macmillan.

Chauncey, George. 1994. *Gay New York: Gender, Urban Culture, and the Making of the Gay Male World 1890–1940*. New York: Basic Books.

Clarke, Eric O. 1999. "Queer Publicity at the Limits of Inclusion." *GLQ* 5 (1): 84–9.

– 2000. *Virtuous Vice: Homoeroticism and the Public Sphere*. Durham, NC: Duke University Press Books.

Clendinen, Dudley, and Adam Nagourney. 1999. *Out for Good: The Struggle to Build a Gay Rights Movement in America*. New York: Simon & Schuster.

Cohen, Cathy J. 1999. *The Boundaries of Blackness:* AIDS *and the Breakdown of Black Politics*. Chicago: University of Chicago Press.

D'Acci, Julie. 1994. "A Woman's Program." *Defining Women: Television and the Case of Cagney and Lacey*. Chapel Hill, NC: University of North Carolina Press.

Dauvergne, Peter, and Genevieve LeBaron. 2014. *Protest Inc.: The Corporatization of Activism*. Cambridge, UK: Polity.

Davidson, Craig J., and Michael G. Valentini. 1992. "Cultural Advocacy: A Non-legal Approach to Fighting Defamation of Lesbians and Gays." *Law and Sexuality: A Review of Lesbian and Gay Legal Issues* 2 (1992): 103–29.

Dávila, Arlene. 2001. *Latinos, Inc.: The Marketing and Making of a People*. Berkeley, CA: University of California Press.

D'Emilio, John. 2012. *Sexual Politics, Sexual Communities*. 2nd ed. Chicago: University of Chicago Press.

– 2000. "Cycles of Change, Questions of Strategy: The Gay and Lesbian Movement after Fifty Years." In *The Politics of Gay Rights*, edited by Craig A. Rimmerman, Kenneth D. Wald, and Clyde Wilcox. Chicago: University of Chicago Press.

de Certeau, Michel. 2011. *The Practice of Everyday Life*. Berkeley, CA: University of California Press.

Dornfeld, Barry. 1998. *Producing Public Television, Producing Public Culture*. Princeton, NJ: Princeton University Press.

Duggan, Lisa. 2003. *The Twilight of Equality? Neoliberalism, Cultural Politics, and the Attack on Democracy*. Boston: Beacon Press.

Dyer, Richard. 1993. *The Matter of Images: Essays on Representations*. New York: Routledge.

Edwards, Lee, and Caroline E.M. Hodges, eds. 2011. *Public Relations, Society & Culture: Theoretical and Empirical Explorations*. New York: Routledge.

Edwards, Lee. 2011. "Public Relations and Society: A Bourdieuvian Perspective." In Edwards and Hodges, *Public Relations, Society & Culture*, 61–74.

English, James F. 2009. *The Economy of Prestige: Prizes, Awards, and the Circulation of Cultural Value*. Cambridge, MA: Harvard University Press.

Escoffier, Jeffrey. 1995. "Community and Academic Intellectuals: The Contest for Cultural Authority in Identity Politics." In *Cultural Politics and Social Movements*, edited by Marcy Darnovsky, Barbara Epstein, and Richard Flacks. Philadelphia: Temple University Press.

Espinosa, Paul. 1982. "The Audience in the Text: Ethnographic Observations of a Hollywood Story Conference." *Media, Culture and Society* 4 (1): 77–86.

Gamson, Joshua. 1998. *Freaks Talk Back: Tabloid Talk Shows and Sexual Nonconformity*. Chicago: University of Chicago Press.

Ghaziani, Amin. 2008. *The Dividends of Dissent: How Conflict and Culture Work in Lesbian and Gay Marches on Washington*. Chicago: University of Chicago Press.

Gladwell, Malcolm. 2000. *The Tipping Point: How Little Things Can Make a Big Difference*. Boston: Little, Brown and Company.

Goldstein, Richard. 2002. *The Attack Queers: Liberal Society and the Gay Right*. London: Verso.

Gomez, Jewelle. 1995. "The Question." *Oral Tradition: Selected Poems Old & New*. Ithaca, NY: Firebrand Books.

Gray, Mary L. 2009. *Out in the Country: Youth, Media, and Queer Visibility in Rural America*. New York: New York University Press.

Grindstaff, Laura. 2002. *The Money Shot: Trash, Class, and the Making of TV Talk Shows*. Chicago: University of Chicago Press.

Gross, Larry. 1994. "What Is Wrong with This Picture? Lesbian Women and Gay Men on Television." In *Queer Words, Queer Images: Communication and the Construction of Homosexuality*, edited by Ronald Jeffrey Ringer. New York: New York University Press.

– 2001. *Up from Invisibility: Lesbians, Gay Men, and the Media in America*. New York: Columbia University Press.

Grossberg, Lawrence. 1997. *Bringing It All back Home: Essays on Cultural Studies*. Durham, NC: Duke University Press.

Hall, Stuart. 1997. "The Work of Representation." In *Representation: Cultural Representations and Signifying Practices*, edited by Stuart Hall. Thousand Oaks: SAGE, in association with the Open University.

– 1996. "New Ethnicities." In *Stuart Hall: Critical Dialogues in Cultural Studies*, edited by Kuan-Hsing Chen and David Morley. New York: Routledge.

– 2011. "The Neo-liberal Revolution." *Cultural Studies* 25 (6): 705–28.

Hanson, Ellis. 1999. "Introduction." In *Out Takes: Essays on Queer Theory and Film*, edited by Ellis Hanson. Durham, NC: Duke University Press.

Harvey, David. 2007. *A Brief History of Neoliberalism*. New York: Oxford University Press.

Henderson, Lisa. 1995. "Directorial Intention and Persona in Film School." In *On the Margins of Art Worlds*, edited by Larry Gross, 149–66. Boulder: Westview Press.

– 1999. "Storyline and the Multicultural Middlebrow: Reading Women's Culture on National Public Radio." *Critical Studies in Mass Communication* 16 (3): 329–49.

Henderson, Lisa. 2013. *Love and Money: Queers, Class, and Cultural Production*. New York: New York University Press. Kindle edition.

Hequembourg, A., and Arditi, J. 1999. "Fractured Resistances: The Debate over Assimilationism among Gays and Lesbians in the United States." *Sociological Quarterly* 40 (4): 663–80.

Hesmondhalgh, David, and Sarah Baker. 2011. *Creative Labour: Media Work in Three Cultural Industries*. New York: Routledge.

Hunter, James Davison. 1992. *Culture Wars: The Struggle to Control the Family, Art, Education, Law, and Politics in America*. New York: Basic Books.

Joseph, Miranda. 2002. *Against the Romance of Community*. Minneapolis: University of Minnesota Press.

Khan, Surina. 2012. "Gay and Lesbian Alliance Against Defamation (GLAAD)." In *Routledge International Encyclopedia of Queer Culture*, edited by David A. Gerstner. New York: Routledge.

King, Samantha. 2008. *Pink Ribbons, Inc.: Breast Cancer and the Politics of Philanthropy*. Minneapolis: University of Minnesota Press. Kindle edition.

Kirk, Marshall K., and Erastes Pill. 1984. "Waging Peace." *Christopher Street*, December 1984, 33–41.

Kirk, Marshall, and Hunter Madsen. 1989. *After the Ball: How America Will Conquer Its Fear and Hatred of Gays in the 90's*. New York: Doubleday.

Klein, Bethany. 2003. "Will the Real Eminem Please Stand Up: The Artist as Polysemic Text." Unpublished essay.

Klein, Naomi. 2001. *No Logo: No Space, No Choice, No Jobs*. London: Flamingo.

Loughery, John. 1998. *The Other Side of Silence: Men's Lives and Gay Identities: A Twentieth Century History*. New York: H. Holt.

Lutz, Catherine, and Jane Lou Collins. 1993. *Reading National Geographic*. Chicago: University of Chicago Press.

Maguire, Jennifer Smith, and Julian Matthews, eds. 2014. *The Cultural Intermediaries Reader*. Thousand Oaks: SAGE Publications Ltd.

Marotta, Toby. 1981. *The Politics of Homosexuality*. Boston: Houghton Mifflin.

Marquis, Jefferson P., Nelson Lim, Lynn M. Scott, Margaret C. Harrell, and Jennifer Erin Kavanagh. 2008. *Managing Diversity in Corporate America: An Exploratory Analysis*. Santa Monica: Rand Corporation.

Mayer, Vicki. 2011. *Below the Line: Producers and Production Studies in the New Television Economy*. Durham, NC: Duke University Press. Kindle edition.

Moe, Albert F. 1966. "'Make out' and Related Usages." *American Speech*, 41 (2): 96–107.

Montgomery, Kathryn C. 1989. *Target, Prime Time: Advocacy Groups and the Struggle over Entertainment Television*. New York: Oxford University Press.

Moscowitz, Leigh. 2013. *The Battle over Marriage: Gay Rights Activism through the Media*. Urbana: University of Illinois Press. Kindle edition.

Pekurny, Joseph. 1977. "Broadcast Self-Regulation: A Participant-Observation Study of the National Broadcasting Company's Broadcast Standards Department." Doctoral dissertation, University of Minnesota.

Radway, Janice A. 1997. *A Feeling for Books: The Book-of-the-Month Club, Literary Taste, and Middle-Class Desire*. Chapel Hill, NC: University of North Carolina Press.

Rayside, David Morton. 1998. *On the Fringe: Gays and Lesbians in Politics*. Ithaca, NY: Cornell University Press.

Reed, Jennifer. 2007. "The Three Phases of Ellen: From Queer to Gay to Postgay." In *Queer Popular Culture: Literature, Media, Film, and Television*, edited by Thomas Peele. Palgrave Macmillan.

Richey, Lisa Ann, and Stefano Ponte. 2011. *Brand Aid: Shopping Well to Save the World.* Minneapolis: University of Minnesota Press. Kindle edition.

Rubin, Gayle S. 1993. "Thinking Sex: Notes for a Radical Theory of the Politics of Sexuality." In *The Lesbian and Gay Reader*, edited by Henry Abelove, Michèle Aina Barale, and David M. Halperin, 3–44. New York: Routledge.

Russo, Vito. 1987. *The Celluloid Closet: Homosexuality in the Movies.* New York: Harper & Row.

Schiavi, Michael. 2011. *Celluloid Activist: The Life and Times of Vito Russo.* Madison: University of Wisconsin Press.

Schilt, Kristen. 2004. "AM/FM Activism." *Journal of Gay & Lesbian Social Services* 16 (3–4): 181–92.

Seidman, Steven. 2002. *Beyond the Closet: The Transformation of Gay and Lesbian Life.* New York: Routledge.

Sender, Katherine. 2005. *Business, Not Politics: The Making of the Gay Market.* New York: Columbia University Press.

Smith, Barbara. 1999. "Blacks and Gays: Healing the Great Divide." In *The Columbia Reader on Lesbians and Gay Men in Media, Society, and Politics*, edited by Larry Gross and James D. Woods, 649–52. New York: Columbia University Press.

Streeter, Thomas. 2000. "What Is an Advocacy Group, Anyway?" In Suman and Rossman, *Advocacy Groups and the Entertainment Industry*, 77–84. Westport, CT: Praeger.

Streitmatter, Rodger. 1995. *Unspeakable: The Rise of the Gay and Lesbian Press in America.* Boston: Faber and Faber.

Sullivan, Andrew. 1996. *Virtually Normal.* New York: Vintage.

Suman, Michael, and Gabriel Rossman. 2000. *Advocacy Groups and the Entertainment Industry.* Westport, CT: Praeger.

Swartz, David. 1997. *Culture and Power: The Sociology of Pierre Bourdieu.* Chicago: University of Chicago Press.

Teal, Donn. 1971. *The Gay Militants.* New York: Stein and Day.

Thomson, Irene Taviss. 2010. *Culture Wars and Enduring American Dilemmas.* Ann Arbor: University of Michigan Press.

Tuchman, Gaye. 1978. *Making News: A Study in the Construction of Reality.* New York: Free Press.

Tyler, Parker. 1972. *Screening the Sexes: Homosexuality in the Movies*. New York: Holt, Rinehart and Winston.

Vaid, Urvashi. 1995. *Virtual Equality: The Mainstreaming of Gay and Lesbian Liberation*. New York: Doubleday.

Valentine, David. 2007. *Imagining Transgender: An Ethnography of a Category*. Durham, NC: Duke University Press.

Walters, Suzanna Danuta. 2001. *All the Rage: The Story of Gay Visibility in America*. Chicago: University of Chicago Press.

Ward, Jane. 2008. *Respectably Queer: Diversity Culture in LGBT Activist Organizations*. Nashville, TN: Vanderbilt University Press.

Warner, Michael. 1999. *The Trouble with Normal: Sex, Politics, and the Ethics of Queer Life*. New York: Free Press.

Wilson, Jeffrey, ed. 2006. *Gale Encyclopedia of Everyday Law*. 2nd ed. Detroit: Gale.

# Index

*Italic page numbers refer to figures*

20/20, 110
*60 Minutes*, 50, 138

ABC, 70, 110, 202
Abercrombie & Fitch, 236
abortion, 158, 219, 244
Absolut Vodka, 78, 100, 102, 104, 106, 111, 222, 224, 264; GLAAD logo ad campaign, 113, 117–20, *118, 119*, 122–3
*Accelerating Acceptance*, 230, 238
*Access Hollywood*, 202
activism, 9, 17, 17–19, 21, 24, 64–5, 67–8, 71, 73, 76, 80, 85–92, 127, 130, 138, 141, 149–50, 152, 155–6, 178, 185, 206–7, 217, 219, 237; corporatization of, 6, 62–3, 79, 82–3, 113, 174–5, 186–7, 191–2, 209, 235, 240–1; direct action, 39, 41, 43, 46, 82–3, 125, 148; intersectional activism, 252–9; media activism, 3–5, 7, 13, 22–3, 27–56, 75, 81, 125, 161–4, 168, 173, 179, 232–4, *233*, 239, 242–50; online activism, 224
Adams, Nick, 101, 162, 168, 201, 203
Adkins, Barry, 38, 47
adoption, 88, 129, 143, 271n11
advertising, 16, 32, 35, 36, 189, 218, 225, 238; Absolut Vodka/GLAAD logo ad, 113, 117–20, *118, 119*, 122; Dr Laura ad campaigns, 29, 134, 139–41, 144–5, 152–4, 157–61, 166–73, 244, 267n9; GLAAD's use of, 42, 53, 94; Hollywood Images campaign, 52; MTV Fight for Your Rights campaign, 199–200; *Queer as Folk* ads, 180, 191–2
*Advertising Age*, 158–60
advocacy, 11, 92, 143, 174, 195, 207, 214, 236, 241, 251; anti-censorship advocacy, 42; child and family advocacy, 130, 141, 169; cultural advocacy, 13–14, 22–3, 30, 45–7; economics of, 181; GLAAD's mission, 145, 178, 193, 225, 242–5, 247, 250, 256, 262n2; GLAAD's

mission of, 3, 17, 20, 43, 50, 82; in
    homophile movement, 31; homo-
    phobic advocacy, 132, 153; of les-
    bian and gay press, 135; politics of
    criticism and, 21; public relations
    and, 35, 191–2
*Advocate*, the, 50, 101, 109, 117,
    125, 148, 152, 183, 216, 271n11
*Adweek*, 158, 160
African Americans, 49, 62, 105, 201,
    203, 211, 217, 219, 222, 227. *See
    also* black communities
*After Ellen*, 262n8, 270n6
Agnos, Art, 48
Agrama, Jehan, 49–51, 53, 55, 103
AIDS, 41, 204, 206; AIDS activism,
    45–8, 53–5, 62, 90, 249; media
    representations of, 3, 28, 37–40,
    83, 97
AIDS Coalition to Unleash Power
    (ACT UP), 46, 63, 75
AIDS-phobia, 55
AIDS Quilt, 105
*Aimee & Jaguar*, 96
Alliance for Gay and Lesbian Artists,
    53
allies, 45, 108, 132, 144, 208, 253
Alwood, Edward, 31–2, 38
*American Beauty*, 105
American Civil Liberties Union, 141
American Express, 225
American Family Association, 47
American Foundation for AIDS Re-
    search, 204
*American Prospect*, 230
Amnesty International: Outfront pro-
    gram, 219
analogies, 116, 151, 197, 219, 251,
    254; sexuality/race analogies, 217
Anderson, Carol, 49
Anderson, Julie, 69, 75, 99, 144, 181
Ang, Ien, 120–1
Aniston, Jennifer, 177

anthropology, 23, 26
Anti-Defamation League of B'nai
    B'rith (ADL), 14, 38–9, 47–8, 51,
    159, 267n10
anti-discrimination law, 35, 55, 72,
    219
anti-gay conservatives, 18, 22, 38,
    45, 72, 105, 143, 146, 169, 240.
    *See also* homophobia
Antigone Rising, 236
anti-Semitism, 141, 221
AOL.com, 126
apartheid, 205
Apple, 229
Arana, Gabriel, 230
Aravosis, John, 141, 161–3, 165,
    171–2, 174
Arditi, Jorge, 12
Arizona, 237, 248
Arizona Human Rights Fund, 227
*Arizona Republic*, 197
Ashcroft, John, 172
Asian Americans, 49, 138, 209–10.
    *See also* Chinese Americans; Fil-
    ipino American
assimilation, 5, 10, 12, 25, 65, 113,
    115–16, 164, 181, 232, 253
Associated Press, 102
Atlanta Braves, 138
*Atlantic*, 229
AT&T, 4–5, 7, 237, 240
audiences, 11, 21–2, 37, 101, 107,
    111, 114, 117, 160, 220–4, 234;
    Dr Laura audiences, 109, 126, 132,
    139, 154, 167, 169; Eminem's au-
    diences, 195–7, 200, 203, 211,
    221; GLAAD's audiences, 218, 246,
    248–50; heterosexist audiences, 70;
    mainstream audiences, 68, 78, 96,
    110; minority audiences, 96;
    straight audiences, 15–16, 84, 96,
    183; studio audiences, 136, 213

Baker, Sarah, 21
Banet-Weiser, Sarah, 270n4
Banks, Miranda, 21
Barnett, Allen, 38
Barnhurst, Kevin, 122
Barrios, Jarrett, 4, 237, 240
*Basic Instinct*, 15, 18, 52–3, 262n8
Bassey, Shirley, 205
*Bay Windows*, 86
B-boy Blues novels, 219
Bean, Billy, 110
*Before Night Falls*, 96
Bell Atlantic, 82, 106
Benson, Rodney, 258
Bergman, Deborah, 49
Berlant, Lauren, 10, 19
Berlanti, Greg: *The Broken Hearts Club*, 96–7
*Best in Show*, 95
Bilerico Project, 240
*Billboard*, 195, 200
*Billy Elliot*, 95
Birch, Elizabeth, 86
*Bird on a Wire*, 52
bisexuals, 4, 14–15, 54, 62, 109, 192, 199, 229, 262n2, 262n8
black communities, 20, 72, 137, 142, 216, 221–2, 235, 249. *See also* African Americans
Blank, Matt, 191–2
blogging, 4, 234, 240
Boehlert, Eric, 196–7
Bohnett, David, 49
Bono, Chastity, 67, 70–1, 81, 88
Bono, Sonny, 67
*Boston Globe*, 4–5, 216
*Boston Herald*, 143
Bourdieu, Pierre, 9–10, 21, 175, 238, 241–2, 258
*Bowers v. Hardwick*, 40, 263n1
boycotts, 44–5, 72–3, 146, 169
Boy George, 105

Boy Scouts of America, 106, 170
*Boys Don't Cry*, 106
*The Boys in the Band*, 105
Brady, Peggy, 59–61, 66
branding, 24, 90, 146–7, 159, 235, 238, 252, 265n7, 266n1, 270n4; GLAAD's brand, 69, 74, 78–9, 112–23, *115, 118, 119*, 227, 247, 266n11, 266n12. *See also* institutionalization
Brand Union. *See* Enterprise IG
Bravo!, 199
Briggs Initiative (CA), 37
*Broadcasting and Cable*, 158
*The Broken Hearts Club*, 96–7
Brooks, Lane, 99–100
Brown, Wendy, 5, 7–8
Brown & Williamson, 104, 146
Bryant, Anita, 37, 105
Buchanan, Patrick, 263n2
*Buffy the Vampire Slayer*, 180
Buford, Howard, 114, 145–7, 158–9, 170, 225, 227
Bunim/Murray productions, 198–9
Burlingame, Jason, 99–101, 144
Bush, Barbara, 110
Bush, George W., 172

Cagle, Van, 23
Caldwell, Chris, 48
California, 37, 48, 72, 248; Los Angeles, 3, 26, 52, 93, 167, 182, 202–3, 207, 225, 227; Sacramento, 48; San Francisco, 24, 37, 57–8, 93, 105, 140, 167, 220. *See also* GLAAD/LA; GLAAD/San Francisco Bay Area
Calvin Klein, 236
camp, 109–10
Canada, 166; Montreal, 80; Ottawa, 80; Toronto, 179
CanWest, 166

capitalism, 6, 8, 10, 19, 21, 24, 27, 241, 253. *See also* class; neoliberalism

Capsuto, Steven, 23, 32, 35, 53

CARE, 113

Carey, Rea, 271n11

Cartagena, Chiqui, 65–6

Carton, Ellen, 58–9, 62

Castle Rock Foundation, 72

CBS, 49–50, 144–6, 153, 156, 203

CBS/Viacom, 131, 152

censorship, 35, 201; anti-censorship campaigns, 42, 206

Center for the Study of Media and Society, 23, 221

Chasin, Alexandra, 7, 24–5, 86, 113, 232, 262n2

Chauncey, George, 31

Che, Cathay, 62–3, 65

Cheney, Dick, 72, 214

Cheney, Lynne, 214–15

Cheney, Mary, 72

Cher, 67, 106

children, 14, 64–5, 82, 84, 88, 91, 95, 107–8, 116–17, 128–31, 141, 169, 172–3, 180, 194–7, 212–18, 230, 234–5, 240, 249, 267n3, 270n6. *See also* adoption

Child Welfare League of America, 141

Chinese Americans, 210

Christianity, 84, 129, 143, 208, 219

*Christopher Street*, 16

citizenship, 8, 19, 25, 113, 253

civil rights, 5, 17–18, 31–2, 129–30, 141, 145, 236

Clarke, Eric O., 18, 122–3

class, 18, 20, 22, 25–6, 31, 36, 45, 81, 154, 192, 193–4, 216, 219–21, 241, 252, 258; GLAAD politics and, 17, 41, 54, 69, 107–8, 111, 122, 209, 248–50, 256; respectability and, 6–8, 231. *See also* capitalism; neoliberalism

Clendinen, Dudley, 23, 32, 35–6, 39–40

Clift, Montgomery, 109

Clinton, Bill, 10, 105, 271n9

closet, 8, 39, 45, 54, 66, 107

CNN, 50, 202, 214, 216, 237; Headline News, 52

Coca-Cola, 199

Cohen, Cathy, 249

Cold War, 263n2

Collins, Jane Lou, 250

Colorado: Denver, 56, 58

Color of Change, 235

coming out, 8, 17, 36, 51, 69–70, 84, 90, 144, 152, 180, 236

communication studies, 17, 22, 80, 122

Communist Party, 31

Condé Nast, 199

Congress, 35, 72, 214

consumption, 8, 10, 12, 21, 25

Cook, Tim, 229

Cooper, Alice, 197

Coors Brewing Company, 44–5, 72–3, 100, 104, 146

copyright, 39

Cornell Gay Liberation, 90

Coronado, Troop, 4

corporate philanthropy, 86, 113

Crain, Chris, 227

cross-dressing, 131, 140, 159

*Cruising*, 176–7, 179

Cultural Interest Media Project, 188, 190, 227

cultural intermediaries, 21, 238

cultural studies, 5, 17, 22, 70, 81, 98, 269n14

culture war, 52, 229–30, 263n2

Cunanan, Andrew, 69

Current TV, 237

D'Acci, Julie, 21

*Daily Variety*, 52, 104, 199

Dale, James, 106

d'Amato, Alfonse, 219

Dangerfield, Rodney, 197

*Darkman*, 52–3

Dauvergne, Peter, 6, 113, 241

Davidson, Craig, 14–17, 23, 44–9, 51, 58

Dávila, Arlene, 24

Davison, Bruce, 54

*Dawson's Creek*, 104–5, 180

Dean, Jimmy, 109

de Certeau, Michel, 254

Decter, Midge, 34

defamation, 13–16, 29, 38–9, 51, 107, 136–7, 139, 143, 154, 159, 170, 177, 201, 218, 267n10

Defense of Marriage Act, 27, 263n3

DeGeneres, Ellen, 69–70, 105, 265n8

DeLaria, Lea, 109

D'Emilio, John, 8–9, 31, 77–8, 230–1

Democratic Party, 4, 90, 219, 237

*Desert Hearts*, 54

developmental narrative, 90–2, 97, 106–7

*The Dick Cavett Show*, 34

Dido, 204

Diller, Barry, 55

Dinkins, David, 53

disability, 142

discrimination, 3, 55, 108, 111, 121, 140, 194, 199, 230, 271n11. *See also* anti-discrimination law

Disney, 52

Divers/Cité, 80

diversity, 16, 23–4, 29–30, 41, 56, 124, 222, 234–5, 240, 258; corporate diversity models, 26–8, 78, 113, 121–2; GLAAD politics and, 60, 62, 90, 112, 177–8, 180, 185, 188–93, 242, 247, 250; in media representations, 20, 64, 96, 188–

93, 209, 224–7, 242; state-managerial diversity, 78, 120–1

Dobbs, Bill, 206

domesticity, 12, 129, 179

domestic partnership benefits, 72

Donahue, Phil, 53

Donohoe, Amanda, 54

donors, 3, 22, 28, 30, 45, 68–9, 74, 78, 93, 99–100, 114, 140, 158, 195, 198, 208, 227, 237, 239, 246, 258, 264n5

Don't Ask, Don't Tell, 27

Dornfeld, Barry, 21

Dostoyevsky, Fyodor, 129

down low, 222

drag, 15, 194

drag queens, 103, 198, 252

Dr Dre, 211

*Dr Laura*: campaign against, 8, 28–9, 106–10, 123–75, 177, 186, 198, 202, 204, 207, 209, 216, 242–6, 250, 255, 266n1, 267n9; *Dr Laura Perspective*, 127

Duggan, Lisa, 5–6, 11–12, 232, 252–3, 257

Dyer, Richard, 18

*Dynasty*, 105


E!, 52, 101, 110, 237

Eddie Bauer, 114

*Edge of Seventeen*, 105–6

Edwards, Lee, 21, 255

Einhorn, Jennifer, 70–1, 73–4

*Election*, 144

*Ellen*, 69–70. *See also* DeGeneres, Ellen

Ellis, Sarah Kate, 232, 235–40, 256, 258, 264n3, 270n6, 271n8

Ellis-Henderson, Kristen, 236, 270n6

Eminem, 8; campaign against *The Marshall Mathers LP*, 29, 177–8, 193–224, 249–50, 254–5

Empire State Pride, 90

empiricism, 22–3, 27, 232

employment discrimination, 18, 31, 36–7, 55, 72, 107–8, 129, 131, 230

English, James F., 92–3, 112

Enterprise IG, 112–15, 117, 265n11, 266n12

*Entertainment Tonight*, 71, 87–8, 101

entrepreneurialism, 5, 7–8, 242

Epstein, Joseph, 33–4

equality, 5–6, 10–12, 25, 27, 116, 163, 182, 214, 229–30, 252, 257, 271

Escoffier, Jeffrey, 19

Espinosa, Paul, 21

Etheridge, Melissa, 105

ethnography, 3, 7, 21–6, 28, 77, 81, 93, 217, 255, 261n1

Evans, Arthur, 34

Everett, Rupert, 95

Facebook, 240

fairness: Fairness Awards, 198–200; in GLAAD mission, 3, 15–17, 92, 95, 97–8, 137, 180–5, 188, 243, 249

Falk, Gene, 62, 71, 83, 144, 188–91

Family Research Council, 208

fantasy, 10, 12, 19, 124–5

*Fargo*, 197

Feder, Don, 143

Federal Bureau of Investigation (FBI), 31

Federal Communications Commission (FCC), 4

Feinstein, Diane, 105

*Felicity*, 180

femininity, 52

feminism, 34, 42, 104, 201–2, 211, 214, 217, 219, 222, 244

field theory, 9, 175, 245, 258

Filipino American, 62

film, 15, 18–20, 49, 52–5, 94–7, 105, 141, 144, 176–7, 185, 197–200, 209–10, 264n4, 270n1. *See also* Motion Picture Association of America; and *individual directors, films, and studios*

film studies, 38

Findle, Bob, 101

Fire Island, 90

First Amendment, 14

Fisher, Carrie, 104

Fisher, Peter, 34

Fleishman-Hillard, 74, 89

Florida, 37; Miami, 227

Ford Motor Company, 199

Fox News, 237

Fox Television, 55

*Frasier*, 69, 97, 144, 246, 267n3

Free Congress Foundation, 72

Friedkin, William: *Cruising*, 176–7, 179

g (bar), 223–4

Galluccio, Jon, 108–9

Galluccio, Michael, 108–9

Gamson, Joshua, 21, 251, 256–7

Garry, Joan, 3, 67–75, 79–93, 99, 106–17, 120, 126–33, 136–9, 142, 144, 147, 161–3, 168–74, 177, 181, 184–8, 192, 195–9, 202, 224–8, 232–40, 243–7, 256, 264n5, 264n10, 269n14

Gay, Lesbian and Straight Education Network, 198, 202

Gay Activists Alliance (GAA), 33–5, 38–40, 43, 83

gay and lesbian community, 7, 14, 19, 25, 39, 44–51, 64, 72, 117, 120, 125, 133, 137–45, 154–6, 162, 166, 170, 173, 175–80, 184, 191, 193, 199, 205, 213–19, 227, 244, 271n11; terminology and, 261n2. *See also* gay men; lesbians

gay and lesbian movement, 3, 8–13,

16, 22–4, 28–30, 32, 82–90, 116,
124–5, 139–41, 149, 163, 170,
178–9, 201–2, 206–7, 217, 230,
233, 248; history of, 31–78; terminology and, 261n2. *See also individual organizations*
gay and lesbian press, 16, 29, 32, 50,
52, 86, 96, 101, 135, 172, 174,
183, 222. *See also individual publications*
Gay and Lesbian Victory Fund, 61
GAYBC Radio Network, 137
Gay.com, 104, 153, 172–3
Gay Liberation Front (GLF), 32–3
Gay Media Task Force, 84
gay men, 4, 31, 33, 51, 90, 108–10,
130, 145, 148, 156, 230, 252, 256,
262n7; class and, 18, 25; discrimination against, 37–8, 107; gay men
politicians, 61; in GLAAD, 47, 56,
61–2, 103, 209, 217, 238, 264n5;
race and, 222–3; representations
of, 8, 15, 20, 29, 32, 43, 52, 54,
64–5, 95, 96–7, 132, 143, 158–9,
162, 166, 172, 176–85, 187–96,
199, 217, 242, 249–50, 255,
264n4; visibility of, 122–3. *See also*
gay and lesbian community; gay
and lesbian movement; gay and lesbian press; homosexuality
gay-straight alliances, 110
gay villages, 80–1, 96, 150
gay villains, 52
gender, 3–6, 20, 26, 49, 56–60, 81,
107, 110–11, 122, 178, 194, 219,
220–2, 231, 241, 249, 252, 259.
*See also* femininity; genderqueer
people; masculinity; men; misogyny; sexism; transgender people;
transphobia; women
genderqueer people, 252
Georgia: Atlanta, 267n9
Ghaziani, Amin, 27

Gibbons, Leeza, 101, 145; Leeza
Gibbons Enterprises, 144; *The
Leeza Show*, 108–9
Giulano, Neil, 237
GLAAD/Atlanta, 47, 56, 58, 66, 75,
226
GLAAD/Chicago, 47, 56, 67
GLAAD/Dallas, 47, 56, 58, 67
GLAAD/Denver, 56, 58
GLAAD Fairness Awards, 198–9
GLAAD/Kansas City, 47, 56, 66, 226
GLAAD/LA, 3, 23, 47–65, 88, 94, 98,
101–12, 127, 144, 161, 192, 198,
201, 212–13, 216–18, 226, 240,
254, 261, 271; Los Angeles Council, 60
GLAAD logo, 114–20, *118*, 159, 173,
266n12
GLAAD Media Awards, 8, 28, 53–8,
78, 90, 92–112, 117, 122, 124,
144–5, 187, 192, 198, 207, 223–4,
227, 240, 255, 261n1, 265, 265n6,
265n8, 271n9
GLAAD/Miami, 227
GLAAD/NY, 3, 45, 48, 50, 53, 56–60,
56–65, 94, 98–9, 110, 117, 142,
192, 219–24, 226, 254, 256,
261n1
GLAAD projects: *Accelerating Acceptance*, 230, 238; Commentator Accountability Project, 239;
GLAAD Alerts, 126, 133, 194; history of, 38–67; MediAlert columns,
65–6; Media Watch columns, 52;
Monitor and Response Project
teams, 63–4, 68; newsletter, 49, 52,
54, 61, 63, 173, 223–4; Program
Steering Committee, 64; Research
and Analysis Program, 23, 75, 220
GLAAD/San Diego, 47, 56
GLAAD/San Francisco Bay Area
(SFBA), 47, 56–7, 60, 64–6, 110,
192, 226–7, 261n1

GLAAD/USA, 56–64
GLAAD/Washington, DC, 56, 58, 66, 73, 94, 98, 192, 207, 226
Gladwell, Malcolm, 215
Goffman, Erving, 11
Gold, Ronald, 35–7
Goldman, Debra, 160–1
Gomez, Jewelle, 38–42, 83
Goodman, John, 264n4
*Good Morning America*, 216
Good Vibrations, 220
Gore, Al, 110, 237
Graddick, Herndon, 237, 239–40, 271n9
Graden, Brian, 195, 199–200
Grammer, Kelsey, 97
Grammy Awards, 202–6, 210–13, 216–18
grassroots organizing, 28, 30, 43, 47, 51, 63–4, 75, 123, 141–2, 147, 156, 173–4
Gray, Mary L., 25–6
Great Britain, 20, 110, 179, 189, 204
Greene, Michael, 202–3, 205, 210–11
Grego, Melissa, 168–9
Grindstaff, Laura, 21
Gross, Larry, 17–18, 23, 32, 37–9, 50, 107, 122, 135
Grossberg, Lawrence, 122
Guns N' Roses, 206

Haley, Bonnie, 65
Hall, Stuart, 5, 20–1, 27, 98
Halm, Will, 53, 59–61
Hansell, Dean, 49, 51, 54, 56
Hanson, Ellis, 19–20
Hapak, Peter, 236
Hardy, James Earl, 219, 221–2, 269n14
*Harper's*, 33–4
Harvey, David, 5
hate crimes, 200

hate lyrics, 195, 200–1, 206, 224
hate speech, 14, 166, 169
Hawaii, 263n3
HBO, 192
health care, 71, 108, 141, 160, 252, 271n11
Heffner, Jason, 63–4, 66, 68–9, 75, 79–81, 114, 264n10
hegemony, 5, 10, 24, 257
Henderson, Lisa, 21
Hequembourg, Amy, 12
Heritage Foundation, 4
Hesmondhalgh, David, 21
heteronormativity, 11–12, 19, 31, 97, 123, 128–32, 231, 251
heterosexism, 56, 70, 128–32, 221
heterosexuality, 7, 39, 115, 124, 128–31, 149, 159, 184, 221, 230, 248, 255; mainstreaming and, 6, 18–19, 31, 43, 77, 85, 263n1; representations of, 17, 70, 95, 97, 142, 180; straight allies, 45, 108, 132, 144, 208, 253; straight audiences, 15–16, 84, 96, 183. *See also* allies; gay-straight alliances
Hill+Knowlton Strategies, 112
hip hop, 178, 193–224, 200, 249–50, 269n14. *See also* Eminem
Hispanics, 24
Hodges, Caroline E.M., 21
*Hollywood Reporter*, 52, 139
Hollywood Supports, 55
homelessness, 252, 271n11
Homie-Sexual Hip-Hop panel, 219–24
homoeroticism, 203–4, 222
homonormativity, 11–12. *See also* mainstreaming
homophile organizations, 31
homophobia, 4, 19, 22, 31–2, 36–7, 45, 52, 72, 105–6, 267n10; of Dr Laura, 28, 109, 123–75, 244; of Eminem, 178, 193–224; GLAAD's

work against, 3, 15, 55–6, 110. *See also* anti-gay conservatives

homosexuality, 14–15, 31–4, 42, 50, 105, 107, 126, 127–31, 176, 244; Dr Laura's views on, 28, 109, 123–75, 244; Eminem's views on, 178, 193–224; mainstreaming of, 6, 8, 11, 51, 77, 85, 230–1; representations of, 19, 38. *See also* gay men; lesbians

Horizons Foundation, 140

*House Party*, 52

Hudson, Rock, 38, 105, 109

Huebner, David, 61, 66

Human Rights Campaign (HRC), 72, 86, 151, 161, 208–9, 218–19, 244; Equality Rocks concert, 207. *See also* Millennium March on Washington

Hunt, Michelle, 133–4

Hutcheson, Rick, 60

Hytner, Nicholas: *The Object of My Affection*, 176–7

ideology, 5, 10, 13, 22, 41, 129, 208, 235, 246, 250–1

*Images* (journal), 221, 269n14

Images Campaign, 64–5

immigration, 271n11

inclusion, 6–10, 25–8, 36, 229–30; GLAAD's work toward, 77–123, 125; limits of, 18, 231, 251. *See also* mainstreaming

institutionalization, 28, 30, 35, 113–14

Interscope Records, 194–5

Intolerance in Music: Town Hall Meeting event, 203

invisibility, 14–17, 25, 38, 122–3, 246, 258. *See also* visibility

Iovine, Jimmy, 206

Ireland, Patricia, 217

Irish Americans, 84, 235

Israel, 170

Italy, 105

Jackson, Joshua, 104

Jackson-Paris, Bob, 65

Jaguar North America, 104

Javier, Loren, 62–3, 188, 210, 220, 222–3, 227

Jennings, Richard, 48–53, 55, 59–60, 63, 210, 212, 214, 218

Jett, Joan, 109

John, Elton, 105, 110, 203–7

Johnson, Debra, 59

Johnson, Marsha P., 105

Joseph, Miranda, 24

Judaism, 14, 48, 142; Orthodox Judaism, 129, 166

Just for Laughs festival, 80

Kameny, Franklin, 31

Kantrowitz, Arnie, 40–1, 47, 83

Keegan, Michael, 61, 65

Kelly, Frank, 134

Ketchum Communications, 89

Kielwasser, Al, 65–6

Kim, Richard, 214, 225

King, Jason, 219, 221–2

King, Rodney, 86

King, Samantha, 113

Kirchick, James, 229–30

Kirk, Marshall, 16–17, 251, 257

*Kiss Me Guido*, 209–10

Klein, Alan, 96, 114, 141, 163, 174

Klein, Bethany, 205

Klein, Naomi, 117

Kolovakos, Gregory, 38, 40–1, 47

Kolzak, Stephen F., 54

Krim, Matilda, 204

Krueger, Freddy, 197

Ku Klux Klan, 217

Kuropat, Rosemary, 42

LA Gay and Lesbian Center, 202

*L.A. Law*, 54
lang, k.d., 105
LaRouche initiative, 40
Lash, Karen, 49
Latino/as, 49, 62, 72, 201, 216
law, 6, 16, 18, 37, 46, 129, 168, 208,
    230; adoption laws, 88, 129,
    271n11; age of consent laws, 182,
    249; anti-discrimination law, 35,
    55, 72, 219; copyright laws, 39;
    defamation law, 13–14; lawyers,
    42, 44–5, 48–9, 75, 225; marriage
    laws, 27, 109, 229, 236, 263n3;
    sodomy laws, 40, 263n1. *See also*
    *Bowers v. Hardwick*; Briggs Initia-
    tive (CA); civil rights; First Amend-
    ment
Lawson, Joel, 141, 174
leather communities, 15, 252
LeBaron, Genevieve, 6, 113, 241
Lee, David, 69, 144, 246
Leeza Gibbons Enterprises, 144
*The Leeza Show*, 108–9
Leno, Jay, 105
Lesbian Community Project, 63
lesbians, 8–12, 24–5, 35, 55, 66, 72,
    80, 82, 108–10, 130, 148, 156,
    167, 179, 188, 214, 230, 236, 252,
    256; in GLAAD, 56, 62; lesbian
    politicians, 61; representations of,
    13–20, 22, 32, 37–9, 43, 46, 48,
    51–2, 54, 64–5, 70, 96, 138, 158–
    9, 162, 166, 169, 180, 184–5, 192–
    4, 199, 217, 249; sexuality and,
    84–5; visibility of, 122–3. *See also*
    gay and lesbian community; gay
    and lesbian movement; gay and les-
    bian press; homosexuality
Leslie Accountancy, 68
liberalism, 4, 7–8, 10, 34, 35. *See
    also* neoliberalism
*Life*, 31
Light, Judith, 54

LinkedIn, 239
Lippincott, 266n12
Lithgow, John, 54
Llewellyn, Richard, 48
lobbying, 4–6, 8, 227, 237
Lobel, Kerry, 247
Loder, Kurt, 195–6
Loe, Dilia, 75, 181, 188, 209–10,
    220, 223, 227, 232, 247–8
*Longtime Companion*, 54
Los Angeles Police Department, 212
*Los Angeles Times*, 32, 49–50, 52,
    135, 140, 158, 167, 205
Los Angeles Unified School District,
    203
Loughery, John, 32
Louis, Karter, 219
Louis-Dreyfus, Julia, 104
Lowry, Brian, 135–6, 167, 267n3
Lucci, Susan, 100
Lucky Strike, 104
Lund, Sean, 101, 135, 162–3, 168,
    173, 214
Lupariello, Joe, 144
Lutz, Catherine, 250

Madonna, 95, 105
Madsen, Hunter (Erastes Pill), 16–
    17, 251, 257
magazines, 16, 34, 47, 50, 69, 94,
    96, 101, 105, 117, 222, 235–6,
    270n6. *See also individual publica-
    tions*
Maguire, Jennifer Smith, 21–2, 238–
    9
Maher, Bill, 107
Mahoney, John, 97
mainstreaming, 6, 8–13, 17, 20, 23–
    4, 26–30, 36, 43, 78, 124–5, 175,
    177–8, 229–33, 242, 253, 256–8.
    *See also* homonormativity; inclu-
    sion; respectability politics
March on Washington, 37, 207

marketing, 22, 24–5, 191, 214, 235–6, 238–9; cause-related marketing, 113; GLAAD politics and, 28, 78, 86, 92–3, 117–23, 145, 216, 233. *See also* branding
Marotta, Toby, 31, 33–5
marriage, 41, 72, 107, 131, 143, 158, 267n3; marriage rights, 8, 10, 27, 71, 108–9, 129, 229–30, 236, 248, 252, 263n3, 271n9, 271n11. *See also* Defense of Marriage Act
*The Marshall Mathers LP*. *See* Eminem
Martin, Steve, 169
masculinity, 110, 195, 252
Massachusetts, 4, 81, 237; Northampton, 79
Mattachine Society, 11, 31, 263n1
Matthews, Julian, 21–2, 238–9
Matthew Shepard Foundation, 202
Mayer, Vicki, 21
MCA/Universal, 52–3, 55
McCain, John, 214
McCarthyism, 31, 54
McCluggage, Kerry, 134, 140, 152
McGill University, 80
McGrath, Judy, 195
media advocacy, 23, 43, 47, 50, 84, 92, 137, 174, 193, 244–5, 256
media literacy, 61, 64
media outlets, 4, 50, 63, 101–2, 134, 210, 216. *See also individual outlets*
media studies, 13, 17, 22–3, 65
*Media Week*, 158
*Men at Work*, 52
methodology, 21–3, 78, 81, 217, 261n1. *See also* ethnography; participant observation
Metropolitan-Duane Methodist Church, 39
Michael, George, 105
Michael-Gelbert, Bruce, 38

Midler, Bette, 105
militancy, 8, 31–2, 41–3, 45–6, 83, 120, 123, 125–6, 128
militarism, 32, 266n13
military, 8, 229
military-industrial complex, 266n13
Milk, Harvey, 37, 72, 105
Millennium March on Washington, 207
Minneapolis Pride, 252–3
*Minneapolis Star-Tribune*, 216
Minnelli, Liza, 205
misogyny, 210, 214, 221
Mitcham, Kerry, 68
Moe, Albert F., 262n7
*Mommie Dearest*, 105
Monette, Paul, 54
monogamy, 65, 85, 107
Montgomery, Kathryn, 23, 92, 174
Montreal Jazz Festival, 80
Morris, Doug, 206
Moscone, George, 37, 105
Motion Picture Association of America, 55
MSNBC, 216
MTV, 3, 67, 103, 145, 177, 180, 195, 197–8, 212; Fight for Your Rights campaign, 199–200. *See also When Lyrics Attack*
*MTV News*, 195
MTV Video Music Awards (VMAS), 195, 197–8, 212
Murdoch, Rupert, 38, 90
Murray, Anne, 167

Nagourney, Adam, 23, 35–6, 38–40
Nardi, Peter M., 51, 54
*The Nation*, 214
National Academy of Recording Arts and Sciences (NARAS), 202–3, 211, 213, 216
National Association for the Advancement of Colored People

(NAACP), 4, 48, 51, 159, 267n10
National Center for Community and Justice, 159
National Education Association, 4
National Endowment for the Humanities, 214
National Gay and Lesbian Task Force (NGLTF), 6, 35–7, 41, 55, 84, 247, 271n11
National Gay and Lesbian Task Force Policy Institute, 228
National Mental Health Association, 141, 159
National Organization for Women, 141, 159, 171, 198, 202
Native Americans, 138
NBC, 161–2, 202, 265, 265n8
NBC News, 162, 224
neoliberalism, 5–8, 10–12, 24, 26–7, 29, 113, 178, 232–3, 236, 252–3, 255–7, 270n4. See also capitalism; class
New Jersey, 82, 88, 107, 185
New Left, 32
New Line Cinema/Fine Line Features, 198
New Republic, 171
new social movements, 36, 120–1
Newsweek, 197
New York (magazine), 117
New York City, 3, 15, 28, 30–2, 35, 39–44, 83, 90, 93, 148, 155, 167, 173, 176, 198, 209, 217, 227, 263n1; Greenwich Village, 38. See also GLAAD/NY
New York Daily News, 34, 162, 179
New York Gay and Lesbian Center, 198, 206, 235
New York Native, 38, 42–3
New York Post, 3, 38, 40, 83, 206
New York State Council for the Arts, 38

New York Times, 34, 40, 83, 140, 148, 158, 236
The Next Best Thing, 95
Nielsen ratings, 166
Nissan North America, 74, 89
non-profits, 5, 24, 60–1, 174, 199, 233–5, 234, 247, 266n13; GLAAD as, 42, 87, 117, 173, 226–7
Noonan, Peggy, 214–15
Normal, Ohio, 201, 264n4
Northrop, Ann, 206

Obama, Barack, 234
The Object of My Affection, 176–7, 179
Ocamb, Karen, 240
O'Donnell, Rosie, 84
Offen, Hal, 38
Ordesky, Mark, 198
Oregon: Portland, 63–4, 66
Oscars, 103, 169
Out, 101
outing, 45, 51
Owles, Jim, 33, 38–9, 41
Oz, 105–6

Pacific Bell, 199
Pacino, Al, 176
Paine, Christopher, 42
Pally, Marcia, 38, 42, 44–7
Paramount Pictures, 95, 144
Paramount Television, 28, 108–9, 131–40, 142–8, 150, 152–6, 161–2, 166, 169, 171–3, 242–3, 246, 267n3
parents, 82, 87, 97, 108, 130, 131, 145, 154, 158, 167, 179, 180, 182, 184–5, 196, 198, 204, 214, 216, 218, 249, 252. See also adoption; Parents and Friends of Lesbians and Gays

Parents and Friends of Lesbians and
   Gays (PFLAG), 179, 202
participant observation, 3, 78–9, 93,
   101–12, 181, 217–18, 261n1
Patterson, Romaine, 198
*PBS News Hour*, 161
pedophilia, 14, 140, 159, 172
Pekurny, Joseph, 92
Pennsylvania, 182, 249; Philadelphia,
   167; Pittsburgh, 179–80
*People*, 102, 104
People for the American Way, 159,
   198
people of colour, 39, 49, 56–8, 62,
   178, 185, 188–93, 218–22, 225–7,
   250, 252, 271. *See also* black communities; Latino/as
Perez, Nancy, 62
Perkins, Star, 219
Perper, Laurie, 4
Peru, Miss Coco, 198
*Philadelphia Gay News*, 42
Philip Morris, 104
Pill, Erastes. *See* Madsen, Hunter
Pillsbury Company, 166
Plum, Jay, 220, 223, 228, 269n14
pluralism, 116, 127, 164
police, 80, 212, 221
*Politically Incorrect*, 107
*Politico*, 4
politics of ambivalence, 252–9,
   270n4
politics of difference, 231
politics of sameness, 231
postgay discourses, 85
post-structuralism, 13
prejudice, 14–15, 18, 31–2, 141, 171
Premiere Radio Network, 140, 168
Prime Access, 145
privilege, 6–7, 10, 25, 26, 41, 108,
   188, 245, 251
Procter & Gamble (P&G), 157–8

professionalization, 8, 26, 62, 90–1,
   125, 174, 178, 193, 238, 254
promiscuity, 178–80, 183–4, 191,
   242, 249, 262n8
Propecia, 104, 265n7
*PR Week*, 167, 173, 246
Pryor, Bill, 212
Pryor, Richard, 197
public relations, 16, 35–6, 141, 144,
   204, 206, 210–11, 228; GLAAD's
   use of, 57, 68, 122, 132, 137, 146,
   173–4, 198, 250, 254–5; public relations firms, 6, 74–5, 86, 89, 112,
   114, 234–5, 239, 246–7
public sphere, 8, 18, 123
*Pulp Fiction*, 197

Queen, 205
*Queer as Folk*, 8, 29, 176–85, 179,
   187–93, 242, 249, 255
queerness, 11–13, 26–7, 54, 65, 110–
   11, 122, 138, 150, 178, 193–4,
   221–2, 226, 230–3, 252–3, 255,
   257, 259, 271n11; queer arts, 20,
   24, 269n14
queer studies, 5, 10, 19, 81

race, 20, 39, 49, 62, 72, 122, 137,
   142, 225–7, 235, 241, 244, 252,
   271; Eminem campaign and, 193–
   224, 249–50; within GLAAD, 41,
   56–60; inclusion and, 6, 26, 29, 81,
   111, 231; representations of, 64,
   178, 180, 185, 188–93, 242. *See
   also* African Americans; black communities; diversity; Latino/as;
   whiteness
racism, 32, 45, 50, 62, 137, 141,
   210, 212, 217, 221–2, 252. *See
   also* apartheid
radicality, 11–12, 17, 28, 33, 35–6,
   41–3, 42–3, 63, 116, 246, 257

radio, 4, 28, 34, 52, 106, 124, 126,
131, 133–4, 136–7, 140, 157, 159–
60, 165, 168–9, 197–8, 212, 244.
*See also* Schlessinger, Laura
Radway, Janice, 21
Rand Corporation, 121, 266n13
rap. *See* hip hop
Rayside, David Morton, 9
Reagan, Ronald, 10–11, 48, 105,
251
realism, 19, 52, 70, 98, 180, 190,
248
*Real Simple*, 235, 270n6
*The Real World*, 105–6, 198–9
Red Cross, 113
Red Wing, Donna, 63–4
Reed, Jennifer, 70, 85
religion, 46, 141, 146, 166, 196,
202, 249, 263n2. *See also* Christianity; Judaism
Renna, Cathy, 73–5, 144, 148, 155,
164, 172, 202, 214–15, 228, 232–
5, 239, 247
reparative therapy, 129, 143
representations: positive v. negative,
13–21, 46, 65, 81, 105, 107, 111,
176, 178, 180–1, 238
Republican National Convention,
263n2
Republican Party, 90, 219, 237,
263n2
respectability politics, 6–11, 16–17,
26–7, 45, 79, 84–5, 92, 109, 178–
9, 184, 224, 231–2, 252, 256–7.
*See also* mainstreaming
Revolting Queers, 252–3, 271n11
Rhue, Sylvia, 54
Riendeau, Danielle, 262n8
Rist, Darrell Yates, 38–40, 42–3, 47,
263n1
Rivera, Sylvia, 105
Robbe, Scott, 141, 174
Robinson, Marty, 33, 38–9

Robinson, Rashad, 235
Rocker, John, 138
Rolling Stones, 197
Rooney, Andy, 50, 138
Rose, Axl, 206
Rossman, Gabriel, 23
Rubin, Gayle, 85, 230
Rudd, Paul, 177
Ru-Paul, 105
Russo, Vito, 19, 38–41, 47, 110,
205–6, 240, 263n1

sadomasochism, 131, 140, 159, 176
*Salon*, 72, 196
*San Francisco Chronicle*, 140, 207
Schiavi, Michael, 38, 41–2, 263n1
Schilt, Kristen, 23, 217
Schlessinger, John: *The Next Best
Thing*, 95
Schlessinger, Laura. *See Dr Laura*
Schrader, Rand, 49
Schwartz, Karin, 44
Seidman, Steven, 12, 257
*Seinfeld*, 104
Sender, Katherine, 24–5
Seomin, Scott, 87–9, 101–2, 106–7,
151, 176–7, 209, 228, 249; during
Dr Laura campaign, 133–5, 140,
160, 162, 165; during Eminem
campaign, 194–5, 201–3, 206, 213;
hiring of, 71, 73–4; during *Queer
as Folk* controversy, 179–80, 182–
93
*Sex and the City*, 105–6
sexism, 32, 62, 221. *See also* misogyny
sexual assimilation, 65, 116, 122
sexuality, 3, 20, 25–6, 32, 65, 72, 81,
109, 111, 172, 220, 241, 251–2,
259, 262n7; representations of, 13,
16, 22, 29, 69, 176–85, 187, 191,
193–4, 214, 219, 236, 242, 249,
257; sexual privacy, 8, 40; sexual

shame, 11, 84–5, 178–9. *See also* heterosexuality; homoeroticism; homophobia; homosexuality; monogamy; promiscuity
sexual orientation, 3, 69, 72, 84, 140
sexual violence, 88, 106, 197
Shales, Tom, 165
shame, 11, 39, 84–5, 126, 152, 178–9, 182, 184, 187, 206
Shaver, Helen, 54
Sheen, Martin, 169
Sheinberg, Sid, 55
Shepard, Judy, 198, 204
Shepard, Matthew, 74, 105, 189, 200, 202, 204
*The Shield*, 193
Shields, Brooke, 109
Showtime, 3, 29, 62, 67, 83, 88, 145, 177, 179–80, 183, 188–93, 242
Signorile, Michelangelo, 4, 125, 144, 148–9, 151, 153, 172–3, 172–4, 175
Siino, Roseanne, 173
Simon & Schuster, 236
Sinatra, Frank, 205
*Six Feet Under*, 192–3
slander, 14
SlimFast, 102
Smalls, Shanté, 219, 221
Smith, Barbara, 217
Smith, David, 72, 161, 207–9
Smith, Liz, 66
Smith-Low, Carmichael, 49
*Soap*, 105
sociology, 9, 11–12, 17, 23, 26–7, 51, 178, 217
soc.motss, 171
Sony/Columbia, 52
Sony Pictures Classics, 199
Sosnick, Jeffrey, 44, 99
South Africa: Sun City, 205
*South Park*, 105, 197
Spelling, Tori, 198

Spivak, Gayatri, 20
Splash! (bar), 218
Springer, Jerry, 197
Spurgeon, Steve, 74–5, 83–9, 101–3, 228, 232, 239, 246–7, 265n8; during Dr Laura campaign, 132–6, 140–1, 144, 148–55, 161–8, 171–3, 244; during Eminem campaign, 197–218, 254; during *Queer as Folk* controversy, 181–91, 249
stereotypes, 14–15, 19, 52, 88, 179–80, 183–4, 187, 189, 217, 262n8. *See also* gay villains
Stern, Howard, 197
Steward, David, 90–1, 110–11, 144, 208, 244
stigmaphile, 11
stigmaphobe, 11
Stolbach, Michael, 46–7
Stone, Sharon, 88, 102
Stonewall riots, 32, 34, 39, 105–6, 178
StopDrLaura.com (SDL), 28–9, 125, 141–4, 147–9, 152–8, 161–75, 186, 207, 242–4, 267n7
Streeter, Thomas, 174, 244–5
Street Transvestite Action Revolution, 105
*Studio Responsibility Index*, 269n1
Suggs, Donald, 62–3
Suman, Michael, 23
Sun Microsystems, 199
Supreme Court, 40, 229, 263n1
Swartz, David, 245, 258
Swift and Terrible Retribution Committee, 39, 41
Sylvester, 105

Taher, Monica, 227
*Taiwan Today*, 101
Tarantino, Quentin: *Pulp Fiction*, 197
Target Corporation, 252

Taylor, Elizabeth, 102, 109, 265n8
*Teletubbies*, 105
television, 8, 23, 28, 34–7, 45, 49,
    52, 54–5, 69, 88, 94, 97, 102, 186,
    216, 226, 229, 239, 250, 255,
    264n4, 266n1, 267n9, 270n1. *See
    also* Nielsen ratings; Paramount
    Television; and *individual networks
    and shows*
Television Critics Association, 165
Temple, Shirley, 212
Temple Beth Chayim Chadashim, 51
terminology, 261n2
Testone, Glennda, 235
Thomas, Marlo, 53
*Time*, 31, 47, 69, 161, 186, 236
Time Inc., 199, 235–6
T-Mobile, 4, 7
*Today Show*, 161, 202, 216
tolerance, 18, 108, 136–7, 139, 143,
    203, 248
TomPaine.com, 140
*Total Request Live*, 200
transgender people, 4, 14, 26, 62,
    192, 194, 199, 201, 217, 230, 252,
    262n2, 271n11
transphobia, 178
*Trick*, 198
Tuchman, Gaye, 246
TV Guide, 90
Twitter, 240
Tyler, Parker, 19
Tyler, Robin, 141, 217
Tyson, Mike, 88

*Undressed*, 103
UNICEF, 113
Universal Music Group, 206
University of Massachusetts,
    Amherst, 81
University of Pennsylvania: Annen-
    berg School for Communication,
    234
University of Wyoming: LGBTA, 74

UPN, 144, 153, 165
*Urbania*, 96–7
USA *Today*, 84

Vaid, Urvashi, 6, 8, 10, 12, 116, 232,
    242–3, 257
Valenti, Jack, 55
Valentine, David, 26
Valentini, Michael, 14–17, 23, 44–6
*Variety*, 35, 70, 158, 165–9
Verhoeven, Paul: *Basic Instinct*, 15,
    18, 52–3, 262n8
Versace, Gianni, 69
VH1.com, 197
Viacom, 67, 131, 142, 145–6, 152,
    171
*Village Voice*, 32
visibility, 7, 17–18, 23–4, 27–8, 30–
    1, 36, 77, 229, 253, 258; of
    GLAAD, 3, 43, 69, 71, 73–5, 78,
    120, 132, 161, 163, 170, 198,
    208–9, 232, 238, 244; GLAAD's
    mission of, 46, 92, 155, 188; limits
    of, 20, 25–6, 123, 245, 252, 255.
    *See also* invisibility
Voeller, Bruce, 35

Wacquant, Loïc, 10, 242
Wallace, Michelle, 104
*Wall Street Journal*, 40
Walters, Suzanna, 17
Ward, Jane, 26–7, 178
Warner, Michael, 10–12, 19, 84–5,
    87, 89, 91, 178–9, 182, 184, 232
Warner Brothers, 199
Washington, DC, 27, 31, 37, 93, 234,
    267n9. *See also* GLAAD/Washing-
    ton, DC
*Washington Blade*, 227
*Washington Times*, 136
Wayans brothers, 182
Waybourn, William, 61–3, 66–7,
    141, 163, 174
Weber, Bruce, 236

welfare reform, 252
Wentworth, John, 133–4
*The West Wing*, 169
*When Lyrics Attack*, 195–6
White, Dan, 37
whiteness, 25, 107, 159, 201, 216–
    17, 220–3; in GLAAD, 58, 61, 209,
    256; GLAAD's mission and, 17,
    193, 209, 248–50; representations
    of, 188, 192, 196, 211–12
*Who's the Boss*, 54
Widmeyer Group, 62. *See also* Win-
    dow
*Wild at Heart*, 52
Wilks, Eric, 212
*Will and Grace*, 105–6, 181, 265n8
Williams, Michelle, 104
Wilson, Dan, 206
Wilson, Jeffrey, 14
Window Media, 62, 174
*Windy City Times*, 240

Winfrey, Oprah, 166
*The Wire*, 192–3
Wockner, Rex, 161–2
women's health movement, 71
*Wonder Boys*, 95
Woo, Michael, 52
Woo, Wonbo, 148–53
*World News Tonight*, 202
World Wildlife Fund, 113
Wright, Ben, 138
Wyoming: Laramie, 73–4

*Xena: Warrior Princess*, 105

youth, 25–6, 91, 109–10, 182, 197,
    203, 211–12, 215–16, 221, 250,
    252
YouTube, 240

zapping, 33, 39